ALSO BY RON SILVER

Bubby's Homemade Pies
with Jen Bervin

BALLANTINE BOOKS
NEW YORK

Bubby's
BRUNCH COOKBOOK

RECIPES AND MENUS
FROM NEW YORK'S FAVORITE
COMFORT FOOD RESTAURANT

RON SILVER

WITH ROSEMARY BLACK

Published in the United States by Ballantine Books, an imprint of
The Random House Publishing Group, a division of Random House, Inc., New York.

BALLANTINE and colophon are registered trademarks of Random House, Inc.

Interior photographs: Ben Fink Photography

ISBN 978-0-345-51163-8

Printed in the United States of America on acid-free paper

www.ballantinebooks.com

2 4 6 8 9 7 5 3 1

First Edition

Book design by Susan Turner

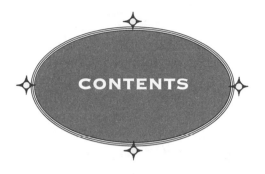

CONTENTS

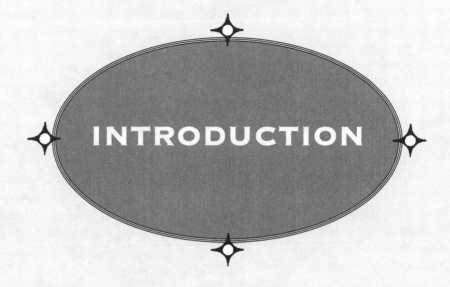

INTRODUCTION

Brunch brings back wonderful memories for me. Before people went out to restaurants all the time, folks cooked at home. Our family— my sister, brother, our mother, and I—looked forward to weekend breakfasts together. There was no rush. There were no pressing deadlines, as opposed to weekday dinners when the topic was often homework, or chores, or whether or not things had gotten done, and if not, when they would get done. Brunch was almost bucolic.

For us, brunch was often about what was growing in our backyard in a suburb of Salt Lake City, Utah. We would go out and pick raspberries off the thorny bushes, or apricots, or apples, and Mom would whip up something from the things we brought her. No one thought of "seasonal" then. Brunch was what we had fresh in the yard. But we also had perennial favorites: During the holiday season, we had crispy potato pancakes—with homemade applesauce. And blintzes, which we understood were an enormous effort that required two days' preparation, at the end of which our entire freezer was packed with aluminum foil packages labeled BLINTZES. We also had sourdough starter developing in the fridge, and many weekends Mom made spongy, tangy sourdough pancakes dripping with butter and maple syrup. As a special treat once every few years, we would go for brunch to a place up Millcreek Canyon called Log Haven, where men in tall white hats would make omelets and pancakes to order. And while I enjoyed watching the food get made, Mom's brunch fare was always better.

Inspired by the cooking of my mother and grandmother, I have, as a chef, always been motivated to search out the best of American home cooking, and to serve that at Bubby's. It has never been my aim to be fancy; let folks go to a fancier place for fancy food. My goal has been to create, with a few changes, home cooking the way I remember it from my childhood. It's important to me that people have a place to go where they can relax and enjoy unfussy, plain-old good cooking. It's also been important to me to encourage people to actually make these same delicious dishes at home.

I'd been cooking professionally and perfecting the art of brunch for years before Bubby's Pie Company first opened its doors in 1990. Bubby's—an old Yiddish word for "grandmother"—was named in honor of both my grandmothers, Miriam Silver and Pearl Stahl. I told each grandmother individually that Bubby's was named for her. I know, sneaky. . . .

The brunch comfort food offered at Bubby's was in high demand right from the start, and brunch continues to be our most popular meal. People want a brunch that their mother may have prepared or that they might make for themselves, and Bubby's menu bridges the gap between home cooking and food that was chef created.

Recommended in national magazines and travel and dining guides as the go-to place for brunch in New York City, Bubby's is where celebrities and everyday folk from all over the country flock to eat. With only a hundred seats in Tribeca, Bubby's still serves brunch to more than fourteen hundred people each weekend. And we serve about the same-size crowd in our DUMBO, Brooklyn, restaurant. Of course, many of these customers have asked for recipes and have wished that they could buy a copy of a book like this one. I always give my recipes to anyone who asks, and I always encourage people to cook at home because I believe eating together is one of the most important things that families and friends can do.

Bubby's is a homelike haven for everyone who loves home cooking, which is why it has evolved over the years from a tiny storefront into two bustling restaurants in New York City (and one opening in Yokohama, Japan!). On any given day, you'll find neighborhood regulars sitting elbow to elbow with artists, chefs, actors, politicians, and truck drivers. It is not uncommon to be reading the newspaper and look up to see some celebrity you are reading about sitting right in front of you. One of the customers who lived in our neighborhood was the late John F. Kennedy, Jr., and I often caught him reading about himself over my shoulder from my paper. Sometimes I even said, "Get your own paper, John! They're right over there."

Admittedly, I'm obsessive when it comes to food and to brunch in particular. I've drawn inspiration from assorted cookbooks—early American, Junior League, regional church groups—as well as from memorable recipes from someone's grandmother or aunt. I've researched, read, traveled, and corresponded in order to seek out the best brunch recipes and techniques and to bring them all together in this book.

There aren't any concrete rules for what to serve for brunch. It's not a meal you have to prepare on a day-to-day basis. Brunch is by its very nature a relaxing repast that everyone looks forward to and likes to linger over.

OF ALL THE MEALS YOU'LL EVER MAKE, BRUNCH IS THE MOST FLEXIBLE, THE MOST FORGIVING—AND THE MOST FUN.

Whether you are cooking for two or for twenty, whether it is served as a picnic in the yard, on fine china at a linen-covered table, or at a casual, self-serve buffet, brunch is a meal where you can let your creative side shine and where you can do as much or as little as you want—and still end up with that warm, contented feeling that comes from spending time around good food, good friends, and family.

Brunch is a middle-of-the-day affair; it can replace breakfast or function as lunch just as easily as it can shine as the main meal of the entire day. Guests anticipate a good brunch by having a skimpy or skipped breakfast and treating dinner almost as an afterthought.

Brunch is also a perfect meal for lovers or would-be lovers to make together. There's something romantic about preparing a feast on a weekend morning and then savoring it together while reading the Sunday paper. It's also the perfect meal for unattached twentysomethings just starting out on their own and entertaining friends: There's a lot less pressure connected with having a brunch than having a dinner party. It's a meal meant for fun.

Besides weekend days, many occasions arise where a brunch is appropriate: small gatherings such as engagement parties, postwedding breakfasts, holiday meals, family get-togethers—a bris or a christening—or even occasions as solemn as wakes or postfuneral receptions. In the book you'll find a chapter called Menus for Special Occasions (page 1) that offers a range of themed menus for twenty-five occasions. There's also a chapter on How to Plan and Pull Off the Perfect Brunch (page 21). Included here are step-by-step instructions and information on prep times for getting everything together for even the biggest brunches in an orderly way.

Just as flexible as the timing of a brunch is the menu for this meal. At Bubby's, we offer lots of choices, ranging from house-smoked salmon to eggs Benedict to a Croque Monsieur sandwich. Cheese grits, Swedish pancakes, and baskets of assorted homemade muffins and quick breads are among the myriad selections. Freshly squeezed fruit juices in many flavors, freshly brewed fair trade coffee, and spicy Bloody Marys give everyone plenty of beverage options.

Brunch at home, like brunch at Bubby's, can be as complex or as basic as you like. A simple omelet for two can be leisurely, understated, and romantic. A brunch for thirty to celebrate a christening or an engagement becomes a bountiful and even boisterous buffet at which the Bloody Marys are mixed by the gallon and fluffy pancakes disappear by the platterful.

Unlike a pressure-filled dinner party, brunch is more fun for everyone, host and guest alike. The rules for entertaining are waived at brunch. No one even has to wear shoes. If you and your guests love traditional brunch fare, this book offers more than two dozen omelet fillings to try, and you can round out the menu with some fresh fruit drinks (fresh squeezed cranberry mimosa, anyone?) and specialty coffee drinks. If you're hosting a group for whom carbs are a primary food group, Blueberry Buttermilk Pancakes (page 121), Crunchy French Toast Stuffed with Cream Cheese and Blackberry Jam (page 134), and Pecan Waffles with Maple Butter (pages 139 and 274) are just a few offerings.

Bubby's Brunch Cookbook is organized so that you've got choices that are easy to make. Eggs (the backbone of most brunches) get their own chapter because there are just so many ways to serve them. All the griddle options—pancakes, waffles, blintzes, crêpes, French toast—are in one chapter. Proteins (meat, bacon, sausages, smoked fish, and more) are grouped together, as are starters and sides. The idea is for you to mix and match whatever dishes you like best. That is the wondrous thing about brunch: Whatever you serve is what works for you and for your guests.

THE RECIPES IN THIS BOOK OFFER INSPIRATION AND SHOW THE WAY TO A SUCCESSFUL HOMEMADE BRUNCH.

All across the country, people are returning to their kitchens in hopes of re-creating the simple, traditional foods that bring back nostalgic and happy memories of their childhoods. For some, success could be as sweet as Blueberry Scones (page 51) and Raisin Challah French Toast (page 132), while for others, an ideal brunch consists of savory dishes—Chopped Cobb Salad and Savory Bacon and Cheese Bread Pudding (pages 162 and 112), for instance. All of these are Bubby's signature dishes, which make brunch a truly special meal. We've noted our most requested signature dishes with this icon next to the recipe title throughout the book. I hope *Bubby's Brunch Cookbook* will be an invaluable resource for everyone interested in preparing great brunches. For beginning cooks and experts alike, my goal is to demystify this most rewarding of meals and to inspire you to take brunch to a whole new level.

MENUS
FOR SPECIAL
OCCASIONS

Besides being the perfect meal for every weekend of the year, brunch is also the perfect special-occasion repast. It can be served most anytime, day or night. Don't limit yourself to just between the hours of 10:00 a.m. and 2:00 p.m. Think midnight pancakes in bed for someone special or an early-morning feast on a sandy beach. A lazy, late-afternoon brunch with friends is a fine way to banish those Sunday, end-of-the-weekend blues.

Brunch is also great for special occasions of every ilk and every size gathering. Sometimes it's planned and sometimes it's not: for example, New Year's Day versus when someone suddenly passes away. Brunch works whenever you want it to. It's your call when to serve it, and what to cook, and whether to offer the meal in a casual setting (like in bed), an elegant venue (a formally set dining table with a silver buffet service), or somewhere in between.

Though you never need an excuse to host a brunch, there are innumerable special occasions that are especially appropriate for serving a satisfying and varied group of dishes. It can be a rather intimate meal, much more so than a lunch or a dinner, so you may want to plan a Valentine's Day or birthday brunch. Before we were married, making brunch for my wife certainly helped draw attention away from my substantial list of flaws and cheflike personality blemishes, and it continues to help them matter less as time goes by. Not to say that cooking buttermilk pancakes for her means I get away with anything, but it doesn't hurt.

Brunch feels right when served on a breezy morning at the lake, high noon at the park, or when it's gray all day long on winter's first official snow day, when everyone's huddled inside by a fire. As a way to show off the fall harvest or the spring offerings at the farmers' market, this meal is also ideal. It goes without saying that a brunch to highlight a particular food—oysters, for instance, or crabs, or some tasty seasonal treat, such as rhubarb after a long winter of potatoes and squash—is certainly one of the more unique and special ways to entertain.

Those intending to spend a day of relaxation outside with friends and family may find brunch a more inviting and leisurely option than lunch. Home cooks in possession of a basket of fresh produce from local farmstands or neighbors with extra-bountiful gardens may want to invite guests to hang out in the backyard for a healthy vegetarian brunch with freshly grown produce as the centerpiece.

Many annual celebrations offer beautiful reasons to invite friends and family over for a brunch. You may want to plan an intimate New Year's Day brunch for just a few close friends, or a lavish Easter brunch for a crowd, or a Christmas brunch to set the festive tone for the day's excitement.

Some brunches take on a more serious tone and can offer comfort and solace to those in need. Following a funeral or during the period of sitting shiva, a brunch can be a wonderful way to feed those in mourning, and it's a much more personal way for family to spend time with one another than at a restaurant. And there are plenty of ways to prepare sustaining, substantial dishes that can sit for hours without your having to fuss over them.

Families get together for reasons both happy and sad, and a reunion can be one of the happiest (or the most annoying, depending on how you look at it). For a memorable meal to mark this event, a brunch offers something for everyone. It works especially well with a variety of dishes—some last-minute and others made ahead of time. The same principles apply for a bar mitzvah or a first communion brunch, or a brunch to celebrate a baby's christening or bris. These types of occasions can end up being more of a crowd than one might choose if only because of the family nature of them and the obligation to invite twenty people for fear of offending one of them (everyone has a cousin Mel or aunt Esther, right?).

The following twenty-five menus are the perfect way to mark a variety of special occasions. You can dou-

REMEMBER, THE BEAUTY OF BRUNCH IS ITS SPONTANEOUS NATURE.

ble, triple, or even split any of the recipes in half to accommodate the size of your crowd. Look through the various menu choices and feel free to mix and match items. In the absence of hard-and-fast rules and fussy formality, brunch is what you want it to be and, as such, will be dictated by your budget, personal time constraints, and the size of your kitchen. If you live in a teensy city apartment with a teensier kitchen, you obviously will want to pass on hosting a large holiday brunch. But that mini kitchen is just intimate enough to whip up a midnight brunch for two or even six, or to make a takeout picnic to enjoy in a sunny park or an impressive Mother's Day brunch for the immediate family. Add family and friends, and you've just cooked up the perfect meal.

MENUS

NEW YEAR'S DAY BRUNCH *(Ideal for serving 6 to 20)*

Welcome in the New Year with an eye-opening brunch that will appeal to everyone, regardless of how they spent the previous evening. Coffee is a must, as are Bloody Marys (page 245). Tradition has it that if you eat the southern-style black-eyed pea dish called Hoppin' John on New Year's Day, you'll have good luck all year long. This is a substantial brunch guaranteed to make guests feel better no matter what their post–New Year's Eve condition. Serve buffet style to allow guests to come and go as they please.

Apple Streusel Coffee Cake (page 63)

Sausage and Mushroom Casserole (page 107)

Bagels and Smoked Salmon–Scallion Cream Cheese (page 275)

Black-Eyed Peas and Andouille Sausage Hoppin' John (page 225)

Blood oranges and pineapples

Pitchers of Bloody Mary (page 245)

Why wait until dinnertime to tempt your sweetheart? Start the morning off with a romantic brunch for just the two of you, and you'll both be glowing for the rest of the day. Champagne and chocolate are front and center on this menu, which is make-ahead so you can devote your time to each other. A single beautiful rose in a bud vase makes a nice centerpiece, though it also looks nice on a tray if the two of you share this feast in bed. Have a box of your sweetheart's favorite chocolates on hand for dessert.

Strawberry Muffins (page 42) with butter and jam

Raisin Challah French Toast (page 132) with maple syrup

Pink Grapefruit and Champagne Cocktail (page 247)

French-pressed coffee (page 257)

✧ ✦ ✧

PANCAKE LOVER'S BRUNCH *(Ideal for serving 6 to 10)*

If your guests think of brunch as an excuse to eat pancakes, why bother with protein? Set out several different kinds of pancakes and accompany them with an assortment of home-made syrups, butters, and conserves. One of the brunches most eagerly anticipated by kids of all ages, this one needs little else except maybe a generous platter of maple-glazed slab bacon (page 177).

Potato Pancakes (page 213) with Pear Sauce (page 279)

Buckwheat Pancakes (page 125) with apples and maple syrup

Blueberry/Blackberry/Raspberry Buttermilk Pancakes (each separate or mix
    the berries and make mixed berry pancakes; page 121)

Maple-Glazed Bacon (page 177)

Chocolate Chip Silver Dollar Pancakes (page 120)

Mulled Spiced Cider (page 251)

OYSTER BREAKFAST: THE HANGTOWN FRY *(Ideal for serving 2 to 10)*

If you like the idea of a brunch that has an actual theme, why not transport your guests back to California during the gold rush, when this hearty meal was created? At the time, the man who requested it thought it was the most decadent breakfast imaginable. Even if your guests couldn't give a hang about history, it's difficult to go wrong with cornmeal-crusted fried oysters, paired with bacon and eggs. The Bubby's version of a Hangtown Fry also includes johnnycakes bursting with blueberries, and we glaze the bacon with maple syrup. This is a good brunch to plan on when you've got time to prepare the oysters to order, though some of the items can be made ahead of time.

Blueberry Johnnycakes (page 130)

Scrambled Eggs (page 75)

Cornmeal-Crusted Fried Oysters (page 197)

Maple-Glazed Bacon (page 177)

PICKLED AND SMOKED FISH BREAKFAST *(Ideal for serving 6 to 30)*

A bris is an important Jewish family occasion that calls for a traditional menu all the relatives will savor and appreciate. Arrange the pickled herrings in large bowls, garnish your homemade smoked salmon with lemon wedges and fresh dill sprigs, and pick up plenty of rye bread and assorted bagels to have on hand for the salmon and the smoked trout mousse.

Pickled herrings: in white sauce, in wine sauce, and matjes herring (page 196)

Thinly sliced homemade Smoked Salmon (page 191) with dill and lemon

Smoked Trout and Scallion Mousse (page 196)

Creamy Buttermilk New Potato Salad (page 223)

Dark rye toast, bagels, and cream cheese

Blood Orange Mimosas (page 246)

NEW GIRLFRIEND/BOYFRIEND/FRIEND BRUNCH *(Ideal for serving 2)*

First (and second) impressions really do count, so when you're new at a relationship and maybe even a little nervous cooking for the two of you, make a delicious statement with this fresh and fabulous menu. Keep the preparation stress-free by making the blackberry compote and fruit salad ahead of time, and whip up the pancake batter in advance, too. The coffee ice cubes in the iced coffee definitely must be made the day before. All you need to do once that very special guest rings the bell is make the pancakes and sprinkle them with confectioners' sugar. It doesn't get any sweeter than this.

German Skillet-Baked Pancakes (page 129) with lemon, confectioners' sugar,

and Blackberry Compote (page 276)

Fruit Salad with Lemon–Poppy Dipping Sauce (page 229)

Sweet Italian sausage links (page 175)

Brewed iced coffee with coffee ice cubes (page 259)

HONEYMOON BREAKFAST *(Ideal for serving 2)*

You'll be cooking together for a lifetime, but the beautiful beginning of your marriage is an ideal time to start preparing and sharing really romantic brunches. The strategy behind a perfect honeymoon brunch is that it should be ready quickly, since you may have other things in mind. This one doesn't take long at all to prepare—three-minute eggs really are ready in three minutes. If you make the crêpes the day before and keep them in the refrigerator, the vegetable and cheese crêpes take just a few minutes. To finish off, slice and get ready your fruit offerings while the crêpes are warming up, and have plenty of fresh coffee on hand. This meal is best eaten in bed, with no interruptions.

Three-Minute Eggs (page 75) on buttered sourdough toast

Crêpes with Zucchini, Spinach, and Onions (page 143)

Sliced Melon and Raspberries with Port Syrup (page 228)

Blood Orange Mimosas (page 246)

MEMORIAL BRUNCH FOLLOWING A FUNERAL *(Ideal for serving 4 to 60)*

During difficult times, family and friends feel cherished when a carefully chosen buffet of homemade food is at the ready to nourish and to comfort. It's so much more personal than being at a noisy restaurant and it can help lift everyone's spirits as you all gather together. What's very nice about this meal is that it can be assembled well in advance and served when your guests are ready. It's an eclectic menu with a little something for everyone. Since none of the dishes are difficult to make, it's easy to pull this meal together during a stressful period.

Apple Streusel Coffee Cake (page 63)

Savory Bacon and Cheese Bread Pudding (page 112)

Assorted sandwiches

Creamy Buttermilk New Potato Salad (page 223)

Fruit Salad with Lemon–Poppy Dipping Sauce (page 229)

Assorted cookies

FRESH CRAB BREAKFAST *(Ideal for serving 4 to 10)*

An elegant brunch for a very special occasion, this is a beautiful menu to feature in spring-time when asparagus is in season. It's delicious with crusty sourdough toast. Because all the components of the menu will hold for a little while, this works well as a buffet. Consider serving this outside on a patio, or poolside, or at a beach house. It's festive and yet sophisticated, just the right offerings for when you're having guests you need to impress.

Scrambled Eggs (page 75)

Crispy Crab Cakes (page 198)

Asparagus Potato Hash (page 210)

Blood Orange Mimosas (page 246)

EASTER BRUNCH *(Ideal for serving 10 to 20)*

Besides visits to church, Easter is also marked by egg hunts, parades to show off bonnets and other finery, and baskets filled with chocolate and jelly beans for the kids. Follow it all up with a lavish brunch that's not too trying on the cook. For a perfect feast, a smoked ham accompanied by a frittata filled with seasonal vegetables is easy and perfect for a larger gathering. Both cream biscuits and silver dollar pancakes are popular with kids on sugar overload, and the rhubarb coffee cake, served with plenty of coffee, makes a not-too-sweet dessert for grown-ups. Take advantage of spring flowers by using them in table centerpieces, and offer a guests a celebratory mimosa as they arrive.

Rhubarb Coffee Cake (page 65)

Bubby's Variation on Mr. Beard's Cream Biscuits (page 54)

Maple-Glazed Smoked Ham (page 187)

Roasted Asparagus and Leek Frittata (page 96)

Chocolate Chip Silver Dollar Pancakes (page 120)

BIRTHDAY BRUNCH *(Ideal for serving 6 to 12)*

You can never have too many candles at a birthday bash, so why not start and finish this brunch by having the guest of honor blow out the candles twice? In between the muffins and the guest's favorite birthday cake is a power brunch: steak and eggs. The port syrup for the fruit can be made ahead of time, leaving you with plenty of time to lavish on the birthday girl or boy.

Blueberry Muffins (page 37)

Gingered Sweet Potato Home Fries (page 215)

Roasted New York Strip Steak (page 190) and eggs

Sliced mixed melons with Port Syrup (page 228)

Lemon–Poppy Seed Cake (page 66) with candles

✧ ✦ ✧

SPRINGTIME IN THE PARK BRUNCH *(Ideal for serving 2 to 6)*

That first unseasonably and unexpectedly warm day is always a cause for celebration, and what better way to put some spring into your step than with an alfresco brunch? Keep things simple with sandwiches and homemade granola with a berry topping. Pack sandwiches, loosely covered, in an insulated hamper and pack the topping separately from the granola so the granola stays nice and crunchy. Thermoses come in handy for drinks, and don't forget a Frisbee!

Creamy Buttermilk New Potato Salad (page 223)

Cucumber and tomato salad

Open-Face Grilled Chicken, Maytag Blue Cheese, and Toasted Pecan Sandwiches (page 156)

Fruity Clafouti (page 113)

CINCO DE MAYO BRUNCH *(Ideal for serving 4 to 10)*

Brunches with a theme are always fun, and this is no exception, because Mexican fare by nature is casual, flexible, and universally appealing. You can make the dishes ahead of time and serve them buffet-style. Even the sangría can be served in big pitchers, so your guests can help themselves. To create a festive mood, put on some mariachi music and get out your most colorful serving dishes.

Huevos Rancheros (page 111)

Chorizo sausages (page 79)

Home Fries with Peppers (page 209)

Watermelon Lemonade (*Jugo de Sandía*) (page 242)

Sangría (page 248)

FIRST COMMUNION BRUNCH *(Ideal for serving 6 to 20)*

Once Mass is over and everyone changes out of their church clothes, it's time for a family-centered celebration guaranteed to please guests ages three to ninety-three. Arrange this feast on a table spread with a white cloth and let guests help themselves. Cut the zucchini bread and coffee cake into small squares and arrange them in napkin-lined baskets. Pour the beverage into pretty glass pitchers and let everyone help him- or herself while waiting for the salads and omelets to be ready.

Zucchini Bread with Zucchini Flowers (page 48)

Roasted Pear and Goat Cheese Omelets (page 89)

Crab Salad (page 199)

Creamy sliced Brie with sourdough baguette toast

Apple Streusel Coffee Cake (page 63)

Cantaloupe skewers tossed in Port Syrup (page 228)

Cranberry and Lime Press (page 239)

EARLY-SUMMER FARMERS' MARKET BRUNCH *(Ideal for serving 6 to 20)*

How to structure a brunch that celebrates the bounty of the farmers' market will depend upon the season. In this case, the flavors to be showcased are at their best in early June. Wait to plan your menu until after you've strolled through the stalls, taking a look at what's fresh and beautiful and bursting with flavor. Figure that you'll want to serve one egg dish, a muffin or quick bread filled with fresh fruit or berries, and maybe an omelet or frittata featuring in-season vegetables. (Make the omelets ahead to serve at room temperature.) This menu works beautifully in a picnic or beach venue, so throw a red checked tablecloth and some sturdy flatware into an insulated cooler and head outside.

Strawberry Rhubarb Muffins (page 42)

Ramp (or leek) and goat cheese scramble (page 99)

Butter and Parsley Potatoes (page 222)

Sourdough baguette toast with roasted spring garlic

Fresh strawberries

Pink Lemonade Cosmopolitans (page 248)

GRADUATION BRUNCH *(Ideal for serving 6 to 20)*

You're justifiably proud of your little scholar, whether he or she is graduating from kinder-garten or law school. If your buffet brunch is following on the heels of one of those marathon, many-hours-long ceremonies, everyone is sure to be famished, so plan to serve a filling meal of casual dishes that guests can eat sitting or standing up as soon as you get home. In order to mingle and enjoy everyone's company yourself, prepare the brunch ahead of time and just warm everything up at the last minute. Don't forget a special cake to honor your star student.

Blackberry Corn Muffins (page 39)

Spinach and Brie Omelet (page 83)

Roasted new potatoes with rosemary and sea salt

Mixed Greens with Shallot Vinaigrette (page 169)

Chocolate and Sautéed Banana Crêpes (page 145)

Fruit Salad with Lemon–Poppy Dipping Sauce (page 229)

MOTHER'S DAY BRUNCH *(Ideal for serving 4 to 12)*

The one day of the year that Mom vacates the kitchen is a fine occasion for you to show how much you love her by whipping up her favorite dishes. Since most moms like to pick at, rather than to finish off, one heavy main course, offer a selection of small bites. Cut the fruit-filled coffee cake into small pieces so that it's nearly bite size, and make the delectable chocolate pancakes into silver dollar size. To tempt Mom out of bed with this meal, put fresh flowers and candles on the table and set the table with fine dishes. It's your once-a-year chance to spoil the woman who loved you first.

Rhubarb Coffee Cake (page 65)

Chocolate Chip Silver Dollar Pancakes (page 120)

Smoked Salmon and Goat Cheese Roses (page 193)

Fruit Salad with Lemon–Poppy Dipping Sauce (page 229)

Rose Hip and Mint Arnold Palmers (page 243)

FATHER'S DAY BRUNCH *(Ideal for serving 4 to 12)*

This is a manly feast for a guy who may love commandeering the grill later on in the afternoon, but who wants to savor the first meal of the day with his family. The options here are meaty enough to please any dad, but they include lighter dishes for the rest of the family, too. Since the homemade corned beef takes some time to make from scratch (up to a week), be sure to plan far enough in advance. Dad will be impressed. This is a nice menu to serve outside at the picnic table or after Dad returns from an early-morning fishing trip, run, or round of golf on his special day.

Blueberry Muffins (page 37)

Deviled Eggs (page 78)

Homemade Corned Beef Hash (page 183)

Asparagus with Orange Vinaigrette (page 291)

Buttery thick-cut sourdough toast

POST-SLEEPOVER BRUNCH FOR TEENS *(Ideal for serving 4 to 10)*

The day after a sleepover party, expect big appetites and satisfy everyone with a super-easy brunch. (You may not be feeling too frisky yourself, depending upon at what time—or whether—the kids fell asleep.) So do yourself a favor and have this menu prepped by making the waffle batter ahead, baking the muffins, and having the bacon all glazed and ready to pop into the oven. Here's one occasion where it's probably fine to let everyone watch TV during the meal.

Blackberry Corn Muffins (page 39)

Eggs in the Hole ("One-Eyed Sailors") (page 76)

Blueberry Buttermilk Waffles (page 135) with blackberry syrup

   (Black and Blue Waffles) (page 282)

Maple-Glazed Bacon (page 177)

Assorted fresh juices (page 238)

Fresh Fruit Salad (page 229)

VEGETARIAN BRUNCH *(Ideal for serving 2 to 12)*

If it sometimes seems as if half your friends are vegetarians, invite them all over for a meat-free feast that won't have anyone missing the bacon. Here's the chance to turn an abundant supply of fresh seasonal produce into a giant and colorful frittata. Most vegetarians love salads and, depending on the number of guests, you may want to serve two or three different kinds. Though salads must be tossed at the last minute, the greens can be washed and crisped ahead of time, and the dressings can be made and refrigerated up to three days in advance.

Cranberry-Pecan Scones (page 51) with fresh fruit jam

Farmer's Frittata (page 92)

Smothered Hash Browns with local Cheddar and onions (page 211)

Green Goddess Salad (page 167)

Local yogurt with fresh berry compote (page 276)

Fruit Salad with Lemon–Poppy Dipping Sauce (page 229)

Seven-grain toast

It's amazing what an appetite you can work up in the wee hours. This menu, elegant but not fussy, is perfect for a couple. Serve it on a candlelit table, on the sofa, or even on the floor; switch on some soft music; and be prepared to sleep late the next day. With a feast like this, you won't feel the need for an early breakfast.

Tomato Eggs in the Hole (page 76)

Maple-Glazed Bacon (page 177)

Buttery crusty toast

Fresh peaches, strawberries, and raspberries in Lemon Syrup (page 282)

Cranmosas (page 247)

FAMILY REUNION BRUNCH *(Ideal for serving 6 to 40)*

When three or four generations of one family meet for a meal, the best choice for a crowd-pleasing menu is comfort food, and plenty of it. That means old-fashioned dishes like deviled eggs and potato pancakes, along with some homemade breads and muffins and make-ahead casseroles. Most reunions are in the summer, in which case great pitchers of watermelon lemonade will keep guests happy and hydrated.

Orange Chocolate Chip Muffins (page 41)

Crawfish Deviled Eggs (page 78)

Bacon, Leek, and Onion Casserole (page 105)

Potato Pancakes (page 213) with homemade Applesauce (page 279)

Whole Grain Banana Bread (page 46)

Iced coffee with Coffee Ice Cubes (page 259)

Icy Watermelon Lemonade (page 242)

FALL HARVEST BRUNCH *(Ideal for serving 4 to 12)*

On a perfect, crisp autumn day, start guests off with apple cider and fresh coffee, along with small wedges of aromatic apple coffee cake. Other fall fruits—pears and pumpkins—are nicely showcased in homemade waffles, and the omelet has a welcome kick to it. If the day is mild, you could turn this meal into an alfresco brunch and take advantage of one of the season's last outdoor dining opportunities. Otherwise, serve indoors and plan on a brisk postbrunch walk to crunch through the falling leaves, and maybe organize a game of touch football on the lawn.

Apple Streusel Coffee Cake (page 63)

Pumpkin Waffles (page 138) with Cinnamon Pear Compote (page 277)

Venison Sausages (page 185)

Apple, Cheddar, and Bacon Omelet (page 88)

Mulled Spiced Cider (page 251)

CHRISTMAS DAY BRUNCH *(Ideal for serving 6 to 12)*

The time between when you unwrap the gifts and dinner is perfectly suited to a festive holiday brunch, preferably one that could be prepared mostly ahead of time. With the exception of the sweet potato home fries, just about all these dishes can be made on Christmas Eve. In fact, the batter for the waffles *must* be made the night before. Eat this meal in front of a cozy fire, in pajamas if you are so inclined, and savor each moment of this most special of holidays. Brew plenty of coffee for the grown-ups and offer rich hot chocolate for the kids (marshmallows are optional), and everyone can enjoy the eggnog.

Banana and Cranberry Bran Muffins (page 44)

Sizzling Ham and Gruyère Omelet (page 82)

Yeasted Buckwheat Waffles (page 136)

Assorted pickled herrings (page 196) and toasts

Gingered Sweet Potato Home Fries (page 215)

Warm Eggnog (page 252)

SNOW DAY BRUNCH *(Ideal for serving 2 to 10)*

Brighten those unexpected and eagerly anticipated days off with a brunch that takes the chill away. After a morning of sledding, ice skating, and snow shoveling, everyone has worked up a ravenous appetite. This buffet is a spirit-lifting, energizing meal that can be made with just a few additions to what you probably already have in your cupboards. If the roads are too impassable for you to go out for ingredients, make some creative substitutions. You can always serve plain scones rather than apricot ones, and replace strawberry butter with cinnamon butter. Hot chocolate is essential, and it's easy to make if you've got cinnamon and heavy cream on hand.

Apricot Scones (page 52) with Strawberry Butter (page 271)

Sizzling Ham and Cheddar Scramble (page 97)

Classic French Toast (page 131) with Maple Butter (page 274)

Serious Hot Chocolate (page 249)

Hot Rum Toddy (page 254)

HOW TO PLAN AND PULL OFF THE PERFECT BRUNCH

Whether you're serving two or twenty, whether your kitchen is the size of a broom closet or a state-of-the-art chef's paradise with an eight-burner stove and Sub-Zero refrigerator, the key to a successful brunch is to have a plan. Not that it can't change, but if you have a basic strategy, from shopping to cooking to serving, you'll have fun, which is what brunch is about. Your guests take their mood cue from you, so if you are having a good time, they will, too. (Both good and bad moods are infectious, so you want to be calm and relaxed.) Before you even get started, here are some questions to ask yourself.

How many guests do I want to have?

Sometimes, the number of guests is decided for you—as when you host a family function and it's not so easy to leave anyone out. Other times, it's up to you whether to keep it intimate or make it big. Though you can't squeeze two dozen people into a four-hundred-square-foot studio apartment, you can have a big party by taking it outside to the roof, a park, a beach, or a patio—even to someone else's house in some instances.

What time of day works best?

If you're the kind of person who doesn't really get moving until you've been up for a couple of hours, you'll probably want to invite guests to come slightly later than if you're a morning person who's organized, motivated, and focused at sunrise. We can hope your guests will be on time, but that's a subject for a different book.

How can I keep from getting stressed out?

Planning and flexibility are key. You can mix and match, not be locked into appetizers and main courses, and change or add to a menu at will. That said, brunch still calls for some organization. Think about how each item will be cooked or prepared. Consider how many things you can make ahead of time and how many things you will have to do once your guests arrive. When cooking for a lot of people, it's best to have everything on the menu in a state of readiness so all you need to do is heat things up. Or, if you are so inclined, leave one thing to the end, like pancakes. If you prefer to be completely finished with the heavy cooking, you can still choose something like French toast, which keeps well in a 200°F oven.

If you're making omelets that call for some pretty intense hands-on time right before you eat, make sure guests have something to snack on while they wait. This could be a basket of muffins and quick breads that you've baked ahead (and even frozen and rewarmed) or a fruit salad or berries with a dipping sauce. And keep in mind that the ingredients of most omelets make great frittatas or casseroles, which are easier to prep in advance than cooking omelets to order.

What if my kitchen is tiny?

If you've got a small space to work in, just tailor the menu to fit. Plan one dish that needs to be baked and one that can be done on the stove top. Bake muffins a couple days ahead of time and freeze them. Frozen muffins heat up in a preheated 300°F oven, and they taste almost as good as freshly baked ones.

What are some of my options if I'm on a tight budget?

It's no fun making a brunch if you know you're spending money that you don't have. So decide in advance what you can afford and plan your menu around that amount. Fortunately, many quintessential brunch items are also very affordable. Eggs, for instance, are a low-cost item that can be whipped up into everything from omelets to frittatas. Home-made muffins and quick breads take minimal time to prepare, and they also start with in-gredients that are definitely budget friendly. And if you think seasonally when deciding what fruits and vegetables to serve, you'll not only have a brunch that is affordable, but one that features great-tasting dishes. That's because seasonal food, grown locally, tends to be fresher. To keep from overspending, you may want to avoid serving dishes that feature meat and fish as the main course. But even if you have to forgo New York strip steak or a platter of homemade smoked salmon, you can still use meat and seafood in small amounts. For instance, Smoked Salmon and Goat Cheese Roses (page 193) uses just four ounces of salmon to make a dozen beautiful appetizers.

How many dishes should I offer in total?

There's no set rule here, which means that you should plan on whatever number of dishes you feel most comfortable with. One strategy that makes your life as a brunch chef a lot easier, especially if you have a small oven, is to plan for some hot dishes, some cold dishes, and some room temperature dishes. This is much easier than it sounds. A salad could serve as the cold dish, and it could be prepped in advance and refrigerated. The oven could be reserved for making one hot dish, say, a frittata or a casserole. And your room tempera-ture dish could be the muffins or rolls that you made the day before. Not only does taking temperature into account help you maximize your kitchen space, it also keeps the brunch menu more interesting.

Are there any parts of the brunch preparation that really have to be done at the last minute?

Yes, but not to worry. There isn't so much last-minute work that you'll end up feeling overwhelmed. And most of the prep can be done in advance, leaving you feeling relaxed and ready to meet your guests. An hour or so before people come is a good time to start reheating any dishes that you've made ahead of time, and you can also slice and arrange quick breads at this point. Butter and preserves can be put into the appropriate dishes and arranged on the table. Right before serving, toss salads with dressings, slice meats and arrange them on platters, and make coffee so it'll be freshly brewed.

COOKING FOR A CROWD

The space issue is prime among many considerations when you're called upon to cook for a crowd. If you're cooking for thirty people and you don't have adequate refrigerator space, steer clear of foods that spoil quickly while at room temperature. Summertime is more difficult than winter for easily spoiled foods because the bacteria count in the air is much higher in the summer than in the winter. It is important to think of safety first when cooking. And avoid making dishes that call for a couple hours' chilling time when your fridge is already full of other dishes that need to stay cold.

If your stove is small, you can increase your heating capacity by simultaneously using the stove top, the oven, the microwave, and maybe an electric griddle (for pancakes), waffle iron (waffles), and electric skillet (sausages, bacon, and fried sandwiches).

Always make a checklist for prep and service. There is nothing worse than buying ingredients and forgetting to prepare them, except maybe preparing something and forgetting to serve it. I have done this more than twice . . . and I'm still mad about it.

In order to have a stress-free meal, refer to the following questions and answers to help you plan a foolproof brunch for a large group.

Should I have a buffet and, if so, what are the best foods to serve?

A buffet works well when you're serving many, but take into consideration the fact that guests may need to balance plates on their laps and serve foods that are easy to handle, as opposed to too saucy or messy. Foods that require little or no cutting are ideal for big groups.

For the most attractive presentation, plan to have two platters for each dish you are serving. As one platter becomes empty, fix the next one and quickly switch them. A full platter of food just looks more appetizing than a half-full platter.

Where will everyone sit?

Think about seating arrangements in advance and have a chair (or a spot on the floor) for everyone. It doesn't have to be fancy, but ideally there should be a place to sit for each and every guest, even at a buffet.

What are some dishes that work really well for a crowd?
Which should I avoid?

Casseroles work well because they can be made in advance and reheated. A large platter of sandwiches can be prepared in advance and kept, loosely wrapped in waxed paper, until it's time for brunch. And recipes for some of Bubby's salads can be doubled or tripled (even octupled) for a crowd. Take into consideration the seating arrangements when you plan a brunch menu. If your guests will be sitting around with plates on their laps, don't prepare dishes that involve a lot of meat cutting. Keep it simple, so guests will feel comfortable. Doing this is also great for minimizing spillage in your living room.

What drinks work well for a large gathering?

Here's one area where just about everything can be done in advance. Squeeze the fruit juices up to a day ahead of time and keep them refrigerated. Make Bloody Marys or other cocktails in large pitchers so guests can help themselves.

What equipment will I need to use in order to serve lots of guests?

Make a checklist well in advance, so you'll be sure to have on hand platters, large serving spoons, big bowls, and plenty of glasses, napkins, plates, and silverware. If you have more guests than you do place settings, don't be afraid to use good, solid paper plates and plastic serving utensils. If you don't like paper plates, don't be shy about asking to borrow plates from a friend or relative, or even some of your guests. If you're having a really big party, consider renting some of the essentials, or even everything you need. One good thing about rentals is that everything can be returned unwashed.

Can I have a buffet and still use the same table to seat guests?

If you've decided to have your brunch be buffet style, make sure everything can be eaten with a fork or is "finger food." Arrange drinks at a separate table that is large enough to hold an ice bucket, glasses, and garnishes such as orange and lemon wedges, in addition to the beverages. Assuming you are having a larger buffet, you might want to orchestrate a two-sided buffet line so guests can move through more quickly. This eliminates having guests wait in one long, slow line while their friends are already seated and enjoying their food. If you have only one big table and plan to use it as both a buffet and dining table, either plan to have everything in the middle, family style, or all on one side, leaving the other side available for a first round of seating. Then, clear the buffet so the rest of your guests can sit down on the other side of the table.

What if I don't have giant serving platters?

You don't have to go out and buy colossal platters and serving dishes. Instead, plan to portion the food onto two smaller platters or dinner plates. Keep an eye on the food, and when it looks as if it needs replenishing, just replace the nearly empty one with the full one. If you're having a sit-down affair, consider whether the platter you're planning on using is too heavy to be passed around.

Whom can I get to help cook? Serve? Clean up?

Plan your time well. It takes twice as long to prepare six leeks as three leeks, to peel twelve apples rather than six, and to peel two pounds of carrots rather than one pound. That's not to say that you can't do it, but be aware that it will take extra time, so plan for this or ask for help. You may want to enlist the assistance of a good friend who can help with the cooking, and a couple of other friends who wouldn't mind hanging around to help with the cleanup.

EQUIPMENT

Having the right equipment is most important for making the cook's life easier. Here's a guide to some of the basics to have on hand.

BAKING PANS: Since you'll be whipping up muffins, quick breads, and biscuits, be sure you have two loaf pans (9 x 5 x 3 inches is the most common size), along with standard 12-cup muffin tins, 9-inch layer cake pans, and a 9- or 10-inch pie plate.

FOOD PROCESSOR: You will use this kitchen staple for sauces, doughs, purées, soups, and more. Food processors come in various sizes, from 2 cups to 6 quarts. Get one that holds at least 7 cups.

GADGETS: A sturdy box grater for cheese, a vegetable peeler, a zester for removing zest in long ribbons from citrus fruit, a timer, an instant-read thermometer, brushes for spreading butter and oil, a rolling pin for dough, a salad spinner, measuring spoons and cups, a slotted spoon, a ladle, and rubber and silicone spatulas. If possible, have an offset spatula for loosening quick breads and cakes and a standard spatula for flipping omelets, French toast, and pancakes.

GRIDDLE: I like using an 18-inch rectangular cast-iron griddle.

KNIVES: You don't need a huge repertoire, but plan to have a good 8-inch chef's knife, a paring knife for trimming and peeling, and a serrated bread knife. Stainless steel is good because it's durable, it keeps an edge, it's easy to clean, and it's easy to sharpen.

MIXER: A stand mixer is especially helpful when it comes to baking. If you don't have one, you can get away with a less powerful but more portable handheld mixer. Both mixers make whipping up muffins, cakes, and cookies simple.

MIXING BOWLS: These are cheap and easy to stack. I like to use stainless steel, but glass bowls would work well, too. Make sure to have several in different sizes.

STOCK POTS: A 6- to 8-quart stainless steel pot can be used for everything from making stock to blanching lots of vegetables.

SAUCEPANS: A set of three saucepans (1-quart, 1½-quart, and 3-quart) should meet most of your needs. Avoid uncoated aluminum pots since the metal can react with acidic ingredients as you cook.

SKILLETS: A 10-inch skillet and a 12-inch skillet are really essential, and a nonstick 8-inch skillet is incredibly handy for making egg dishes including omelets. The skillets themselves can be made of various materials. The nonstick heavy-duty aluminum cookware is durable and easy to care for, but stainless steel with a layer of copper or aluminum is even better—though pricier. Cast-iron skillets have their place, though you wouldn't want to use them for everything because they are quite heavy.

WHISK: You will use it constantly for everything from beating egg whites to combining ingredients in a batter.

BAKED TREATS:
QUICK BREADS, MUFFINS, SCONES, AND MORE

When I was a boy, the smell of freshly baked blueberry muffins was enough to send me sprinting into the kitchen. Not much has changed now: The aroma of just-out-of-the-oven muffins is the first thing I smell every morning when I come to work at Bubby's, and I can't get through the door fast enough.

A basket filled with warm muffins, plump scones, and slices of a flavorful, buttery quick bread is the ideal way to begin a brunch. It holds the promise of dishes to come, teasing the appetite without leaving one fully sated. On occasion, of course, these treats could make a light breakfast on their own, accompanied by freshly brewed coffee or a fragrant pot of tea, some homemade preserves, and some fresh fruit.

The cream biscuits featured in this chapter can be split and used for strawberry shortcake, placed atop a sweet or savory cobbler, or served for breakfast alongside eggs. The basis for my all-time favorite biscuit is actually borrowed from James Beard, the dean of American cookery, known for his truly superior biscuits, which he made with heavy cream. They're also easy because there's no cutting in butter or fat: The cream has all the fat you need.

When breads are leavened with baking powder and/or baking soda rather than yeast, they are called quick breads, simply because they're much faster to prepare than yeast-raised breads. They're also a lot easier: no waiting around for the dough to rise; no need to spend time kneading, shaping, and baking loaves. Quick breads typically are mixed in one bowl and take no more than about ten minutes to assemble. There's not too much effort involved: Sugar and butter are creamed, then flour, baking soda, and baking powder are added, along with oil or butter, milk, and usually a fruit (and sometimes a vegetable). Nuts and dried fruits can really enhance muffins and quick breads, too, adding texture, intense pockets of flavor, and many a grandma's "secret ingredient goodness." Usually baked in a loaf pan, quick breads can also be baked in round or square ones. If you're new to baking, quick breads and muffins are an ideal place to start because they're simple to mix up, and the results are always delectable and appreciated.

At Bubby's, we serve a selection of quick breads, including an unusual Zucchini Bread with Zucchini Flowers (page 48) and Pumpkin Spice Bread (page 50). Every diner who sits down at Bubby's is offered a basket filled with our Honey Jalapeño Corn Bread (page 49). Served with your brunch at home, this corn bread will be a hit. It goes perfectly with savory omelets and frittatas and has a little bit of heat that's balanced by sweetness.

Try topping these baked goods with Strawberry or Blackberry Butter (page 271), or your own homemade jams and preserves. Either way, the selection of Bubby's fresh-from-the-oven treats offered here will start off brunch with a very special touch.

Muffins are quick breads baked into individual portions and are also wonderful served with spreads like freshly made preserves, nice soft butter, or flavored butter such as Maple Butter (page 274) or Apple Butter (page 272), which is not butter at all, but rather a cooked-down essence of the fruit with a heightened concentration of flavor. These single-serving treats are ideal for busy brunch hosts because they take just minutes to stir together and minutes to bake, and they are a welcoming sight (and smell) for your guests as they arrive.

ALL OF THESE BAKED TREATS ARE GOOD ON THEIR OWN, BUT IF YOU WANT TO PUSH IT OVER THE TOP, TRY THEM WITH FRESH PRESERVES OR A SWEET FRUIT BUTTER.

Though quick breads may be about as simple as baking gets, there are a few tricks of the trade that will ensure that your baked goods emerge from the oven perfectly moist, flavorful, and light. Some of the recipes call for sifted flour, which aerates the mixture and can make for a lighter crumb. Combine dry and wet ingredients only until blended. The secret to tender muffins is to beat the batter less, not more. If you are too heavy-handed with your mixing, you may end up with a quick bread that is oily and dense, coarse and flat. A standard muffin tin holds twelve muffins. Whether you use fluted paper baking cups or greased tins is up to you. Muffins baked in paper baking cups will stay fresh a little longer. Still, the best time to eat a muffin is when it is warm from the oven.

Most quick breads are leavened with baking powder, so it's important that yours is fresh. To be sure, date the can when you buy it and toss it after six months. Sometimes quick breads rely on baking soda or a combination of baking soda and baking powder in order to rise. Whenever you use baking soda, you need an acid ingredient, too, such as yogurt, sour cream, or buttermilk to help activate it. When combined with one of these ingredients, the baking soda foams up and helps the bread rise. Baking powder is baking soda with cream of tartar. The cream of tartar is an acidifying agent that helps the baking soda react with liquid.

Nuts and dried fruit have a couple of functions in quick breads and muffins: They provide flavor, of course, but they also offer texture, a little moisture, and a wonder-inspiring surprise. Most nuts and dried fruits are interchangeable, so if a recipe calls for pecans and you've got only walnuts in the cupboard, use the walnuts instead. Dried cranberries, dried apricots, or dried sour cherries can be used in place of raisins, or you can use chopped dates as well.

Quick bread batter is typically spooned into a cake pan, loaf pan, or muffin pans (if using a muffin pan, use a ¼ cup ice cream scoop to evenly and neatly distribute the batter among the cups). Be sure to grease (and flour if directed) the pans in order to prevent the breads and muffins from sticking. And though you may be tempted to fill a loaf pan three-quarters full so you'll get an impressively sized loaf, just fill it two-thirds of the way up with batter. More batter than this may mean an unpleasant overflow into the oven (not fun to clean up) or a loaf that's underdone in the middle and dry and tough at the edges.

Bake quick breads and muffins on a rack set in the middle of the oven, and make sure the oven is preheated before you slide in the pans. Rotating the pan two-thirds of the way through the baking also helps to ensure even browning. Even convection ovens have hot spots, so know your oven!

You'll notice that a typical quick bread emerges from the oven practically doubled in volume from how it went in. And it may have a crack across the top, which is caused by steam escaping but is certainly nothing to worry about.

Baked quick breads may be frozen for up to three months. Be sure to use freezer-quality resealable plastic bags or plastic wrap, which are best at keeping out the air. Reheated in a 300°F oven for a few minutes, quick breads taste as delicious as when first baked.

Scones, once relegated to afternoon tea, are a brunch essential. These tender, biscuit-like pastries can be plain or flecked with chocolate chips, assorted fruits, or cheeses. I like to use cream in our scones so that they are richly dense inside and crisp and golden on top.

The scones and muffins in this chapter are versatile enough to change with the season: Fresh blueberries can easily be exchanged for raspberries, raisins, or chocolate chips; rhubarb can be combined with strawberries or blackberries in a recipe. Having the kind of flexibility these breads offer keeps things interesting all year round. Try out various combinations of butters and preserves to serve alongside.

When you make a batch of scones, be sure not to overmix the dough once you add the liquid, which may be heavy cream or sour cream. That's the best way I know to avoid leaden lumpy scones. The dough can be either patted out and cut with a dough cutter, biscuit style, or it may be formed into a round disk, then scored and cut into triangular wedges. You can also make free-form scones by mounding the dough with your hands, which is how we do it at Bubby's. It really depends on how refined you like your scones to look. We like to keep things rustic, but you may want a more polished end result. Either way, you'll end up with something delicious.

WHETHER HOME STYLE OR REFINED, ALL OF BUBBY'S BAKED GOODS ARE CROWD PLEASERS THAT WILL GIVE A VERY WELCOME TOUCH OF SWEETNESS TO YOUR BRUNCH.

BLUEBERRY MUFFINS

MAKES 16 MUFFINS

These classic muffins are simple to make and taste great with just about any brunch dish. They have a generous proportion of berries to batter, which makes them extra appealing. Use fresh blueberries picked at the peak of the season or frozen ones that you were smart enough to pop into the freezer when they were abundant in the summer. You can also use good-quality store-bought frozen berries. Frozen berries tend to be juicy and very flavorful because they are picked and flash-frozen on the spot. These muffins freeze well and can be rewarmed in a 250°F oven for 15 minutes or so. They are delicious plain or with fresh fruit preserves.

2½ cups all-purpose flour	3 extra-large eggs, at room
½ teaspoon baking soda	temperature
½ teaspoon kosher salt	1½ teaspoons pure vanilla extract
12 tablespoons (1½ sticks) unsalted	1 cup sour cream
butter, at room temperature	¼ cup milk
1½ cups sugar	2 cups fresh or frozen blueberries

1. Position an oven rack in the middle of the oven. Preheat the oven to 350°F. Line two standard muffin pans with 16 paper baking cups or lightly butter the muffin cups.

2. Combine the flour, baking soda, and salt in a large bowl and set aside.

3. Using a mixer set on high speed, cream the butter and sugar in a medium mixing bowl for about 3 minutes, or until light and fluffy. Beat in the eggs, one at a time, beating well after each addition. Add the vanilla, sour cream, and milk and beat until well combined.

4. Turn the mixer to low and combine the flour mixture with the butter mixture, beating just until incorporated, with no streaks of flour remaining. Gently fold in the blueberries with a rubber spatula or wooden spoon.

5. Spoon the batter evenly among the muffin cups, filling them two-thirds full. Bake the muffins for 20 to 25 minutes, or until the tops spring back when pressed lightly and a toothpick inserted into the center comes out clean.

6. Remove the muffins from the oven and allow to cool in the pan for 5 minutes. Remove the muffins from the pan, transfer to a wire rack, and allow to cool for 15 minutes.

CORN MUFFINS

MAKES 20 MUFFINS

Buttermilk gives these muffins a tender crumb and light texture, and they really need no accompaniment—though they're even more irresistible topped with butter or one of the delicious flavored butters in the Toppings and Sauces chapter. If you like a fruity muffin, add fresh raspberries or any other berry, and for a cheese flavor, stir in grated sharp white Cheddar (see variations). You can also add a zing by adding black pepper or jalapeño peppers.

2 cups all-purpose flour	¾ cup sugar
1 cup cornmeal	2 extra-large eggs, at room
1½ tablespoons baking powder	temperature
½ teaspoon kosher salt	1¼ cups buttermilk
½ pound (2 sticks) unsalted butter, at room temperature	

1. Position an oven rack in the middle of the oven. Preheat the oven to 350°F. Line two standard muffin pans with 20 paper baking cups or lightly butter the muffin cups.

2. Combine the flour, cornmeal, baking powder, and salt in a large bowl and set aside.

3. Using a mixer set on high speed, cream the butter and sugar in a medium mixing bowl for about 5 minutes, or until light and fluffy. Beat in the eggs, one at a time, beating well after each addition.

4. Turn the mixer to low and combine the flour mixture with the butter mixture in three additions, alternating with the buttermilk; beat just until incorporated, with no streaks of flour remaining.

5. Spoon the batter into the muffin cups, filling them two-thirds full. Bake the muffins for 20 to 25 minutes, or until the tops spring back when pressed lightly and a toothpick inserted into the center comes out clean.

6. Remove the muffins from the oven and allow to cool in the pan for 5 minutes. Remove the muffins from the pan, transfer to a wire rack, and allow to cool for 15 minutes.

CHEDDAR CHEESE CORN MUFFINS VARIATION: Add 1 cup grated sharp white Cheddar cheese to the batter after all the other ingredients have been combined.

RASPBERRY CORN MUFFINS VARIATION: Add 1 cup fresh or frozen raspberries to the batter after all the other ingredients have been combined.

BLACKBERRY CORN MUFFINS

MAKES 12 MUFFINS

*J*uicy blackberries garnish these moist, flavorful corn muffins, which have a soft and rich interior. Not overly sweet, these muffins go especially well with cheese omelets. Try substituting raspberries or blueberries for the blackberries.

1½ cups cornmeal

1 cup sifted all-purpose flour

⅓ cup sugar

1 tablespoon baking powder

1 teaspoon kosher salt

2 extra-large eggs, at room temperature

1½ cups milk

12 tablespoons (1½ sticks) unsalted butter, melted and cooled

½ cup fresh or frozen corn kernels

1 cup blackberries, plus 3 blackberries for the top of each muffin

1. Position an oven rack in the middle of the oven. Preheat the oven to 375°F. Line a standard muffin pan with paper baking cups or lightly butter the muffin cups.

2. Combine the cornmeal, flour, sugar, baking powder, and salt in a large bowl; set aside.

3. Using a mixer set on medium speed, beat the eggs briefly in a large mixing bowl. Add the milk and butter and beat for 1 minute.

4. Turn the mixer to low. Combine the flour mixture with the milk mixture and beat the batter briefly, just until the flour is incorporated, with no streaks of flour remaining. Fold in the corn kernels and 1 cup blackberries. Don't worry if the berries break apart. No need to be too careful about it.

5. Spoon the batter into the muffin cups, filling them two-thirds full. Place 3 blackberries on top of each muffin. Bake the muffins for 18 to 20 minutes, or until the tops spring back when pressed lightly or a toothpick inserted into the center comes out clean.

6. Remove the muffins from the oven and allow to cool in the pan for 5 minutes. Remove the muffins from the pan, transfer to a wire rack, and allow to cool for 15 minutes.

RED CURRANT MUFFINS

MAKES 16 MUFFINS

*F*resh currants come into season in August, but they also can keep for months in the freezer. You can substitute frozen or more widely available dried currants for fresh, making these muffins a year-round indulgence.

2½ cups all-purpose flour	3 extra-large eggs, at room
½ teaspoon baking soda	temperature
¼ teaspoon ground cinnamon	1½ teaspoons pure vanilla extract
½ teaspoon kosher salt	1 cup sour cream
12 tablespoons (1½ sticks) unsalted	¼ cup milk
butter, at room temperature	1 cup fresh, frozen, or dried red
1½ cups sugar	currants

1. Position an oven rack in the middle of the oven. Preheat the oven to 350°F. Line two standard muffin pans with 16 paper baking cups or lightly butter the muffin cups.

2. Combine the flour, baking soda, cinnamon, and salt in a large bowl; set aside.

3. Using a mixer set on high speed, cream the butter with the sugar in a large mixing bowl for 3 minutes, or until light and fluffy. Beat in the eggs, one at a time, beating well after each addition. Add the vanilla, sour cream, and milk, and beat until smooth.

4. Turn the mixer to low and add the flour mixture to the butter mixture, beating just until incorporated, with no streaks of flour remaining. Gently stir in the currants.

5. Spoon the batter into the muffin cups, filling them two-thirds full. Bake the muffins for 20 to 25 minutes, or until the tops spring back when pressed lightly or a toothpick inserted into the center comes out clean.

6. Remove the muffins from the oven and allow to cool in the pan for 5 minutes. Remove the muffins from the pan, transfer to a wire rack, and allow to cool for about 15 minutes.

CURRANT CARE

To remove the stems from fresh currants, place the currants in the freezer for 1 hour. Take them out of the freezer and pull off their stems over a bowl. The currants will come off the stem clean, for the most part. Just pick out any sticks that may be left behind and discard.

ORANGE CHOCOLATE CHIP MUFFINS

MAKES 16 MUFFINS

*C*itrus and chocolate is a classic flavor combination. It's your call whether to use semisweet chocolate chips or bittersweet chocolate chips. You could also leave the chips out entirely, or substitute a half cup of chopped nuts of your choice instead.

2½ cups all-purpose flour	1½ teaspoons pure vanilla extract
½ teaspoon baking soda	1 cup sour cream
¼ teaspoon ground cinnamon	¼ cup milk
½ teaspoon kosher salt	2 tablespoons freshly grated orange
12 tablespoons (1½ sticks) unsalted	zest
butter, at room temperature	1½ cups semisweet or bittersweet
1½ cups sugar	chocolate chips
3 extra-large eggs, at room	
temperature	

1. Position an oven rack in the middle of the oven. Preheat the oven to 350°F. Line two standard muffin pans with 16 paper baking cups or lightly butter the muffin cups.

2. Combine the flour, baking soda, cinnamon, and salt in a large bowl and set aside.

3. Using a mixer set on high speed, cream the butter and sugar in a large mixing bowl for 5 minutes, or until light and fluffy. Beat in the eggs, one at a time, beating well after each addition. Add the vanilla, sour cream, milk, and orange zest, and beat until smooth, occasionally scraping down the sides of the bowl.

4. Turn the mixer to low and combine the flour mixture with the butter mixture, beating just until incorporated, with no streaks of flour remaining. Fold in the chocolate chips.

5. Spoon the batter into the muffin cups, filling them two-thirds full. Bake the muffins for 20 to 25 minutes, or until the tops spring back when pressed lightly and are a light golden color, or a toothpick inserted into the center comes out clean.

6. Remove the muffins from the oven and allow to cool in the pan for 5 minutes. Remove the muffins from the pan, transfer to a wire rack, and allow to cool for 15 minutes.

RHUBARB MUFFINS

I n springtime at the farmers' market, rhubarb is a gloriously welcome sight after a winter of squash and potatoes. If possible, buy rhubarb at a farm stand or farmers' market. If you are craving rhubarb when it's not in season, frozen rhubarb is available at most supermarkets. Remember, if you pick your own rhubarb, use only the stalks, not the leaves as they are poisonous.

2½ cups all-purpose flour	1½ teaspoons pure vanilla extract
½ teaspoon baking soda	1 cup sour cream
¼ teaspoon ground cinnamon	¼ cup milk
½ teaspoon kosher salt	1 tablespoon freshly grated orange
12 tablespoons (1½ sticks) unsalted	zest
butter, at room temperature	2 cups chopped rhubarb (½-inch
1½ cups sugar	pieces)
3 extra-large eggs, at room	
temperature	

1. Position an oven rack in the middle of the oven. Preheat the oven to 350°F. Line two standard muffin pans with 16 paper baking cups or lightly butter the muffin cups.

2. Combine the flour, baking soda, cinnamon, and salt in a large bowl and set aside.

3. Using a mixer set on high speed, cream the butter and sugar in a large mixing bowl for about 5 minutes, or until light and fluffy. Add the eggs, one at a time, beating well after each addition. Add the vanilla, sour cream, milk, and orange zest and beat for 5 minutes.

4. Turn mixer to low and combine the flour mixture with the butter mixture, beating just until incorporated, with no streaks of flour remaining. Fold in the rhubarb.

5. Spoon the batter into the muffin cups, filling them two-thirds full. Bake the muffins for 20 to 25 minutes, or until a toothpick inserted in the center comes out clean, the tops spring back when pressed lightly, and they are a light golden color.

6. Remove the muffins from the oven and allow to cool in the pans for 5 minutes. Remove the muffins from the pans, transfer to a wire rack, and allow to cool for about 15 minutes.

STRAWBERRY MUFFINS VARIATION: Substitute 2 cups chopped strawberries for the rhubarb.

STRAWBERRY RHUBARB MUFFINS VARIATION: Substitute 1 cup chopped strawberries for 1 cup rhubarb.

WHY YOU SHOULD SHOP AT FARMERS' MARKETS

Need some convincing that shopping for fresh local produce is the way to go? Take a bite out of a supermarket carrot and then sample one from a farmers' market. The first one tastes more like wood or cardboard than carrot, and the second tastes like you just plucked it out of the garden. Now try the same thing with a locally grown apple versus an apple that was trucked all the way across the country. One tastes mealy and flavorless, and the other encompasses all the flavors and aromas of fall.

Taste is a compelling reason to shop locally for in-season produce. So is getting in touch with what grows in your area and the fact that you're supporting local farmers. You're also using less energy, since local crops don't have to be transported across the country and refrigerated in storage for days or weeks or even months. You can conserve fuel and eat well at the same time.

Then there's the excitement of becoming involved in and familiar with the growing season—and taking advantage of it by showing off seasonal specialties in brunch dishes as different as omelets, salads, muffins, and preserves. Once you start shopping at farmers' markets, your awareness of the growing season will expand dramatically. You'll start anticipating what's coming next and how you'll use it. After a winter of hard-shelled squash and potatoes, it's refreshing to see that first rhubarb. And just when you're starting to tire of rhubarb, the first strawberries start showing up, and then other berries come along, followed by peaches, until the farmers' tables are literally heaped with a bounty of lush, colorful fruit.

It's the same with vegetables. In May, you start seeing ramps and asparagus, spring onions and garlic, then beet greens and beets. June ushers in crunchy, translucent fresh garlic and tender, crisp early broccoli. Carrots and cauliflower follow in July, joined by string beans and peas. As you watch the seasons and the market offerings change, it's almost like a walk back in time, before genetic engineering, pesticides, and modern transportation systems brought us year-round everything. Peaches in December, honeydews in February, tomatoes in December—they're all available, but they certainly don't taste as good as they look.

Their appearance, by the way, belies what's beneath the skin. One of the drawbacks of our modern food supply is that much of what we buy is heavy in pesticide residues. Buying locally lets us avoid a lot of these artificial substances and brings us closer to real, actual food.

When you shop at farmers' markets, you may find yourself being more creative, too. It's not a given that you'll always get to buy what you've come for. If something is unavailable, you can learn how to quickly improvise and substitute. It might mean making watermelon lemonade instead of a blackberry press. Or using leeks instead of wild ramps in an omelet. It all boils down to being creative and flexible. The end result will no doubt be seasonal and delicious.

BANANA AND CRANBERRY BRAN MUFFINS

MAKES 12 MUFFINS

*G*ood, ripe bananas lend plenty of natural sweetness to these muffins. Feel free to substitute another nut for the pecans if you like. I like using All-Bran for these muffins, as opposed to bran flakes, because it holds up very well during baking and lends a great nutty bran flavor to the muffins.

2 cups all-purpose flour	¾ cup milk
1 tablespoon baking powder	½ cup packed dark brown sugar
½ teaspoon kosher salt	⅓ cup vegetable oil
½ teaspoon ground cinnamon	1½ cups All-Bran cereal
1 extra-large egg	½ cup chopped pecans
1 cup mashed very ripe banana	¾ cup dried cranberries

1. Position an oven rack in the middle of the oven. Preheat the oven to 400°F. Line a standard muffin pan with paper baking cups or lightly butter the muffin cups.

2. Combine the flour, baking powder, salt, and cinnamon in a large bowl and set aside.

3. Using a mixer set on medium speed, beat the egg, banana, milk, brown sugar, and vegetable oil in a large mixing bowl for 1 minute, or until smooth and creamy. Stir in the All-Bran and set the batter aside for about 10 minutes.

4. Turn the mixer to low and combine the flour mixture with the banana mixture, beating just until incorporated, with no streaks of flour remaining. Fold in the pecans and cranberries.

5. Spoon the batter into the muffin cups, filling them two-thirds full. Bake the muffins for 20 to 25 minutes, or until the tops spring back when pressed lightly or a toothpick inserted into the center comes out clean.

6. Remove the muffins from the oven and allow to cool in the pan for 5 minutes. Remove the muffins from the pan, transfer to a wire rack, and allow to cool for 15 minutes.

BUCKWHEAT, BANANA, AND ZUCCHINI MUFFINS

MAKES 12 MUFFINS

Packed with all kinds of good ingredients, these muffins make a densely flavorful treat that, if paired with yogurt, could almost be a light meal on its own. Buckwheat flour is made from the dry fruit seeds of the buckwheat plant, and is available at most health food stores.

1 cup all-purpose flour	¼ teaspoon baking soda
¾ cup buckwheat flour	⅛ teaspoon kosher salt
½ cup mashed very ripe banana	¾ cup buttermilk
1 cup grated zucchini	3 tablespoons honey
½ cup raisins	2 tablespoons vegetable oil
½ cup packed dark brown sugar	1 extra-large egg, lightly beaten
½ teaspoon ground cinnamon	½ cup chopped walnuts
1½ teaspoons baking powder	

1. Position an oven rack in the middle of the oven. Preheat the oven to 375°F. Line a standard muffin pan with paper baking cups or lightly butter the muffin cups.

2. Combine the all-purpose flour, buckwheat flour, banana, zucchini, raisins, brown sugar, cinnamon, baking powder, baking soda, and salt in a large mixing bowl.

3. Combine the buttermilk, honey, vegetable oil, and egg in a mixing bowl and whisk vigorously.

4. Form a deep "well" in the center of the flour mixture with a large wooden spoon. Pour the buttermilk mixture and the nuts right into this well. Immediately stir the mixture with the wooden spoon so that all the ingredients are well blended.

5. Spoon the batter into the muffin cups, filling them two-thirds full. Bake the muffins for 18 to 20 minutes, or until the tops spring back when pressed lightly or a toothpick inserted into the center comes out clean.

6. Remove the muffins from the oven and allow to cool in the pan for 5 minutes. Remove the muffins from the pan, transfer to a wire rack, and allow to cool for 15 minutes.

WHOLE GRAIN BANANA BREAD

MAKES ONE 8 x 4 x 3-INCH LOAF

*T*his recipe could almost be labeled a health bread, except that it tastes too good. It's packed with a generous quantity of bananas, plus an assortment of mix-and-match dried fruit. Spread the bread with any of our fruit butters (pages 270–272) and serve at a fall or winter brunch.

½ cup buckwheat flour

½ cup brown rice flour

1 ½ teaspoons baking powder

2 extra-large eggs

½ cup vegetable oil, preferably canola

2 ½ large very ripe bananas, peeled and cut into large chunks

1 teaspoon ground cinnamon

⅛ teaspoon ground allspice

⅛ teaspoon ground nutmeg

¼ teaspoon kosher salt

1 cup diced mixed dried fruit, such as raisins, apricots, prunes, apples, or cherries

½ cup chopped walnuts

1 tablespoon honey

1. Position an oven rack in the middle of the oven. Preheat the oven to 350°F. Lightly butter and flour an 8 x 4 x 3-inch loaf pan, tapping out any excess flour.

2. Combine the buckwheat flour, brown rice flour, and baking powder in a large bowl and set aside.

3. In the work bowl of a food processor fitted with the metal blade, combine the eggs, vegetable oil, bananas, cinnamon, allspice, nutmeg, and salt. Purée until smooth. Add the dried fruit, walnuts, and honey. Pulse just to combine.

4. Add the flour mixture to the batter in the food processor. Pulse a few times, just until the flour is incorporated.

5. Pour the batter into the prepared pan. Bake the loaf for 35 to 40 minutes, or until the top of the loaf is golden brown and a toothpick inserted into the center comes out clean.

6. Remove the loaf from the oven and cool in the pan for 10 minutes. Use a sharp knife to loosen the edges of the loaf from the pan, and cool in the pan for another 10 minutes. Remove the loaf from the pan and transfer to a wire rack to finish cooling.

CRANBERRY-PECAN BANANA BREAD

MAKES ONE 8 x 4 x 3-INCH LOAF

Banana bread was one of the great rewards for not eating all the bananas Mom bought for our lunch boxes. This hearty loaf is full of crimson berries and pecan chunks. When sliced and served in a napkin-lined basket, it rounds out any brunch. Leftovers are equally good for breakfast the next day. You can also bake the batter in muffin pans.

2 cups all-purpose flour
1 cup sugar
1 teaspoon baking soda
¼ teaspoon kosher salt
½ tablespoon ground cinnamon
¼ teaspoon ground nutmeg
8 tablespoons (1 stick) unsalted
   butter, at room temperature

2 extra-large eggs
3 to 4 ripe medium bananas
   (about 1 pound), peeled and
   mashed
1 cup fresh or frozen cranberries
½ cup coarsely chopped pecans

1. Position an oven rack in the middle of the oven. Preheat the oven to 350°F. Lightly butter and flour an 8 x 4 x 3-inch loaf pan, tapping out any excess flour.

2. Combine the flour, sugar, baking soda, salt, cinnamon, and nutmeg in a large bowl.

3. Using a mixer set on medium speed, beat the butter in a large mixing bowl for 3 minutes, or until light and fluffy. Add the eggs, one at a time, beating well after each addition.

4. Mix the flour mixture into the butter mixture and beat just until incorporated, with no streaks of flour remaining. Don't overbeat this batter or the bread will be tough. Fold in the bananas, cranberries, and pecans.

5. Pour the batter into the prepared pan. Bake the loaf for 35 to 45 minutes, or until a toothpick inserted into the center comes out clean.

6. Remove the loaf from the oven and cool in the pan for 10 minutes. Use a sharp knife to loosen the edges of the loaf from the pan and cool for another 10 minutes. Remove the loaf from the pan and transfer to a wire rack to finish cooling.

ZUCCHINI BREAD WITH ZUCCHINI FLOWERS

This rich, dense bread is flecked with green from the zucchini and adorned with delicate zucchini blossoms on top. The flowers, which are available at gourmet specialty stores, are a beautiful addition, but the loaf is equally delicious with or without them. You can also use this batter for muffins, in which case you'll have about twenty-four muffins and you'll need to bake them for 20 to 25 minutes.

3 cups all-purpose flour

1 tablespoon ground cinnamon

⅛ teaspoon ground nutmeg

1 teaspoon baking soda

½ teaspoon baking powder

1 teaspoon kosher salt

3 extra-large eggs

1 cup vegetable oil

1¾ cups sugar

2 cups grated zucchini (about 1 medium zucchini)

2 teaspoons pure vanilla extract

1 cup chopped fresh zucchini flowers or squash blossoms, plus 8 small whole flowers, split lengthwise (optional)

½ cup chopped walnuts, pecans, or pistachios (optional)

1 cup dried cranberries or raisins

1. Position an oven rack in the middle of the oven. Preheat the oven to 350°F. Lightly butter and flour two 9 x 5 x 3-inch loaf pans, tapping out any excess flour.

2. Combine the flour, cinnamon, nutmeg, baking soda, baking powder, and salt in a large bowl and set aside.

3. Beat the eggs with a whisk in a large mixing bowl until frothy and light. Whisk in the vegetable oil and sugar. Stir in the zucchini and vanilla.

4. Stir the flour mixture into the egg mixture and mix just until incorporated, with no streaks of flour remaining. Fold in the chopped zucchini flowers, the nuts, and the dried cranberries.

5. Divide the batter between the two prepared pans, spreading it evenly in the pans. Arrange the whole split flowers on top of each loaf. Bake the loaves for 50 to 60 minutes, or until a toothpick inserted into the centers comes out clean.

6. Remove the loaves from the oven and cool in the pans for 10 minutes. Use a sharp knife to loosen the edges of the loaves from the pans and cool for another 10 minutes. Remove the loaves from the pans and transfer to a wire rack to finish cooling.

HONEY JALAPEÑO CORN BREAD

MAKES ONE 8-INCH PAN OF CORN BREAD

*T*he sweetness of the honey and the spiciness of the jalapeños make for an intriguing flavor combination in this rich corn bread. Wear rubber or plastic gloves when handling and chopping hot chile peppers—the chiles can make your fingers sting—and wash your hands thoroughly afterward. Serve with butter, honey butter, Maple Butter (page 274), or jam.

1⅓ cups all-purpose flour

1 cup plus 2 tablespoons cornmeal

5 teaspoons baking powder

½ teaspoon kosher salt

¾ cup honey

1⅓ cups buttermilk

5 tablespoons unsalted butter, melted and cooled

1 extra-large egg, lightly beaten

2 fresh jalapeño peppers, seeded and chopped

1. Position an oven rack in the middle of the oven. Preheat the oven to 375°F. Lightly butter and flour an 8-inch square baking pan, tapping out any excess flour.

2. Combine the flour, cornmeal, baking powder, and salt in a large mixing bowl; set aside.

3. Whisk together the honey, buttermilk, butter, and egg in a mixing bowl.

4. Add the egg mixture to the flour mixture. Using a mixer set on medium speed, beat for just a minute, or until just incorporated, with no streaks of flour remaining. Don't overmix the dough. Fold in the jalapeños.

5. Pour the batter into the prepared pan. Bake the corn bread for 45 to 50 minutes, or until a toothpick inserted into the center comes out clean.

6. Remove from the oven and cool in the pan for 15 minutes. When the corn bread is thoroughly cool, cut into squares.

PUMPKIN SPICE BREAD

MAKES TWO 8 x 4 x 3-INCH LOAVES

*T*hanks to a combination of aromatic spices, this is an extraordinarily good pumpkin bread, and it's also easy to make. Be sure to use plain canned pumpkin and not the pumpkin pie version, which has spices already added to it.

3½ cups all-purpose flour
2 teaspoons baking soda
1½ teaspoons kosher salt
1 teaspoon ground cinnamon
½ teaspoon ground nutmeg
¼ teaspoon ground cloves
½ teaspoon ground ginger

One 15-ounce can pumpkin purée
4 extra-large eggs, at room
  temperature
8 tablespoons (1 stick) unsalted
  butter, melted and cooled
½ cup vegetable oil
3 cups sugar

1. Position an oven rack in the middle of the oven. Preheat the oven to 350°F. Lightly butter and flour two 8 x 4 x 3-inch loaf pans, tapping out any excess flour.

2. Combine the flour, baking soda, salt, cinnamon, nutmeg, cloves, and ginger in a large bowl and set aside.

3. Using a mixer set on medium speed, beat the pumpkin purée, eggs, butter, vegetable oil, sugar, and ⅔ cup water for 3 minutes, or until well blended, occasionally scraping down the sides of the bowl.

4. Turn the mixer to low and combine the flour mixture with the pumpkin mixture, beating just until incorporated, with no streaks of flour remaining.

5. Pour the batter into the prepared pans. Bake the loaves for 45 to 50 minutes, or until a toothpick inserted into the centers comes out clean.

6. Remove the loaves from the oven and cool in the pans for 10 minutes. Use a sharp knife to loosen the edges of the loaves from the pans and cool for another 10 minutes. Remove the loaves from the pans, transfer to a wire rack, and allow to cool for 15 minutes.

BLUEBERRY SCONES

MAKES 12 SCONES

These scones are easy to make and can be rewarmed quickly in a 300°F oven for about 10 minutes. They work well with either fresh or frozen berries.

3 cups all-purpose flour, plus more
  for the work surface
1½ tablespoons baking powder
½ cup sugar, plus 2 tablespoons for
  sprinkling on top of the scones

½ teaspoon kosher salt
1 cup fresh or frozen blueberries
2 cups heavy cream, plus more for
  brushing the tops of the scones

1. Position an oven rack in the middle of the oven. Preheat the oven to 375°F. Line a large baking sheet with parchment paper.

2. Stir together the flour, baking powder, ½ cup sugar, and salt in a large mixing bowl. Fold in the blueberries. Stir in the heavy cream.

3. Use a large rubber spatula or your hands to form a soft dough. Don't overmix the dough. There should be a few lumps of dry ingredients throughout.

4. Turn out the dough onto a lightly floured work surface. Knead the dough very briefly, about 30 seconds, just until it sticks together. There should be as little handling as possible. Gently form the dough into a ball and lightly dust it with a little flour. Sprinkle a little more flour on the work surface and using a floured rolling pin, roll out the dough into a 1-inch-thick round that is 8 to 9 inches in diameter.

5. Cut the dough into desired shapes. Gather up the scraps, reroll them, and cut out more scones until the dough is used up. Pat the scones lightly to smooth the tops.

6. Place the scones about 2 inches apart on the prepared baking sheet. Brush the tops of the scones with cream and sprinkle with the extra sugar. Bake for 10 to 12 minutes, or until the tops spring back when pressed lightly and the bottoms are golden brown.

7. Remove the scones from the oven and cool on the baking sheet for 5 minutes. Transfer the scones to a wire rack to cool for at least 5 minutes before serving.

CURRANT SCONES VARIATION: Substitute 2 cups fresh or frozen red currants for the blueberries.

RAISIN SCONES VARIATION: Substitute 2 cups dark or golden raisins for the blueberries.

CRANBERRY-PECAN SCONES VARIATION: Substitute 1 cup fresh or dried cranberries and ½ cup coarsely chopped pecans for the blueberries.

CHOCOLATE CHIP SCONES

MAKES 12 TO 14 SCONES

*C*rumbly and rich, these scones need no adornment at all to be a delicious indulgence.

2 cups all-purpose flour, plus more
for the work surface
1 tablespoon baking powder
1 teaspoon kosher salt
2 teaspoons sugar, plus 2 to
3 tablespoons for sprinkling
on top of the scones

½ cup buttersweet chocolate
chips
¾ to 1 cup heavy cream, plus ¼ cup
for brushing the tops of the
scones

1. Position an oven rack in the middle of the oven. Preheat the oven to 425°F. Line a baking sheet with parchment paper.

2. Combine the flour, baking powder, salt, and 2 teaspoons sugar in a large bowl and stir well. Add the chocolate chips and toss to combine.

3. Add ¾ cup of the cream and stir well, using a large spatula or your hands. Add more cream, a teaspoon at a time, until a soft, manageable dough forms. You may not need to use the entire cup of cream.

4. Turn out the dough onto a lightly floured work surface. Knead the dough very briefly, about 30 seconds, just until it sticks together. There should be as little handling as possible. Gently form the dough into a ball and lightly dust it with a little flour. Sprinkle a little more flour on the work surface and using a floured rolling pin, roll out the dough into a 1-inch-thick round that is 8 to 9 inches in diameter.

5. Cut the dough into desired shapes. Gather up the scraps, reroll them, and cut out more scones until the dough is used up. Pat the scones lightly to smooth the tops.

6. Place the scones about 2 inches apart on the prepared baking sheet. Using a small pastry brush, brush the tops of the scones with cream and sprinkle with the extra sugar. Bake the scones for 15 to 18 minutes, or until the tops spring back when pressed lightly and the bottoms are golden brown.

7. Remove the scones from the oven and cool on the baking sheet for 5 minutes. Transfer the scones to a wire rack to cool for at least 5 minutes before serving.

APRICOT OR RAISIN SCONES VARIATIONS: Substitute chopped dried apricots or raisins for the chocolate chips.

Savory Whole Wheat, Spinach, and Cheddar Scones

MAKES 12 SCONES

*T*hese colorful scones are crumbly and rich from the combination of Cheddar cheese and spinach. A more substantial scone than some of the sweet ones, these go well with just about any salad and are also good with a frittata.

3 cups whole wheat flour, plus more for the work surface	1½ cups heavy cream
1½ tablespoons baking powder	¾ cup steamed spinach, squeezed dry and chopped
1½ teaspoons kosher salt	¾ cup grated sharp Cheddar cheese
¾ cup honey	

1. Position a rack in the middle of the oven. Preheat the oven to 425°F. Line a baking sheet with parchment paper.

2. Combine the flour, baking powder, and salt in a large mixing bowl and set aside.

3. Whisk the honey and cream in a separate bowl until smooth.

4. Stir together the spinach and Cheddar cheese in a small bowl and set aside.

5. Whisk the cream mixture into the flour mixture. Stir in the spinach mixture until smooth. Don't overmix the dough. It's okay if a few lumps of dry ingredients are visible.

6. Turn out the dough onto a lightly floured work surface. Knead the dough very briefly, about 30 seconds, just until it sticks together. There should be as little handling as possible. Gently form the dough into a ball and lightly dust it with a little flour. Sprinkle a little more flour on the work surface and using a floured rolling pin, roll out the dough into a 1-inch-thick round that is 8 to 9 inches in diameter.

7. Cut the dough into desired shapes. Gather up the scraps, reroll them, and cut out more scones until the dough is used up. Pat the scones lightly to smooth the tops.

8. Place the scones about 2 inches apart on the prepared baking sheet. Bake the scones for 12 to 14 minutes, or until the tops spring back when pressed lightly and they are golden brown on the top and bottom.

9. Remove the scones from the oven and cool for 5 minutes on the baking sheet. Transfer the scones to a wire rack to cool for at least 5 minutes before serving.

BUBBY'S VARIATION ON MR. BEARD'S CREAM BISCUITS

MAKES 20 BISCUITS

*J*ames Beard's excellent biscuit recipe can hardly be improved upon. But by using sour cream in the recipe, we feel the biscuits are a little creamier. If you prefer the original Beard biscuits, just omit the sour cream and double the heavy cream.

5 cups all-purpose flour, plus more for the work surface	1 cup heavy cream
1 teaspoon kosher salt	1 cup sour cream
2½ tablespoons baking powder	12 tablespoons (1½ sticks) unsalted butter, melted and cooled
⅓ cup sugar	

1. Preheat the oven to 425°F. Line two large baking sheets with parchment paper.

2. Combine the flour, salt, baking powder, and sugar in a large bowl. Add the cream and sour cream and stir until a dough forms. Don't overmix the dough. Form the dough into a flattened ball.

3. Using a lightly floured rolling pin, roll out the dough on a lightly floured work surface until it is about ½ inch thick. Using a biscuit cutter, cut out rounds that are about 2 inches in diameter. Dip them into the melted butter to coat all over. Reroll the scraps with the rolling pin and cut out more biscuits until the dough has been used up.

4. Place the biscuits on the prepared baking sheets. Bake the biscuits for 8 to 12 minutes, or until golden brown. Rotate the pans once during the baking so that the biscuits brown evenly.

5. Remove the biscuits from the oven and cool on the baking sheets for 5 minutes. Transfer the biscuits to a wire rack to cool for at least 5 minutes before serving.

POPOVERS

MAKES 6 TO 8 POPOVERS

My adopted grandmother, called Mema by dozens of grandkids, step-grandkids, and us adopted grandkids alike, as well as scores of great-grandkids, always made these popovers for Christmas dinner. They are just as tasty for brunch. Popovers rise in the oven due to steam, not a leavener such as yeast, and then they deflate somewhat after baking. Good with butter, jam, or honey, they are best eaten warm. I like using a cast-iron popover pan, but you can also use a good, solid muffin pan. For the puffiest, airiest popovers, make the batter at least 2 hours ahead of time. Refrigerate the batter for 1 hour, and then let it sit out at room temperature for 1 hour.

2 extra-large eggs	1 cup all-purpose flour
1 cup milk	½ teaspoon kosher salt
1 tablespoon unsalted butter, melted and cooled, plus 2 tablespoons, softened	

1. Whisk together the eggs, milk, and melted butter in a large mixing bowl. Stir in the flour and salt. Using a mixer set on medium speed, beat the batter for 1 minute, or until very smooth.

2. Refrigerate the batter for at least 1 hour. Remove it from the refrigerator about an hour before you plan to bake the popovers.

3. Position an oven rack in the lower third of the oven. Preheat the oven to 400°F. Generously grease a popover pan or muffin pan with the softened butter.

4. Pour the batter into the prepared pan, filling each cup one-half to two-thirds full. Bake the popovers for 35 to 40 minutes, or until puffed and golden brown. Do not open the oven door for the first 35 minutes of baking or the popovers may collapse.

5. Remove the popovers from the oven and run a knife around the edges to loosen them from the pan. Pop them out of the pan and serve immediately.

PARKER HOUSE ROLLS

*S*oft, *slightly sweet rolls are an American dinnertime tradition, but they certainly have their rightful place at the brunch table, too. From this basic recipe, you can shape many rolls, including round rolls, cloverleaf rolls, and twists.*

16 tablespoons (2 sticks) unsalted butter	2 packages (4 teaspoons) quick-rising yeast
1½ cups milk	½ cup lukewarm water (90° to 100°F)
3 tablespoons sugar	5 to 5½ cups all-purpose flour
1 teaspoon kosher salt	

1. Melt 8 tablespoons butter in a saucepan over low heat. Stir in the milk, sugar, and salt and cook over medium heat, stirring, until simmering. Remove the mixture from the heat and allow it to cool.

2. In the work bowl of a stand mixer fitted with a dough hook, combine the yeast and warm water. Stir until the yeast is dissolved. Allow to stand for about 10 minutes, until bubbly.

3. Stir the cooled milk mixture into the yeast mixture. Add 5 cups of the flour and beat until smooth. Add a little more flour as needed if the dough seems sticky. When the dough starts to pull away from the sides of the bowl, turn off the mixer and transfer the dough to a lightly floured work surface.

4. Knead the dough for a minute or two with your hands, just until smooth. Place the dough into a large, well-buttered bowl and allow it to rise in a warm place for about 30 minutes, or until doubled in size.

5. Melt the remaining 8 tablespoons of butter.

6. To shape the rolls, pull off ¼-cup pieces of dough and roll them into about 16 balls about 2½ inches in diameter. Flatten each ball slightly and make an indentation down the middle with a spatula. For each ball, butter one half with about 1½ teaspoons of the melted butter and fold the other half over it, lightly pressing on the edges.

7. Preheat the oven to 400°F. Butter a baking sheet.

8. Place the rolls at least 1 inch apart on the prepared baking sheet. Cover the rolls with a clean kitchen towel and allow them to rise again for about 30 minutes, or until doubled in size.

9. Bake the rolls for about 15 minutes, or until lightly browned. Remove the rolls from the oven and cool on the baking sheet for 5 minutes. Transfer the rolls to a wire rack and cool for at least 15 minutes before serving.

STICKY BUNS

*D*eliciously gooey and sweet, these delectable breakfast pastries immediately put everyone in a good mood. Be sure to start a few hours in advance of serving to give the dough time to rise. You can also start them the night before.

1 recipe Parker House Rolls (page 56), prepared through step 4

½ cup raisins
¾ cup pecan pieces, toasted

For the filling
1 cup plus 6 tablespoons packed dark brown sugar
1 tablespoon ground cinnamon
¼ teaspoon ground cloves
Pinch of kosher salt
11 tablespoons unsalted butter, melted and cooled

For the glaze
4 tablespoons (½ stick) unsalted butter, at room temperature
1 cup packed dark brown sugar
½ cup honey

1. After the dough has doubled in size, use a rolling pin to roll out a 9 x 15-inch rectangle on a lightly floured work surface.

2. Combine 1 cup of the brown sugar, the cinnamon, cloves, and salt in a small bowl; set aside.

3. Pour ½ cup of the melted butter over the dough, spreading it evenly from edge to edge with a pastry brush. Sprinkle the brown sugar mixture over the buttered dough. Sprinkle evenly with the raisins and pecans.

4. Starting with one long side of the dough, roll up the dough. The filling and the dough should create a pinwheel spiral, like a jelly roll. Pinch together the edges to seal in the filling. Using a sharp knife, cut the roll into 12 slices, each about ¾ inch thick.

5. Coat the bottom of a 9 x 13 x 2-inch baking pan with the remaining 3 tablespoons melted butter. Sprinkle the pan evenly with the remaining 6 tablespoons brown sugar.

6. Place the sticky bun slices close together in the pan. Place the end pieces cut side down. Cover with a towel and allow the slices to rise in a warm place until doubled in bulk, about 45 minutes.

7. Preheat the oven to 350°F.

8. Bake the buns for about 30 minutes, or until nicely browned. Remove the buns from the oven and cool in the pan for 5 minutes. Using a spatula, gently loosen them from the sides of the pan and carefully transfer them to a large platter to finish cooling.

9. Make the glaze: Using an electric mixer set on medium speed, beat together the butter, brown sugar, and honey in a small bowl.

10. Spread the glaze over the slightly cooled sticky buns with a narrow spatula or a table knife. You can also drizzle on the glaze with a spoon.

FRESH TALK ABOUT DRIED FRUIT

Dark raisins are sun-dried for a few weeks, which gives them their characteristic color, while golden raisins are dried with artificial heat. Both varieties, along with currants, will keep at room temperature for a few months when tightly wrapped. In the refrigerator, they will keep for a year when in a sealed plastic bag.

If your raisins are a little past their prime, it's easy to plump them up again. Put them into a saucepan, cover with water, and bring to a boil. Drain well, and allow to cool before using. The technique works with dark raisins, golden raisins, and currants, too. And if you use dates, apricots, or prunes in your baking, you may plump these up, too.

Pick over pitted fruit such as dates before stirring them into baked goods to make sure that they are all pitted. (The pitting is done mechanically.) And when you use dried figs in your baked goods remove the stems before stirring them into a batter since these can become quite hard after baking.

CREAM CHEESE CINNAMON ROLLS

When our neighbors made this recipe on Saturday mornings when we were growing up, the entire neighborhood smelled like cinnamon heaven. These frosted cinnamon rolls are a little more complicated to make than scones or muffins, but they are definitely worth the effort. The cream cheese makes the dough flakier than that of many cinnamon rolls, and the filling is rich and delicious. You can prepare these the night before and let them rise for an hour before baking them in the morning. The uncooked cinnamon rolls also freeze very well for a couple of weeks.

For the dough
One ¼-ounce package active dry yeast
¼ cup plus ½ teaspoon granulated sugar
¼ cup warm water (100°F)
½ cup lukewarm milk (90° to 100°F)
2 tablespoons packed dark brown sugar
½ teaspoon pure vanilla extract
1 extra-large egg
1 extra-large egg yolk
2¾ to 3¼ cups all-purpose flour
¾ teaspoon kosher salt
8 tablespoons (1 stick) unsalted butter, at room temperature

For the filling
¼ cup granulated sugar
½ cup packed light brown sugar
½ cup finely chopped pecans
¼ cup raisins
2 teaspoons ground cinnamon
½ teaspoon kosher salt
Big pinch of ground cloves
2 tablespoons honey or maple syrup
4 ounces cream cheese, at room temperature
8 tablespoons (1 stick) unsalted butter, melted and cooled

For the icing
2 cups confectioners' sugar
¼ cup milk or buttermilk

1. Make the dough: In the work bowl of an electric stand mixer fitted with a dough hook, combine the yeast, ½ teaspoon of the granulated sugar, and the warm water. Stir until the yeast is dissolved. Allow to stand for about 10 minutes, until bubbly.

2. Add the remaining ¼ cup granulated sugar, the milk, brown sugar, vanilla, egg, and egg yolk. Mix on low speed until thoroughly combined.

3. Turn the mixer off and add 2¾ cups flour and the salt. Turn the mixer back on and mix on medium speed until the dough comes together. Turn the mixer to high speed and continue to mix for 4 more minutes.

4. Turn the mixer off again and add the butter. Turn on the mixer once more and beat on medium speed for 5 to 7 minutes, until the dough is smooth and pulls away from the sides of the bowl. Remove the bowl from the mixer, cover it with plastic wrap, and set it aside in a warm place. Allow the dough to rise until it has doubled in size, 1½ to 2 hours.

5. Make the filling: Stir together the granulated sugar, brown sugar, pecans, raisins, cinnamon, salt, and cloves in a large bowl. Stir in the honey; set aside.

6. When the dough has doubled in size, punch it down and turn it out onto a heavily floured work surface. Gently knead the dough for about 1 minute, until it's no longer sticky, adding more flour as necessary.

7. Using a floured rolling pin, roll the dough into a 10-inch square. Butter a 9 x 13 x 2-inch light-colored metal baking pan.

8. In another bowl, beat the cream cheese with a wooden spoon until smooth and easy to spread. Spread the cream cheese evenly over the dough with the wooden spoon. Fold the square into thirds as you would fold a business letter. You will now have a rectangle. Take the open ends and fold them inward into thirds again, making a small square. Flip the dough so that the seam is facing down. Using the well-floured rolling pin, gently roll the dough into a 10 x 20-inch rectangle.

9. Turn the dough so that the short sides are parallel to you. Brush the dough with half of the melted butter. Drizzle the reserved filling over the dough, leaving a 1-inch border at the edge farthest away from you. Lightly press the filling into the dough.

10. Lift up the bottom edge of the dough with your hands and roll it forward into a tight cylinder. Place the cylinder seam side down on a lightly floured work surface. Using a sharp knife, trim off the ends. Cut the cylinder crosswise into 8 equal-size slices. Nestle the slices, cut sides up and evenly spaced from one another, in the prepared baking pan. Cover the pan with a clean kitchen towel and set it aside in a warm place to rise until doubled in bulk, about 2 hours. Alternatively, the rolls may be refrigerated overnight.

11. Preheat the oven to 375°F.

12. Uncover the rolls. (If refrigerated, let the rolls sit at room temperature for 1 hour.) Bake the rolls for about 30 minutes, or until they are golden brown. Give the rolls a little thump and if they sound hollow, they're done.

13. Make the icing: While the rolls are baking, whisk together the confectioners' sugar and milk in a small bowl until smooth.

14. Remove the cinnamon rolls from the oven and transfer to a wire rack. Brush the rolls with the remaining melted butter left over from the filling. Cool for 5 minutes. Using a wire whisk to scoop up the icing, drizzle it over the rolls. Serve immediately.

RAISIN CHALLAH BREAD

MAKES TWO 9 x 5 x 3-INCH LOAVES

*H*omemade raisin challah bread is a real treat. Slice this light, egg-rich loaf thick for toast or use it to make a memorable French toast. This bread can be frozen for up to two weeks.

For the dough
One ¼-ounce package active dry
  yeast
1½ cups lukewarm water (90° to
  100°F)
¼ cup sugar
1½ tablespoons kosher salt
⅓ cup vegetable oil, plus more to
  grease the bowls and loaf pans

2 extra-large eggs, lightly beaten
4⅓ cups bread flour, plus more if
  needed
1¼ cups raisins

For the topping
2 teaspoons ground cinnamon
¼ cup sugar

1. Make the dough: In the work bowl of a stand mixer fitted with a dough hook, combine the yeast and the warm water. Stir until the yeast is dissolved. When the water begins to bubble, stir in the sugar, salt, vegetable oil, and eggs.

2. Add about one-third of the flour. Beat the dough on medium speed for about 5 minutes, adding the remaining flour in two more batches and occasionally scraping down the sides of the bowl. Add the raisins, and beat for another 5 minutes on medium speed. Don't worry that the raisins will get pulverized: that won't happen when you use the dough hook.

3. Stop beating and check the consistency of the dough. It should be starting to come together, but not be overly sticky. If it is too sticky, add a couple more tablespoons of flour and beat for another minute or so.

4. Brush two large stainless steel bowls with some vegetable oil. Divide the dough into 2 equal-size balls. Place 1 ball of dough into each of the bowls. Cover each bowl with a clean kitchen towel and allow the dough to rise in a warm place until it doubles in size, about 1 hour.

5. Lightly oil two 9 x 5 x 3-inch loaf pans.

6. Place the balls into the greased pans, cover them with a clean kitchen towel, and allow them to rise in a warm place for about 1 hour, or until doubled in size.

7. Preheat the oven to 350°F.

8. Make the topping: Stir together the cinnamon and sugar in a small bowl. Sprinkle the topping evenly over the loaves.

9. Bake the loaves for 30 to 35 minutes, or until they are golden brown and sound hollow when tapped on the bottom.

10. Remove the loaves from the oven and cool in the pans for 15 minutes. Remove the loaves from the pans and transfer to a wire rack. Cool for at least 1 hour before slicing.

CLASSIC HOLIDAY BREAD

Challah is a traditional Jewish bread, served on the Sabbath and other holidays as well. Very often it is braided, but it can be formed into many other shapes as well. At the Sabbath table, the head of the family sits down before a cloth-covered braided challah. The cloth is removed and a prayer is said before the loaf is sliced and served.

APPLE STREUSEL COFFEE CAKE

MAKES ONE 9 x 13 x 2-INCH COFFEE CAKE

My family goes crazy for this coffee cake, one of the most requested items in my recipe box. This moist, tender cake is delicious cut into squares and served either warm or at room temperature, perhaps in a basket alongside muffins and slices of quick bread. It works especially well with a tart apple such as Granny Smith, though at apple picking time, it is a joy to go to the market to find the tartest, crispiest apple you can. Mutsu, Jonagold, Honeycrisps, and Winesaps are just a few examples. Well wrapped, this cake can be frozen for up to three months. Thaw it overnight at room temperature before serving, and store it, covered, at room temperature.

For the topping

1½ cups coarsely chopped walnuts

½ cup packed light brown sugar

½ teaspoon ground cinnamon

¼ teaspoon kosher salt

1 tablespoon unsalted butter, at
room temperature

For the cake

2½ cups all-purpose flour

1 teaspoon baking powder

1 teaspoon baking soda

½ teaspoon kosher salt

½ pound (2 sticks) unsalted butter,
at room temperature

1 cup granulated sugar

3 extra-large eggs, at room
temperature

1 cup sour cream

1 tablespoon pure vanilla extract

2 large apples, peeled, cored, and
cut into ¼-inch dice

1½ cups coarsely chopped walnuts

1. Preheat the oven to 350°F. Lightly butter a 9 x 13 x 2-inch baking pan and line the bottom with parchment paper. Butter the parchment paper.

2. Make the topping: Stir together the walnuts, brown sugar, cinnamon, and salt in a medium mixing bowl. Work in the butter with your fingertips until the mixture is crumbly and moist. Set aside.

3. Make the cake: Combine the flour, baking powder, baking soda, and salt in a large bowl and set aside.

4. Using a mixer set on medium speed, cream the butter in a large mixing bowl for 2 to 3 minutes, or until pale and light. Gradually add the sugar, beating well and occasionally scraping down the sides of the bowl. Beat in the eggs, one at a time, beating well after each addition. Beat in the sour cream and vanilla.

5. Add the flour mixture and beat just until incorporated, with no streaks of flour remaining. Fold in the apples and walnuts.

6. Pour the batter into the prepared baking pan. Sprinkle the topping evenly over the cake.

7. Bake for about 40 minutes, or until a toothpick inserted into the center comes out clean.

8. Remove the cake from the oven and cool in the pan for 10 minutes before cutting the cake into squares to serve.

PICKING APPLES

The best apples for baking aren't necessarily the best for eating raw. Northern Spies are ideal for a pie, cake, or cobbler since they hold their shape during baking and make for a juicy filling. Pippins, with their firm texture and nice tart flavor, are excellent in pies and cakes. Apples to avoid for baking include MacIntosh, Macouns, and Red Delicious. And though Rome Beauties are wonderful baked, they're not so flavorful in a pie.

RHUBARB COFFEE CAKE

MAKES ONE 9 x 13 x 2-INCH COFFEE CAKE

This pink-hued cake is filled with rhubarb, which is in season during the spring and early summer. The cake freezes nicely and has a high ratio of fruit to cake—always good in a brunch sweet. Sliced into wedges, this coffee cake is a nice way to round out a seasonal bread basket of fruit muffins.

For the cake
4 cups all-purpose flour
1 teaspoon kosher salt
2 teaspoons baking soda
3 cups packed dark brown sugar
½ pound (2 sticks) unsalted butter, at room temperature
2 extra-large eggs
1 teaspoon pure vanilla extract
2 cups buttermilk
5 cups diced rhubarb (½-inch pieces)

For the topping
½ cup granulated sugar
2 teaspoons ground cinnamon

1. Preheat the oven to 350°F. Lightly butter a 9 x 13 x 2-inch baking pan and line the bottom with parchment paper. Butter the parchment paper.

2. Make the cake: Stir the flour, salt, and baking soda in a large bowl and set aside.

3. Using a mixer set on medium speed, beat the brown sugar and butter in a large mixing bowl for 3 minutes, or until light and creamy. Beat in the eggs one at a time, beating well after each addition. Beat in the vanilla and buttermilk. Continue to beat for 2 minutes, or until smooth, occasionally scraping down the sides of the bowl.

4. Mix the flour mixture into the batter one-third at a time, beating briefly after each addition. Fold in the rhubarb until it is well distributed.

5. Pour the batter into the prepared baking pan. Use a rubber spatula to smooth it out to the edges of the pan. The batter will be very thick.

6. Make the topping: Stir together the granulated sugar and cinnamon in a small bowl. Sprinkle the topping evenly over the batter.

7. Bake the cake for 40 to 45 minutes, or until a toothpick inserted into the center comes out clean. Remove the cake from the oven and transfer to a wire rack. Cool for 1 hour before cutting the cake into squares to serve.

LEMON–POPPY SEED CAKE

MAKES ONE 9-INCH LAYER CAKE

A buttery soft frosting blankets this tall and sprightly cake, rich with eggs and dotted with lemon zest and poppy seeds throughout. An impressive and showy dessert for lemon lovers, this can be made a day in advance. It's a nice end-of-brunch finale.

For the cake
2½ cups sifted cake flour
2½ teaspoons baking powder
½ teaspoon kosher salt
8 tablespoons (1 stick) unsalted
   butter
1 tablespoon freshly grated lemon
   zest
1¾ cups granulated sugar
6 extra-large egg yolks
1 cup plus 2 tablespoons milk
3 tablespoons poppy seeds

For the frosting
4 cups confectioners' sugar
8 tablespoons (1 stick) unsalted
   butter, softened
2 tablespoons fresh lemon juice
1 teaspoon freshly grated lemon
   zest
2 tablespoons milk

1 tablespoon poppy seeds for the
   top of the cake

1. Preheat the oven to 350°F. Lightly butter two 9-inch round cake pans and line the bottoms with parchment paper. Butter the parchment paper.

2. Make the cake: Combine the flour, baking powder, and salt in a large bowl and set aside.

3. Using a mixer set on medium speed, cream the butter with the lemon zest in a large bowl for about 3 minutes, or until light and fluffy. Gradually add the sugar, beating for 2 minutes. Add the egg yolks, one at a time, beating well after each addition.

4. Add the flour mixture alternately with the milk, beating until smooth after each addition. Fold in the poppy seeds until well combined.

5. Pour the batter into the prepared pans. Bake the layers for 25 to 30 minutes, until a toothpick inserted into the centers comes out clean.

6. Remove the pans from the oven and cool in the pans on a wire rack for 10 minutes.

7. Run a sharp knife around the edges of each pan to loosen the cake layers. Invert the pans over large plates and shake gently, so the layers slide top side down onto the plates. Transfer the layers to wire racks to cool completely. Peel off the parchment paper.

8. Make the frosting: Using an electric mixer set on medium speed, beat the confectioners' sugar, butter, lemon juice, and lemon zest in a large bowl until smooth. Add the milk and increase the mixer speed to high. Continue to beat for 1 minute, or until light and fluffy.

9. Assemble the cake: Using a sharp serrated knife, slice each cake layer in half horizontally. You will have 4 layers.

10. Place 1 layer cut side up on a serving plate or cake stand. Spread with about ½ cup frosting. Top with another layer cut side down, and spread with about ½ cup frosting. Add the third layer cut side up, and spread with about ½ cup frosting. Place the final layer cut side down, and frost the top and sides of the cake with the remaining frosting.

11. Sprinkle the top with the poppy seeds. Refrigerate the cake until serving time. Bring to room temperature before serving.

EGGS OF
ALL KINDS

When it comes to brunch, there is no question which came first, the chicken or the egg: The egg trumps the chicken. Eggs can be prepared in dozens of ways, from the perfectly simple to the very complex. They can be poached and enjoyed with nothing more than a sprinkling of salt and pepper, scrambled, shirred, or baked. The whites can become light as a feather in a soufflé. The yolks can become the airy base of sabayon sauce. Smoked meats, cheeses, vegetables, seafood, and even fruit can be combined with eggs to come up with some of the world's classic dishes such as Eggs Benedict or Huevos Rancheros. Even when they're not center stage, eggs make their way into many brunch dishes, from French toast to quick breads to waffles.

Once thought to be the villains of a bad diet, now eggs are often considered a super food. They contain all nine essential amino acids, vitamins, and enough protein to keep you energized for hours. They are the near-perfect food. Eggs are inexpensive, sold everywhere, and easy to store since they keep a relatively long time in the refrigerator.

That said, it is essential to handle eggs properly. The first, most important thing is to buy fresh eggs. If you are buying farm eggs, know your source, and know that the eggs have been handled properly: washed and brought to market refrigerated.

Eggs that were laid within three days of purchase, or the same morning, are incomparable to store-bought eggs with a sell-by date. Though it's not easy to tell when eggs are fresh (no sniff or squeeze test as when you buy produce), you can increase your odds of getting the best eggs by shopping at farmers' markets. If you buy your eggs at the supermarket, however, make sure to get a carton with the latest possible sell-by date.

Once you get the eggs home, the best way to tell how fresh an egg is is to crack it: The whites should form a gelatinous bubble that holds up around a brightly colored yolk. The whites from store-bought eggs, when cracked, frequently will run like water into the bowl or pan. Often, the yolks from unfresh eggs will break when the eggs are cracked. The shells also tend to be brittle. An unfresh egg is perhaps most annoying and noticeable when you try to separate yolks from whites and the yolks keep breaking into the whites, rendering them useless if your hope is to whip them into a frothy meringue.

ASIDE FROM OMELETS, EGGS ARE GENERALLY BEST COOKED OVER LOW HEAT, CODDLED OR SIMMERED.

Fresh eggs are called for in myriad Bubby's brunch favorites. In this chapter, for instance, are Bubby's popular omelets, scrambles, and frittatas. From coddled eggs (which are simmered until the white is very delicate) to shirred eggs (baked with cream) to poached eggs (simmered in water for just minutes), the recipes here offer endless brunch inspirations.

Though you might think serving made-to-order omelets is too stressful on the cook, it's actually easy if you prep the fillings and toppings ahead of time—and your guests will love that you made their meal to order. Omelets are superfast to make, once you get going. They're one of the few egg dishes that require high (if brief) heat. For an omelet to turn out perfectly, it's important to heat the ingredients in the pan by sautéing them in butter before adding the eggs. Use a whisk or a fork when beating the eggs for omelets. All Bubby's omelets are made with three extra-large eggs.

To make omelets for a crowd, it's usually best not to double or triple recipes. Have all your ingredients at the ready (chopped, grated, sautéed, and peeled) and you can quickly make as many as six omelets in under ten minutes, especially if you are adept at working with two or three burners at a time. If, however, you would like to make a larger batch, you can bake almost any omelet recipe as a frittata or, for an even larger crowd, as a casserole. To bake a frittata, place the eggs into an ovenproof skillet and bake in a preheated 350°F oven for 10 to 20 minutes, or until the eggs are set.

Omelets are best served as soon as they're made, so have plates on hand for when it's time to slide one out of the hot pan. Frittatas and casseroles taste best after resting for a time, which firms up the eggs a little and makes slicing easier.

Classic Eggs Benedict (page 109) is a really simple brunch dish, thanks to the invention of Blender Hollandaise Sauce (page 286), inspired by the great Irma Rombauer, coauthor of *Joy of Cooking*. And yes, also included here is Traditional Hollandaise Sauce (page 285) for purists.

Frittatas, also thought of as Italian egg pies, can be filled with just about anything from seafood to herbs and vegetables. Frittatas are the ideal brunch recipe for a crowd since they can be made ahead, and the recipes can easily be doubled and tripled. When cooking for many guests, egg casseroles—such as Bacon, Leek, and Onion Casserole (page 105) or Sausage and Mushroom Casserole (page 107)—are perfect; they can be prepped in advance, hold up well, and look beautiful on a table.

A central ingredient in dishes that cook in minutes (such as an omelet) or an hour (such as a casserole), and that can be prepared in innumerable ways, eggs are undoubtedly the most versatile brunch food of all. This chapter explains how to prepare them for brunches both big and small, no matter how much time you have to cook.

EGGS 101

CERTAIN EGG DISHES ARE TIME-HONORED classics that taste as good today as they did when we were kids. It's worth learning to master a few basic egg cooking techniques so you can add these traditional favorites to your repertoire. Simple dishes that call for very few ingredients, these can be whipped up in just a few minutes.

EGGS SUNNY-SIDE UP: Place an 8-inch nonstick skillet on medium-low heat and allow it to get hot, but it should not be so hot that it is smoking. Test by flicking a drop of water on the pan. It should sizzle, not disappear immediately. Put 1 teaspoon unsalted butter in the pan and allow it to melt and get bubbling hot. Gently crack 2 extra-large eggs into the pan. The eggs should sizzle a little when they hit the pan, but they should not bubble up, meaning the pan is *too* hot. If they do bubble, remove the pan from the heat and let it cool down just a little (the eggs will take the heat out of the pan). Then place the pan back on the burner. As the whites begin to cook, tilt the pan and slide the eggs back and forth so they don't stick. The whole process takes no more than a minute or two. When the yolks look like they are set and the whites are mostly white (as opposed to clear) all the way through, the eggs are done. Slide them from the pan directly onto the plate. Add salt and pepper to taste.

EGGS OVER EASY: The skill of flipping over easy eggs comes once you master a few simple tricks. First, you must have a good-quality nonstick pan. Second, the pan and the oil have to be sufficiently hot, almost smoking, before the eggs go in. Third, you must be able to flip things in a hot skillet without burning yourself. This is where practice and skill come into play. One way to practice is with a skillet and some dry beans. Start with literally one bean. Tilt the skillet forward by bending your wrist, and gently move the bean to the front of the pan with a wave and flip of the wrist. The bean should float into the air and land with a little *plunk*. Once you master one bean, try two, then five, then ten. Of course, you could also use a flexible spatula to flip the eggs.

When you're ready to try flipping with an actual egg, place a medium nonstick pan over medium-high heat and add 1 teaspoon of butter. Just before the pan is smoking, quickly crack the eggs into the pan. Crack them as close to the surface of the pan as you can so the hot grease doesn't splatter the stove or your arms. Let the eggs sizzle for a minute, until the whites are set and almost cooked through to the top. Then, using your bean-flipping skills (or a flexible spatula), move the eggs to the front of the pan and flip, gently cradling the eggs back into the pan. Place the pan back on the heat. For over easy eggs, it is only 30 seconds and they are done. For over medium, it may be 45 to 60 seconds. Slide the eggs from the pan directly onto the plate. Add salt and pepper to taste. For over hard eggs, keep them in the pan for another minute.

SCRAMBLED EGGS: Perfectly scrambled eggs are a little wet, a little buttery, and seasoned with a little salt and pepper. Scramble the raw eggs in a bowl with a fork, but don't scramble them too much; there should be a little white and a little yolk still separately swimming around. Season the eggs with a little salt and freshly ground black pepper before you begin cooking them. Start your pan on medium heat, add a little butter, and let the butter melt until sizzling. Be careful not to let it brown. Now, add the eggs and continue moving them around in the pan with a rubber spatula or a wire whisk. Cook them only until just set, but still a little wet, about 1 minute. They will continue to cook a little after they come out of the pan.

One thing the cooks at Bubby's always think about is having a very light touch when plating scrambled eggs. Rather than smashing the eggs downward, they use a spatula to ease them out of the pan with extra care. This makes for fluffy, nicely cooked eggs.

POACHED EGGS: Poached eggs are simple and delicious when prepared right. A little dash of acid (white vinegar or lemon juice) will ensure that the eggs won't stick to the bottom of the poaching pan. Although you can poach 6 or 8 eggs at a time, the more you cook at one time, the more difficult it becomes to manage them.

Fill a shallow 2-quart saucepan with water. Add ½ teaspoon white vinegar or fresh lemon juice and bring the liquid to a simmer over medium-high heat. Crack 2 extra-large eggs into the saucepan. Cook the eggs for 3 to 5 minutes, depending on how runny you like them. Once the whites are firm, the eggs are done. Remove the eggs from the saucepan with a slotted spoon. Add salt and pepper to taste before serving.

You can poach eggs the night before a brunch to save time. When you remove the eggs from the pan, place them in a container of icy water to cool them down fast and avoid overcooking. Otherwise, be sure that all the water is drained from the eggs before plating. To reheat them, simply place them gently in simmering water until they are hot, which takes about 1 minute.

BOILED EGGS: When boiling eggs, keep in mind that there are several stages of doneness. Fortunately, they are all marked by the time it takes to cook the eggs. A 3-minute egg is coddled; a 9-minute egg will cool to have a barely liquid center; a 10-minute egg has a very yellow yolk in the center; a 12-minute egg is a hard-boiled egg with a solid center. Anything past 12 minutes is overcooked, and the yolk will have a gray layer at the edge.

Bring a pot of water to a boil. Place the eggs into the boiling water with a slotted spoon and keep careful track of the time. When the boiled eggs have cooked to the desired doneness, either serve them hot in an appropriate egg server or let them cool down to peel later. Unpeeled boiled eggs can keep in the refrigerator for two days.

To peel hard-boiled eggs, crack them against a hard surface, such as the walls of the kitchen sink, and run them under cold water. Make sure all shell particles are removed.

EGGS IN THE HOLE

SERVES 1

*I*n my house, eggs in the hole were also called one-eyed sailors. Whatever they are called in yours, this is a great dish that children will love. It consists of bread with a hole punched in the middle, griddled with butter, and an egg dropped into the hole and then flipped over to griddle the other side. Depending on the thickness of your bread, or the type of bread, you could create a little "eye patch" by griddling the punched-out part and setting it on top of the egg. This dish is quite versatile. For a more sophisticated variation, try adding basil and Parmesan cheese or a smear of anchovy paste, a clove of roasted garlic, a slice of goat cheese, American cheese, or sharp Cheddar. Put a blanket of crispy fried ham over the "little sailor." For a romantic brunch for Valentine's Day, you could use a heart-shaped cookie cutter to punch out the hole in the middle of the bread. For heartier appetites try cutting a larger hole in the bread and cooking two eggs rather than just one.

1 slice bread (white or whole wheat)	1 extra-large egg
1¼ teaspoons unsalted butter	

1. Using a 1½-inch round cutter, cut a hole out of the center of the bread. Reserve the cut-out part.

2. Melt 1 teaspoon of the butter in a cast-iron skillet over medium heat. Place the slice of bread in the pan. Add the remaining ¼ teaspoon butter to the hole and let it melt.

3. Crack the egg directly into the middle of the hole. Let the egg and the bread cook for about 2 minutes. The object is to get the bread brown and the egg cooked just right at the same time.

4. When both the bread and the egg are cooked, use a sturdy spatula to flip over the bread. Cook for another 2 minutes to brown that side of the bread. Use a spatula to transfer it from the pan to a plate.

TOMATO EGGS IN THE HOLE VARIATION: Use a nice crusty sourdough bread cut ½ to ¾-inch thick. Rub the bread with garlic before punching out the hole, and griddle both sides of the bread before adding 3 tablespoons Roasted Tomato Sauce (page 289) to the hole. It will spread around the pan. Crack the egg into the hole. Spoon another tablespoon of sauce on top of the bread and top with a sprinkle of Parmesan cheese. Bake in a preheated 375°F oven for 4 or 5 minutes, until the egg is done to your liking.

SHIRRED EGGS

SERVES 1

*S*ometimes you just need the taste of some eggs cooked in butter or cream. Shirred eggs fit the bill: They're baked in hot fat or heavy cream. At Bubby's, we use either butter or bacon fat. They are baked in the same dish in which they will be served—a 4-inch oval ceramic ramekin is perfect.

2 tablespoons melted unsalted
   butter, bacon fat, or heavy cream
2 extra-large eggs

Good sea salt and freshly ground
   black pepper to taste

1. Preheat the oven to 375°F.

2. Place the melted butter, bacon fat, or heavy cream in a 4-ounce ovenproof oval ceramic ramekin. Place the ramekin in the oven for about 30 seconds to warm it. Crack the eggs into the warm butter, season with salt and pepper, and immediately place the ramekin in the oven.

3. Bake the eggs for 4 to 8 minutes, depending upon how done you like them.

DEVILED EGGS

*T*he beloved picnic classic is updated here with generous dashes of Tabasco and Worcestershire sauce. Be sure to give yourself time to boil the eggs in advance, so they can chill for at least an hour.

6 extra-large eggs, boiled for 12 minutes, drained, and cooled (see page 75)	1 teaspoon minced onion
1 teaspoon Dijon mustard	3 dashes Tabasco
3 tablespoons mayonnaise, homemade (page 284) or store-bought	¼ teaspoon Worcestershire sauce
	Kosher salt and cayenne pepper to taste
	Paprika

1. Peel the eggs under cold running water. Gently cut each egg in half lengthwise. Remove the yolks, being careful not to tear the whites. Place the yolks into a small mixing bowl and set aside the whites.

2. Mash the yolks with a fork. Stir in the mustard, mayonnaise, onion, Tabasco, Worcestershire sauce, salt, and cayenne pepper.

3. Using a teaspoon or a pastry bag fitted with the star tip, fill each half egg white with some of the seasoned yolk mixture. Sprinkle lightly with paprika.

CRAWFISH DEVILED EGGS VARIATION: You will need 4 ounces cooked crawfish tails (fresh and frozen are equally fine), 4 tablespoons chopped scallion greens, and ½ teaspoon Creole seasoning. Make the deviled egg filling through step 2. Roughly chop half the crawfish tails and stir them into the yolk mixture, along with 2 tablespoons of the chopped scallion greens and the Creole seasoning. Fill the eggs and top each with 1 crawfish tail, a sprinkling of chopped scallions, and a little sprinkle of paprika.

SPANISH OMELET WITH CHORIZO AND AVOCADO

SERVES 1

*C*horizo sausage gives this omelet a little kick and is a nice foil to the creamy-smooth avocado. For some extra spice, serve with Pico de Gallo (page 290) and fresh corn tortillas.

2 tablespoons olive oil

2 ounces cured chorizo, cut into
¼-inch dice (¼ cup)

1 small Spanish onion, cut into
¼-inch dice

2 garlic cloves, minced

1 ripe Roma or heirloom tomato,
cut into ¼-inch dice

1 tablespoon fresh lemon juice

3 extra-large eggs

Kosher salt and cayenne pepper to
taste

½ ripe avocado, peeled, pitted, and
sliced lengthwise

1. Heat 1 tablespoon of the olive oil in a 1½-quart saucepan over medium heat. Add the chorizo and sauté for 2 minutes, or until crisp.

2. Add the onion and garlic and cook for 4 to 5 minutes, or until soft and translucent. Stir in the tomato and lemon juice. Cook, stirring, for 3 to 5 minutes, or until thick.

3. Using a whisk or a fork, beat the eggs in a small bowl until frothy. Whisk in some salt and cayenne pepper.

4. Heat the remaining tablespoon of olive oil in an 8-inch nonstick skillet over medium heat. Pour the eggs into the pan, tilting the pan gently to evenly distribute the eggs. Let the eggs cook and set for about 5 seconds.

5. Using a silicone or rubber spatula, gently pull the cooked egg from the edges toward the center of the pan, while allowing the liquid egg to run back underneath and onto the hot pan. The omelet will cook in about 2 minutes. When it is fairly set but not overly firm, spoon about 4 tablespoons of the chorizo-tomato sauce onto one side of the omelet.

6. As you slide the omelet onto the plate, fold it in half to cover the sauce. Top the omelet with a little more of the sauce and the avocado slices.

OMELETS TO FLIP FOR

When it comes to omelets, there are scores of different combinations to try. In addition to using anything that might inspire you at your local farmers' market, you might also want to take a look around your fridge and pantry. Use any cheeses, meats, and vegetables that may be taking up space. Be as creative or simple as you want. Here are three variations on standard omelets that may be of interest.

INSIDE-OUT OMELET

This omelet, which features cheese essentially melted on the outside of the omelet, takes a little bit of skill. It is accomplished by making the omelet as usual, but instead of adding cheese at the end, you flip the omelet once, place the grated cheese on it, and flip it again so the cheese is on the pan. Let the cheese get all melty and a little crisp, then slide the omelet onto the plate, and fold, cheese side up. People go crazy for this little trick. Just be careful that when you flip it before the cheese-side-down flip, cheese doesn't go flying everywhere. Practice makes perfect.

BAKED OMELET

Any omelet can be a baked omelet. Baking is easier than flipping. Just heat the oven to 375°F, melt a little butter in an ovenproof pan, put the filling ingredients in the bottom of the pan, and pour the eggs over the top. If there is cheese in the omelet, put the cheese on top of the eggs and bake for 5 to 7 minutes, until it is done to your liking. The eggs will be slightly fluffy, almost like a soufflé.

CHILLED OMELET

Make a cold omelet using summer vegetables like tomatoes, zucchini, yellow summer squash, eggplant, and assorted baby root vegetables. Roast or sauté the vegetables very well and set aside to cool. Make an omelet as usual. When you are ready to fold the omelet, spoon some of the cooked vegetables onto one side of the omelet and fold the other half over. Refrigerate for an hour or until ready to serve. You might also wish to serve your chilled omelet as an unfolded frittata, in which case you would bake the frittata, slide it onto a plate, and chill it for an hour before serving. You can chill your frittata up to a day in advance. Serve chilled or at room temperature.

ASPARAGUS AND WHITE CHEDDAR OMELET

SERVES 1

*T*his is a springtime treat, when asparagus is at its peak and you can get the young, thin stalks. Making this with thick stalks is fine, though you may want to peel the tougher bottom half of the stalks before cooking. Blanching rather than steaming helps the asparagus retain its bright green color and firm texture. Serve with Niçoise Salad (page 160).

4 stalks asparagus	Kosher salt and freshly ground
3 extra-large eggs	black pepper to taste
1 tablespoon unsalted butter	¼ cup grated sharp white Cheddar
2 tablespoons thinly sliced shallot	cheese (1 ounce)
2 tablespoons chopped scallion	
(white and pale green parts)	

1. Trim the asparagus spears by breaking them off where they snap and discarding the tough bottom stems. Bring a 1- or 2-quart saucepan of lightly salted water to a boil. Blanch the asparagus spears for 1 minute. Drain well. Place the asparagus in a bowl of cold water for 1 minute, then drain again. Cut into 1-inch pieces.

2. Using a wire whisk or a fork, beat the eggs in a small bowl until frothy.

3. Heat the butter in an 8-inch nonstick skillet over medium heat. Add the shallot and sauté for 1 minute, or until fragrant but not brown. Add the asparagus and sauté for 1 minute. Add the scallion and sauté for 1 minute. Season with salt and pepper.

4. Pour the eggs into the pan, tilting the pan gently to evenly distribute the eggs over the vegetables. Let the eggs cook and set for about 5 seconds. Using a silicone or rubber spatula, gently pull the cooked egg from the edges toward the center of the pan, while allowing the liquid egg to run underneath and onto the hot pan. After about 20 seconds, or when the eggs look cooked but are still moist, sprinkle the omelet with the Cheddar cheese.

5. Using the spatula, fold the omelet in half. Cook the omelet for another 30 seconds, or until the cheese is melted. Tip the pan over a serving plate so that the omelet slides onto the plate bottom side up.

SIZZLING HAM AND GRUYÈRE OMELET

SERVES 1

For this luxurious omelet, choose a good-quality lean ham, but avoid pepper ham or maple-glazed ham because you don't want to distract from the flavor of the Gruyère, which has a wonderful taste and melts beautifully. If you don't have Gruyère, you can use Emmenthal or Beaufort. This recipe doesn't call for salt because both the ham and the Gruyère are naturally salty. Serve with Steamed Sesame Spinach (page 216).

3 extra-large eggs
1 tablespoon unsalted butter
½ cup chopped good-quality cooked
    ham slices (2- to 3-inch squares)

¼ cup grated Gruyère cheese
    (1 ounce)

1. Using a whisk or a fork, beat the eggs in a small bowl until frothy.

2. Heat the butter in an 8-inch nonstick skillet over medium heat. Add the ham and sauté for 1 minute, or until crisp.

3. Pour the eggs into the pan, tilting the pan gently to evenly distribute the eggs over the ham. Let the eggs cook and set for about 5 seconds.

4. Using a silicone or rubber spatula, gently pull the cooked egg from the edges toward the center of the pan, while allowing the liquid egg to run underneath and onto the hot pan. After about 20 seconds, or when the eggs look cooked but are still moist, sprinkle the omelet with the Gruyère cheese.

5. Using the spatula, fold the omelet in half. Cook the omelet for another 30 seconds, or until the cheese is melted. Tip the pan over a serving plate so that the omelet slides onto the plate bottom side up.

SPINACH AND BRIE OMELET

SERVES 1

Fresh spinach and creamy Brie make a delectable combination, especially in an omelet. One big bunch of spinach yields only about 1 cup of cooked spinach, but it is enough for three or four omelets. You will need about ⅓ cup of steamed, chopped spinach for each omelet. Serve with Butter and Parsley Potatoes (page 222).

1 bunch fresh spinach	1 tablespoon unsalted butter
3 extra-large eggs	¼ cup thinly sliced Brie (1 ounce),
Kosher salt and freshly ground	rind left on
black pepper to taste	

1. Wash the spinach in plenty of cold water at least twice to get rid of any grit or sand. The easiest way is to swish it around in a bowlful of cold water and lift it out. If there's grit in the bottom of the bowl, change the water and repeat the process. You can leave on the stems if you're using baby spinach. Otherwise, tear off the stems at the base of the large, crinkly leaves and discard.

2. Steam the spinach by tossing it with a little water in a skillet over high heat. Alternatively, microwave it for 1 minute.

3. Cool the spinach by running it under cold water, and drain it well in a colander. Give it a couple of good squeezes with your hands to get rid of as much liquid as possible. Using a sharp knife, roughly chop the spinach into ½-inch pieces.

4. Using a whisk or a fork, beat the eggs with some salt and pepper in a small bowl until frothy.

5. Heat the butter in an 8-inch nonstick skillet over medium heat. Add ⅓ cup of the spinach and sauté for 1 minute, or until very hot.

6. Pour the eggs into the pan, tilting the pan to evenly distribute the eggs over the spinach. Let the eggs cook and set for about 5 seconds.

7. Using a silicone or rubber spatula, gently pull the cooked egg from the edges toward the center of the pan, while allowing the liquid egg to run underneath and onto the hot pan. After about 30 seconds, or when the eggs look cooked but are still moist, arrange the Brie slices on half of the omelet. The cheese is soft and will melt quickly.

8. Using the spatula, fold the omelet in half. Cook the omelet for another 10 seconds. Slide the omelet from the pan onto a serving plate.

CAJUN OMELET

A robust Cajun tomato sauce flecked with bacon and chopped bell peppers blankets this spicy omelet, which is bursting with andouille sausage, crawfish, and sautéed vegetables. You could make the sauce ahead of time, refrigerate it, and reheat it before using.

For the sauce
1 slice bacon, finely diced
½ cup finely chopped onion
1 teaspoon finely diced garlic
¼ cup finely diced red bell pepper
¼ cup finely diced green bell pepper
1 cup diced peeled tomatoes
1 teaspoon Tabasco
1 teaspoon chopped fresh parsley
Pinch of dried thyme
1 bay leaf
Kosher salt and cayenne pepper
   to taste

For the omelet
3 extra-large eggs
1 teaspoon unsalted butter
3 ounces andouille sausage, cut into
   1-inch pieces
2 tablespoons chopped scallion
   (green parts only)
2 ounces fresh or frozen crawfish
   tails, thawed if frozen

1. Make the sauce: Fry the bacon in a small skillet over medium heat until crisp. Use a slotted spoon to transfer the bacon from the skillet to a plate.

2. In the same skillet, sauté the onion and garlic for 2 minutes, or until the onion is translucent. Add the red and green bell peppers and cook for 1 minute, or until soft. Add the tomatoes, breaking them up with a wooden spoon as you stir.

3. Lower the heat to a simmer. Stir in the Tabasco, parsley, thyme, bay leaf, bacon, salt, and cayenne pepper. Simmer for 10 to 15 minutes, or until most of the water has cooked out of the vegetables and the sauce has thickened. Remove and discard the bay leaf. Taste the sauce and adjust the seasoning with salt and cayenne pepper.

4. Make the omelet: Using a whisk or a fork, beat the eggs in a small bowl until frothy.

5. Heat an 8-inch nonstick skillet over medium heat for 30 seconds. Add the butter. Add the andouille sausage and let it cook in the butter for 2 to 3 minutes, until nice and crispy. Stir in half of the scallion and the crawfish.

6. Pour the eggs into the pan, tilting the pan gently to evenly distribute the eggs over the sausage. Let the eggs cook and set for about 5 minutes. Using a silicone or rubber spatula, gently pull the cooked egg from the edges toward the center of the pan, while allowing the liquid egg to run underneath and onto the hot pan. When the sides of the omelet begin to rise up the edges of the pan, flip the omelet. It is done when it is nicely set but not overly firm. There should be a hint of just-cooked egg in the center of the omelet.

7. Using the spatula, fold the omelet in half and slide it onto a serving plate. Spoon about ¼ cup of the sauce over the top of the omelet. Sprinkle with the remaining scallion and serve.

CRAB OMELET

SERVES 1

*I*f you're using fresh crabs, you want to use the meatiest ones you can find, such as Dungeness crabs from the West Coast. The little blue Maryland crabs are good, too, but they are a lot of work to get the meat. I usually figure about one-third of the whole crab weight will be meat. So, for every pound of crab, you might get one-third pound of cleaned meat. If fresh crabs are not available, you can usually find freshly picked lump crabmeat at your fish market. If all else fails, frozen pasteurized canned crab will suffice. Serve with Asparagus Potato Hash (page 210).

3 extra-large eggs
1 tablespoon unsalted butter
2 tablespoons chopped red bell
  pepper
2 tablespoons chopped scallion
  (green parts only)

3 ounces (¼ cup) crabmeat (see
  sidebar)
¼ teaspoon chopped fresh tarragon

1. Using a whisk or a fork, beat the eggs in a small bowl until frothy.

2. Heat the butter in an 8-inch nonstick skillet over medium heat. Add the bell pepper and scallion. Sauté for 3 minutes, or until the vegetables start to soften. Add the crab and sauté for 1 minute.

3. Pour the eggs into the pan, tilting the pan gently to evenly distribute the eggs over the crabmeat. Let the eggs cook and set for about 5 seconds.

4. Using a silicone or rubber spatula, gently pull the cooked egg from the edges toward the center of the pan, while allowing the liquid egg to run underneath and onto the hot pan. When the sides of the omelet begin to rise up the edges of the pan, flip the omelet. It is done when it is nicely set but not overly firm. There should be traces of just-cooked egg in the center of the omelet.

5. Using the spatula, fold the omelet in half and slide it onto a serving plate. Sprinkle with the tarragon and serve.

PREPARING FRESH CRABMEAT

Flavorful, buttery-rich Dungeness crab must be cooked and cleaned before using. It's some work, but it's worth it. Boil the crab first in plenty of seasoned water (I like a good crab boil, like Old Bay) for 15 to 18 minutes, until brightly colored all over. Drain, and stop the cooking by plunging the crab into a bowl of ice water. To clean a whole cooked crab, hold the crab over a bowl to catch the juices. Then find the folding flap on the bottom; pull and twist that off. Take the crab in one hand and place the thumb of your other hand under the shell, right at the midpoint. Lift off the shell, and scrape out and discard the orange-tinted soft organs and feather gills. Holding the crab in both hands, break it in half lengthwise down the center and pull off the legs. Crack the shell with a meat mallet or a small hammer, and remove the meat, using your fingers and a fork. When the meat has been removed, pick through it once more very well with your fingers to make sure all the bits of shell and cartilage have been removed. The crabmeat is now ready to use.

On the East Coast, blue crabs are more readily available (and less expensive). Blue crabs are in season from June to September. They are much smaller, and therefore more work than Dungeness crabs, but folks in the Chesapeake Bay area would argue that they are the tastiest crabs around. Buy jumbo blue crabs, and prepare them using the same method.

APPLE, CHEDDAR, AND BACON OMELET

SERVES 1

*C*heddar and apples are great together, and the combination gets even better when you add some superior-tasting slab bacon. Any sweet-tart apple—Macoun, Mutsu, Greening, Winesap— works well here.

3 extra-large eggs

2 slices thick slab bacon, cut into
   ¼-inch pieces

¼ sweet-tart apple, cored, peeled,
   and thinly sliced

Kosher salt and freshly ground
   black pepper to taste

1 teaspoon unsalted butter

¼ cup grated sharp white Cheddar
   cheese (1 ounce)

1. Using a whisk or a fork, beat the eggs in a small bowl until frothy.

2. Sauté the bacon in an 8-inch nonstick skillet over medium heat for 5 minutes, or until crisp. Transfer the cooked bacon to paper towels; set aside. Drain all but 1 tablespoon of the bacon fat from the skillet and either discard it or reserve it for another use.

3. Sauté the sliced apple in the remaining bacon fat for 3 minutes, or until softened. Season lightly with salt and pepper.

4. Return the bacon to the pan. Sauté the bacon and apple until hot. Add the butter and when sizzling, pour the eggs into the pan, tilting the pan gently to evenly distribute the eggs around the bacon and apple. Let the eggs cook and set for about 5 seconds.

5. Using a silicone or rubber spatula, gently pull the cooked egg from the edges toward the center of the pan, while allowing the liquid egg to run underneath and onto the hot pan. When the sides of the omelet begin to rise up the edge of the pan, flip the omelet. It is done when it's nicely set but not overly firm. There should be a hint of just-cooked egg in the center of the omelet.

6. Sprinkle the Cheddar cheese evenly over the top of the omelet. Using the spatula, fold the omelet in half and slide it onto a serving plate.

ROASTED PEAR AND GOAT CHEESE OMELET

SERVES 1

R oasting pears accentuates their sweetness, making them the perfect match for tangy goat cheese. Allow yourself enough time to prepare the pears and let them cool—about 30 minutes in total. This can be done several hours ahead or even a day before you plan to make the omelet, which takes under 10 minutes to cook. You'll have enough roasted pears for four omelets; if you make only one, use the extra pears to top pancakes or waffles.

Bartlett or Bosc pears are a good choice for this recipe, although you could use apples instead. Be sure your goat cheese is chèvre, which means that it's made entirely from goat's milk. Among the better-known types of chèvre are Montrachet, Banon, and Bucheron.

For the pears	For the omelet
2 sweet ripe pears, peeled, cored, and cut lengthwise into ¼-inch-thick slices	3 extra-large eggs
	1 teaspoon unsalted butter, melted
2 tablespoons unsalted butter, melted	2 ounces good-quality goat cheese, crumbled (¼ cup)
Pinch of kosher salt	1 teaspoon chopped fresh parsley

1. Preheat the oven to 375°F.

2. Toss together the pear slices, melted butter, and salt in a small shallow baking pan. Roast the pears for 5 minutes. Using tongs or a spatula, turn over the pears so they'll cook evenly. Continue to roast for another 10 to 15 minutes, or until browned. Set aside to cool.

3. Using a whisk or a fork, beat the eggs in a small bowl until frothy.

4. For each omelet, sauté 8 pear slices in the butter in an 8-inch nonstick skillet over medium heat for 1 minute. Pour the eggs into the pan, tilting the pan gently to evenly distribute the eggs around the pear slices. Let the eggs cook and set for about 5 seconds.

5. Using a silicone or rubber spatula, gently pull the cooked egg from the edges toward the center of the pan, while allowing the liquid egg to run underneath and onto the hot pan. When the sides of the omelet begin to rise up the edge of the pan, flip the omelet. It is done when it is nicely set but not overly firm. There should be traces of just-cooked egg in the center of the omelet.

6. Sprinkle the goat cheese over half of the omelet. Using the spatula, fold the omelet in half and slide it onto a serving plate. Sprinkle with the parsley and serve.

ROASTING FRUIT

Roasting intensifies a fruit's naturally sweet flavor, softens it, and opens up many serving possibilities. You can top roasted fruit with ice cream or whipped cream, roll it into a crêpe, or serve it with cakes and other pastries. Apples, pears, apricots, plums, and nectarines are especially delicious when roasted.

To roast fruit, preheat the oven to 375°F. Mix the fruit with a little lemon juice in a large bowl. Generously butter a rimmed baking sheet. Place the fruit on the prepared sheet and drizzle with a little melted butter. Roast the fruit for about 20 to 25 minutes, or until soft and golden, turning it with a spatula after 10 minutes. Let the fruit cool on the baking sheet. You can store roasted fruit in the refrigerator for up to 2 days.

Broccoli, Onion, and Cheddar Omelet

SERVES 1

The key to making a great broccoli omelet is to slightly overcook the broccoli. One of the best cheeses to pair with broccoli in many a dish is Cheddar because of its sharp, tangy taste.

1 cup peeled and diced broccoli florets and stems (½-inch pieces)	1½ teaspoons unsalted butter
	Kosher salt and freshly ground black pepper to taste
3 extra-large eggs	¼ cup grated sharp white Cheddar cheese (1 ounce)
¼ cup finely diced red onion	

1. Bring a small pot of salted water to a boil over medium heat. Cook the broccoli for 5 minutes, or until very soft. Drain and set aside to cool.

2. Using a whisk or a fork, beat the eggs in a small bowl until frothy.

3. Sauté the red onion in 1 teaspoon of the butter in an 8-inch nonstick skillet over medium heat for 2 minutes, or until soft and translucent. Add the broccoli and cook for about 1 minute. Season with salt and pepper.

4. Add the remaining ½ teaspoon butter and pour the eggs into the pan, tilting the pan gently to evenly distribute the eggs over the broccoli. Let the eggs cook and set for about 5 seconds.

5. Using a silicone or rubber spatula, gently pull the cooked egg from the edges toward the center of the pan, while allowing the liquid egg to run underneath and onto the hot pan. Continue for 2 to 3 minutes, or until the omelet is set and there are a few traces of just-cooked egg in the center of the omelet.

6. Sprinkle the Cheddar cheese on half of the omelet. Using the spatula, fold the omelet in half, enclosing the cheese. Slide the omelet onto a serving plate and serve immediately.

FARMER'S FRITTATA

Bubby's
SIGNATURE DISH

SERVES 1

*A*s the name implies, this is a workingman's or -woman's omelet, bulging with crispy chunks of slab bacon, potatoes, and onions. It's also great with leeks. There's no need to fold this before serving. It's served as is, flat and round, and right out of the skillet. Serve with Zucchini Bread with Zucchini Flowers (page 48).

4 slices slab bacon	1 tablespoon unsalted butter
3 extra-large eggs	1 cup Home Fries (page 209)

1. Fry the bacon in an 8-inch nonstick skillet over medium heat until crisp. Remove the bacon to a paper towel–lined plate to cool slightly. Cut it into 2-inch pieces.

2. Using a whisk or a fork, beat the eggs in a small bowl until frothy.

3. Heat the butter in a separate skillet over medium-high heat. Add the home fries and cook for 1 minute, or until the fries are nice and crispy. Add the bacon and toss it with the home fries until well combined.

4. Pour the eggs into the pan, tilting the pan to evenly distribute the eggs over the home fries and bacon. Using a silicone or rubber spatula, gently pull the cooked egg from the edges toward the center of the pan, while allowing the liquid egg to run underneath and onto the hot pan. When the sides of the omelet begin to rise up the edge of the pan, flip the omelet. It is done when it is nicely set but not overly firm. There should be traces of just-cooked egg in the center of the frittata. Serve hot.

LOBSTER PECORINO FRITTATA

SERVES 6

This dish tastes like an entire New England clambake all folded into a luxurious frittata. Budget enough time to bake the potato and to steam the lobster. Though this is a little more work than most brunch dishes, it's worth the extra time when you really want to pamper some guests, and yourself. Serve with Spicy Zucchini with Mint (page 218).

1 large Idaho potato

One 1½- to 2-pound live lobster

12 extra-large eggs

½ cup heavy cream

8 tablespoons (1 stick) unsalted butter

Kosher salt and freshly ground black pepper to taste

1 red onion, finely diced

Kernels from 2 ears fresh corn

¼ cup chopped fresh parsley

½ cup freshly grated Pecorino Romano cheese

1. Preheat the oven to 400°F.

2. Scrub the potato and prick it in several places with a fork. Place the potato on the oven rack and bake for 40 to 45 minutes, depending on its size. When the potato is soft, remove it from the oven and set aside to cool. Reduce the oven temperature to 350°F.

3. Set a colander in the bottom of a deep, wide stockpot and fill the stockpot with water to a depth of about 1½ inches. Salt the water generously. Bring the water to a boil over high heat. When the water boils, place the lobster into the colander. Cover the pot, lower the heat to a simmer, and steam the lobster for about 15 minutes. Remove the lobster from the pot and plunge it into cold water to stop the cooking. Let cool completely.

4. Once the lobster has cooled, remove the meat and cut it into bite-size pieces. Set aside.

5. Without removing its skin, cut the potato in half lengthwise. Cut each half into ½-inch-thick half-moon slices.

6. Using a whisk or a fork, beat the eggs in a medium bowl until frothy. Beat in the heavy cream.

7. Heat 4 tablespoons of the butter in a 10-inch nonstick ovenproof skillet over medium heat. Add the potato slices and turn the heat to medium-high. Season with salt and pepper. Cook the potatoes, continuously flipping them with a spatula, until browned. Don't worry—the potatoes won't fall apart from all the handling. Watch carefully and don't allow them to burn.

8. When the potatoes are nicely browned, add the red onion and corn. Cook, stirring, for 2 minutes, or until the vegetables are starting to color. To ensure that the mixture doesn't stick to the bottom of the pan, run a spatula along the edges and bottom to dislodge any vegetables that adhere to the pan.

9. Add the remaining 4 tablespoons butter to the pan and allow to melt and begin to sizzle. Add the lobster and parsley. Season with salt and pepper. Pour the eggs evenly over the mixture in the pan. Sprinkle with the Pecorino cheese.

10. Bake the frittata for 8 to 10 minutes, or until it begins to puff up slightly. It should still be a little runny in the very center. Allow the frittata to stand for 5 minutes. Cut into wedges and serve.

ZUCCHINI, TOMATO, AND PARMESAN FRITTATA

SERVES 1

*T*his late-summer indulgence showcases a harvest of vegetables abundant from August until the end of September. Although you can buy these ingredients year-round, this frittata is at its best when made with ripe in-season produce. This recipe can be doubled, but don't try to make more than two frittatas at a time or you'll end up with runny, undercooked eggs. This is delicious accompanied by garlic toast. Serve with Potato Pancakes (page 213).

½ cup grated unpeeled zucchini	Kosher salt and freshly ground
3 extra-large eggs	black pepper to taste
2 teaspoons olive oil	¼ cup freshly grated Parmesan
½ cup chopped tomato	cheese (1 ounce)
1 teaspoon minced garlic	2 fresh basil leaves, thinly sliced

1. Lightly salt the zucchini and set it aside in a colander to drain for 30 minutes. Rinse under cold water and squeeze dry thoroughly in a kitchen towel.

2. Preheat the oven to 400°F.

3. Using a whisk or a fork, beat the eggs in a small bowl until frothy.

4. Heat 1 teaspoon of the olive oil in an 8-inch ovenproof nonstick skillet over medium-high heat. Add the zucchini, tomato, and garlic and sauté for 3 to 4 minutes, or until softened. Season with salt and pepper.

5. Add the remaining 1 teaspoon olive oil to the skillet and turn up the heat to medium-high for 30 seconds. Pour the eggs into the pan and cook for about 30 seconds, without stirring, until the edges start to bubble. Sprinkle the eggs with half of the Parmesan cheese.

6. Bake the frittata for 10 minutes, or until it is nicely set but not overly firm. There should be traces of just-cooked egg in the center of the frittata. Transfer the frittata to a serving plate. Sprinkle with the remaining Parmesan cheese and the basil. Allow the frittata to stand for 5 minutes. Serve hot.

ROASTED ASPARAGUS AND LEEK FRITTATA

SERVES 2

A fine choice for a spring menu, although good whenever you can find fresh asparagus, this frittata has an especially nice flavor because the asparagus and leeks are roasted and caramelized before being added. If you like, roast the vegetables a day ahead of time and refrigerate them until ready to use.

1 bunch asparagus, trimmed of
   tough bottom stems
¼ cup olive oil
2½ teaspoons kosher salt
1 teaspoon freshly ground black
   pepper
1 tablespoon sliced garlic

2 leeks (white and pale green parts),
   trimmed, halved, and washed
   very well
1 red onion, cut into ½-inch dice
6 extra-large eggs
¼ cup heavy cream

1. Preheat the oven to 450°F.

2. Toss the asparagus with 1 tablespoon of the olive oil, 1 teaspoon of the salt, and ¼ teaspoon of the pepper in a large mixing bowl. Stir in the garlic. Spread out the asparagus on a baking sheet.

3. In the same mixing bowl, toss the leeks with 2 tablespoons of the olive oil, 1 teaspoon of the salt, and ½ teaspoon of the pepper. Spread out the leeks on a separate baking sheet.

4. Put both baking sheets in the oven and roast the asparagus and leeks for 5 minutes. Remove the vegetables from the oven, turn once, and return to the oven for another 5 minutes, or until nicely browned. Remove from the oven and let cool for 5 minutes on the baking sheets.

5. Reduce the oven temperature to 350°F.

6. Chop the asparagus and leeks into 1-inch pieces.

7. Heat the remaining 1 tablespoon olive oil in a 10-inch ovenproof nonstick skillet over medium heat. Add the asparagus, leeks, and red onion and cook for 2 minutes.

8. Using a whisk or a fork, beat the eggs and cream with the remaining ½ teaspoon salt and the remaining ¼ teaspoon pepper in a bowl until frothy. Pour the egg mixture over the asparagus and leeks.

9. Bake the frittata for 10 to 12 minutes, or until it is nicely set but not overly firm. Allow the frittata to stand for 5 minutes. Cut into wedges and serve.

SIZZLING HAM AND CHEDDAR SCRAMBLE

SERVES 1

This egg dish is bursting with generous chunks of ham and scallion and bound with an abundance of sharp Cheddar. Be sure your ham is sizzling nicely before adding the eggs, and don't overcook this scramble: The eggs are just right when they're still a little wet. Serve with Blackberry Corn Muffins (page 39).

3 extra-large eggs

1 tablespoon unsalted butter

3 ounces sliced cooked ham, cut
    into 2-inch squares

2 tablespoons chopped scallion
    (white and pale green parts)

¼ cup grated sharp white Cheddar
    cheese (1 ounce)

Kosher salt and freshly ground
    black pepper to taste

1. Using a whisk or a fork, beat the eggs in a small bowl until frothy.

2. Place an 8-inch nonstick omelet pan or skillet over medium-high heat and preheat for 30 seconds. When the pan is nice and hot, add the butter and ham. Cook, stirring, for about 1 minute.

3. Reduce the heat under the pan to low. Stir in the scallion, the eggs, Cheddar cheese, salt, and pepper and cook, stirring gently and constantly pushing the eggs toward the center of the pan with a rubber spatula, until they are nearly set but still soft and creamy. Season with salt and pepper. Spoon onto a serving plate and serve immediately.

MUSHROOM AND LEEK SCRAMBLE

SERVES 1

*I*n the spring we go to the farmers' market for morels and in the fall for chanterelles. Either mushroom is wonderful in this dish, as are cremini, oysters, hen o' the woods, trumpets, porcini, and portobellos. One cautionary note: Know your mushrooms, and never eat any that you pick yourself unless you are absolutely certain they're edible. See Alice in Wonderland for the effects of eating the wrong mushrooms or speak to someone at your local emergency room for details.*

3 extra-large eggs
3 tablespoons unsalted butter
2 small leeks (white and pale green
    parts), trimmed (see sidebar),
    cut into ½-inch pieces, and
    washed very well (about 1 cup)

4 ounces wild mushrooms, such as
    morels or chanterelles, cleaned
Kosher salt and freshly ground
    black pepper to taste

1. Using a whisk or a fork, beat the eggs in a small bowl until frothy.

2. Heat the butter in an 8-inch nonstick skillet over medium heat. Add the leeks and cook for 2 minutes, or until they start to soften. Add the mushrooms and sauté for another 2 or 3 minutes, or until the mushrooms are soft and the liquid has evaporated.

3. Reduce the heat under the pan to low. Pour the eggs into the pan and cook, stirring gently, until they are nearly set but still soft and creamy. Season with salt and pepper. Spoon onto a serving plate and serve immediately.

A LESSON ON LEEKS

Since a lot of recipes call for just the white part of the leek, always look for leeks with the largest amount of white on them. Trim away the hairy root where it joins the white section of the leek and pull off the outer membranes. Also cut away the outer, dark green leaves. Underneath, the pale green or white interior is what you'll want to use. To get rid of sand, slice or chop the leeks first. Soak the pieces in a large bowl of cold water, changing the water at least twice.

WILD RAMPS AND PARMESAN SCRAMBLE

SERVES 1

*O*ur friend Gerry has a farm in upstate New York, in Delaware County, and it is a trove of little wildly growing goodies. Each spring, around the end of April through the end of May, little leafy wild leeks, called ramps, spring up (ahead of the rhubarb, ahead of the asparagus) in patches on the side of streamlets. These wild leeks taste amazingly good with eggs, though we often pickle the bulbs and use just the leaves for scrambled eggs. At our local farmers' market in Manhattan's Union Square, ramps are one of the first green things to fill the winter-barren tables. If you can't find ramps, leeks make a good substitute. Use one-quarter of a well-washed, chopped leek per serving. Also try substituting goat cheese for the Parmesan for a slightly different flavor. Serve with Skillet Hash Browns (page 211).

4 ounces ramps

3 extra-large eggs

2 tablespoons unsalted butter

1 ounce Parmesan cheese, shaved
    with a carrot peeler (¼ cup)

Kosher salt and freshly ground
    black pepper to taste

1. Wash the ramps very well under cold running water. Trim and chop them into 1- or 2-inch pieces. You should have about ½ cup of chopped ramps.

2. Using a whisk or a fork, beat the eggs in a small bowl until frothy.

3. Heat the butter in an 8-inch nonstick skillet over medium heat. Add the ramps and sauté for 3 minutes, or until they begin to soften.

4. Reduce the heat under the pan to low. Pour the eggs into the pan. Cook, constantly pushing the eggs toward the center of the pan with a rubber spatula, until the eggs begin to thicken. Sprinkle with the Parmesan cheese and season with salt and pepper. Continue to cook and stir the eggs over low heat for another minute, or until nearly set but still soft and creamy. Spoon the eggs onto a serving plate and serve immediately.

JALAPEÑO AND CHEDDAR SCRAMBLE

SERVES 1

*T*hose who like a little extra kick in their eggs will enjoy this dish. Customize it by adding a little extra jalapeño, which will increase the heat. The clean, bright flavor of cilantro is excellent here, and it adds color as well.

3 extra-large eggs
1 tablespoon unsalted butter
½ to 1 jarred pickled jalapeño
    pepper, thinly sliced into
    rounds, seeds intact
¼ cup grated sharp white Cheddar
    cheese (1 ounce)

1 teaspoon chopped fresh
    cilantro
Kosher salt and freshly ground
    black pepper to taste

1. Using a whisk or a fork, beat the eggs in a small bowl until frothy.

2. Heat the butter in an 8-inch nonstick skillet over medium heat. Add the jalapeño slices and sauté for 1 minute, or until hot.

3. Pour the eggs into the pan. Cook over medium heat, constantly pushing them toward the center of the pan with a rubber spatula, until they begin to thicken. Sprinkle with the Cheddar cheese and half the cilantro. Season with salt and pepper.

4. Continue to cook and stir the eggs for another minute or so, until nearly set but still soft and creamy. Spoon the eggs onto a serving plate, sprinkle with the remaining cilantro, and serve immediately.

ANDOUILLE AND CRAWFISH SCRAMBLE

SERVES 1

Andouille, a spicy Cajun sausage, is a must in dishes like jambalaya. Here, along with another favorite Louisiana ingredient, crawfish, it flavors a delectable scramble that will make you think of New Orleans. You may use either fresh or frozen crawfish tails. In case you've never eaten them, crawfish tails have a flavor that is somewhat like shrimp, only sweeter.

3 extra-large eggs

1 tablespoon olive oil

2 ounces andouille sausage, cut into
    ¼-inch-thick slices

1 tablespoon unsalted butter

2 ounces fresh or frozen crawfish
    tails, thawed if frozen

2 tablespoons sliced scallion (white
    and pale green parts)

Kosher salt and freshly ground
    black pepper to taste

Dash of paprika

1. Using a whisk or a fork, beat the eggs in a small bowl until frothy.

2. Heat the olive oil in an 8-inch nonstick skillet over medium heat. Add the andouille sausage and sauté for 1 to 2 minutes, or until crisp. Reduce the heat to low. Add the butter, crawfish tails, and scallion. Stir to combine.

3. Pour the eggs into the pan and cook, stirring gently and constantly pushing the eggs toward the center of the pan with a rubber spatula, until they are nearly set but still soft and creamy. Season with salt and pepper and sprinkle with the paprika. Spoon onto a serving plate and serve immediately.

SMOKED TROUT SCRAMBLE VARIATION. Omit the sausage and crawfish. Stir ½ cup smoked trout chunks into the egg mixture as the eggs start to thicken. Continue to cook until the eggs are soft but still creamy. Spoon the eggs onto a serving plate and top with Horseradish Cream (page 157).

TOMATO, BASIL, AND BUFFALO MOZZARELLA SCRAMBLE

SERVES 1

*M*ade in summer at the height of tomato season, this scramble is wonderful with fresh mozzarella or burrata, a delicious, buttery-textured Italian cheese. It's important not to overcook the tomatoes or the basil, which will keep its bright green color when added toward the end.

3 extra-large eggs
1 tablespoon olive oil
½ teaspoon minced garlic
Kosher salt and freshly ground
    black pepper to taste
¼ cup chopped tomato

1 or 2 fresh basil leaves, thinly
    sliced
1 ounce fresh buffalo mozzarella or
    burrata cheese, cut into ¼-inch
    cubes

1. Using a whisk or a fork, beat the eggs in a small bowl until frothy.

2. Heat the olive oil in an 8-inch nonstick skillet over medium heat. Add the garlic and sauté for 1 minute, or until just starting to color.

3. Reduce the heat under the pan to low. Pour the eggs into the pan and cook, stirring gently and constantly pushing the eggs toward the center of the pan with a rubber spatula, until they are nearly set but still soft and creamy.

4. Season with salt and pepper. Stir in the tomato, basil, and mozzarella cheese. Cook and stir for 30 seconds, or until the cheese is barely melted. Spoon onto a serving plate and serve immediately.

GREEN EGGS AND HAM

(BASIL PARMESAN SCRAMBLED EGGS WITH SEARED HAM STEAK)

SERVES 1

This Bubby's version of Dr. Seuss's whimsical creation will satisfy kids and adults alike. Serve this children's classic with Home Fries (page 209) or Stone-Ground Hominy Grits (page 207).

For the basil purée
1 cup packed fresh basil leaves
½ cup fresh parsley leaves
1 small garlic clove
2 tablespoons olive oil

For the eggs
3 extra-large eggs
One 4- to 6-ounce ham slice
1 teaspoon unsalted butter
2 tablespoons freshly grated
  Parmesan cheese

1. Make the basil purée: In the work bowl of a food processor or blender, purée the basil, parsley, garlic, olive oil, and 2 tablespoons of water until smooth.

2. Make the eggs: Using a whisk or a fork, beat the eggs in a small bowl until frothy.

3. Sear the ham in a hot 8-inch nonstick skillet for 1 minute, or until crispy.

4. Heat the skillet over medium heat for 1 minute. Add the butter and lower the heat slightly. Pour the eggs into the pan. Cook, constantly pushing the eggs toward the center of the pan with a rubber spatula, until they begin to thicken. Stir in 2 tablespoons of the basil purée and 1½ tablespoons of the Parmesan cheese. Continue to cook and stir the eggs until they are nearly set but still soft and creamy. Arrange the eggs and ham on a serving plate. Sprinkle the remaining Parmesan cheese over the eggs and serve immediately.

CARAMELIZED ONION AND PEPPER TORTA

SERVES 2

Torta—*Spanish for "cake," "loaf," or "sandwich"—is also a substantial brunch entrée in which the eggs are baked, often with vegetables. In this version, caramelizing brings out the natural sweetness in the onion and red bell pepper. Serve this torta either hot or at room temperature with sourdough toast and slab bacon.*

3 tablespoons unsalted butter
½ red onion, cut lengthwise into
   thin slices
1 red bell pepper, cored, halved,
   seeded, and cut into thin strips

Kosher salt and freshly ground
   black pepper to taste
6 extra-large eggs

1. Heat 1 tablespoon of the butter in an 8-inch ovenproof nonstick skillet over low heat. Add the onion and bell pepper. Sauté, stirring often, for 20 to 30 minutes, or until caramelized. Season with salt and pepper.

2. Preheat the oven to 375°F.

3. Using a whisk or a fork, beat the eggs in a medium bowl until frothy.

4. Add the remaining 2 tablespoons of butter to the pan with the onion and pepper.

5. Pour the eggs over the onion and pepper, tilting the pan gently to evenly distribute the eggs around the onion and pepper.

6. Bake for about 10 minutes, or until the middle is slightly soft and the edges are rising up the edges of the pan. Allow the torta to stand for 10 minutes. Cut into wedges and serve immediately.

BACON, LEEK, AND ONION CASSEROLE

SERVES 4

This layered, all-in-one brunch casserole is great for when you're serving four or more people because it can be prepped before your guests arrive. It's an old-time casserole with the added flavor of leeks and some delicious homemade fried onion straws on top.

For the onion straws
1 onion, very thinly sliced into
   rings
3 tablespoons salt
1 cup all-purpose flour
1 teaspoon freshly ground black
   pepper
1 teaspoon paprika
½ teaspoon garlic powder
4 cups vegetable oil

For the casserole
1 pound bacon, cut into 2-inch
   pieces
2 leeks (white and pale green parts),
   trimmed, chopped, and washed
   very well
12 extra-large eggs
1 cup milk
1 tablespoon kosher salt
1 teaspoon freshly ground black
   pepper
3 cups grated Gruyère cheese
   (12 ounces)
3 tablespoons chopped fresh parsley

1. Make the onion straws: Gently separate the onion rings in a colander and sprinkle with 2 tablespoons of the salt. Let sit for 30 minutes to extract the water.

2. Combine the flour, the remaining 1 tablespoon salt, pepper, paprika, and garlic powder in a small bowl; set aside.

3. Heat the vegetable oil in a 4-quart saucepan over medium-high heat until the temperature reaches 365°F on a food thermometer.

4. Toss half the onion slices in the flour, shaking off any excess before carefully placing them in the hot oil. As they cook, turn them carefully with a spider or tongs until light golden brown. Remove the onion straws to a paper towel–lined plate. Do the same with the remaining onion slices. Make sure not to flour the slices until just before frying or they will get gooey.

5. Preheat the oven to 325°F. Lightly butter a 2-quart casserole dish.

6. Make the casserole: Cook the bacon in a skillet over medium heat until crispy. Remove the bacon and drain it on paper towels. Drain off all but 2 tablespoons of the bacon fat from the pan. Sauté the leeks in the bacon fat for 4 or 5 minutes, until soft.

7. Using a whisk or a fork, beat the eggs, milk, salt, and pepper in a large bowl until frothy.

8. Spread the leeks in an even layer in the prepared casserole. Top with 1 cup of the Gruyère cheese, then the bacon, then another cup of the cheese, and then the egg mixture. Sprinkle the top with the remaining 1 cup Gruyère cheese. Arrange the onion straws on top.

9. Bake the casserole for 40 minutes, or until the eggs are firm in the center. Remove the casserole from the oven and sprinkle the top with the parsley. Allow to stand for 10 minutes before serving.

SAUSAGE AND MUSHROOM CASSEROLE

SERVES 4

Traditionally made by my stepmother, Sue, for New Year's Day brunch, this is a wonderful make-ahead dish. It can be prepared with canned cream of mushroom soup or leftover home-made cream of mushroom soup, and you can substitute various kinds of sausage, according to your taste. Serve with Mimosas (pages 246–247) or Bloody Marys (page 245).

For the casserole
1 pound breakfast sausage links
8 slices white bread, cut into cubes
1 cup grated Cheddar cheese
    (4 ounces)
4 extra-large eggs
1½ cups milk
1 tablespoon dry mustard
Kosher salt and freshly ground
    black pepper to taste

For the sauce
One 14¾-ounce can condensed
    cream of mushroom soup mixed
    with ¼ cup milk, or 1½ cups
    homemade cream of mushroom
    soup

1. Cook the sausage in an 8-inch nonstick skillet over medium heat. Turn it a couple of times so that it browns evenly. Remove the sausage from the skillet and cut into 2-inch pieces.

2. Lightly butter a 9 x 13 x 2-inch baking pan. Pour the bread cubes over the bottom of the pan. Sprinkle evenly with the sausage and Cheddar cheese.

3. Whisk together the eggs, milk, and dry mustard in a large bowl. Pour the egg mixture over the sausage mixture. Cover tightly with aluminum foil and refrigerate overnight.

4. Preheat the oven to 300°F.

5. Remove the pan from the refrigerator, uncover, and pour the mushroom soup mixture over the casserole.

6. Bake the casserole, uncovered, for about 1½ hours or until fairly firm inside and lightly golden on top. Let stand for 5 minutes. Serve warm.

MAKING EGGS BENEDICT IN ADVANCE

When people think about brunch, they often think first of that quintessential brunch dish, eggs Benedict. Believed to have been created in the late 1890s at Delmonico's, the celebrated restaurant that was frequented by everyone from John L. Sullivan and Diamond Jim Brady to Frank Sinatra, it's a classic that is one of Bubby's most requested brunch items. The original recipe is often said to have come about when Delmonico's patrons Mr. and Mrs. Le Grand Benedict complained that there was little to eat on the lunch menu. In response, the chefs topped a poached egg, ham, and English muffin concoction with hollandaise sauce, and one of the country's long-standing brunch specialties was born.

Eggs Benedict can be prepared ahead of time as long as you stay on top of the various steps. Keep in mind that it all has to happen quickly for the dish to arrive at the table properly. Make the hollandaise sauce ahead of everything else. It is also important to have the Canadian bacon sliced and seared. It's easy to keep it hot on top of the stove or covered with a damp kitchen towel in a very low (warm) oven. Generally, if you are making just a couple servings of Benedicts, you can put the English muffins in the toaster at about the same time you place the eggs in the poaching water. Having all the components done will make eggs Benedict easy to serve.

One trick of the trade, if you are preparing eggs Benedict for a crowd, is to poach the eggs in advance. Just follow the instructions for poached eggs on page 75. You can also toast the English muffins and sear the Canadian bacon ahead of time. This way, you can put a platter or individual plates together very quickly, placing the muffins on the platter or plate and the bacon on all the muffins. Use a slotted spoon to place the eggs on the bacon (it is good to use your thumb or a spoon to make an indentation in the bacon for the eggs to rest in), and then a ladle to top it all with sauce.

If you are working ahead, make sure everything is the right temperature and texture when you serve it. The eggs need to be hot; the English muffins need to be toasty and hot and springy, not like crackers; the hollandaise needs to be flowing, as opposed to broken or congealed. This is a dish that can win high marks if prepared properly, and it can be very disappointing if not.

Baked Treats: Quick Breads, Muffins, Scones, and More. *Clockwise from top:* Cream Cheese Cinnamon Rolls *(page 59),* Blueberry Scones *(page 51),* Lemon–Poppy Seed Cake *(page 66),* Honey Jalapeño Corn Bread *(page 49),* Raisin Challah Bread *(page 61),* Bubby's Variation on Mr. Beard's Cream Biscuits *(page 54)*

Lobster Pecorino Frittata *(page 93)*

Green Eggs and Ham *(page 103)*
with Stone-Ground Hominy Grits *(page 207)*

Bacon, Leek, and Onion
Casserole *(page 105)*
with Potato Pancakes *(page 213)*

Huevos Rancheros *(page 111)*

Blueberry Johnnycakes *(page 130)*

German Skillet-Baked Pancakes *(page 129)*
with Venison Sausages *(page 185)* and
Blueberry Syrup *(page 282)*

Crunchy French Toast Stuffed with Cream Cheese and Blackberry Jam *(page 134)* and Mixed Summer Berry Parfait *(page 231)*

Pecan Waffles *(page 139)* with Maple Butter *(page 274)*
and a Cranmosa *(page 247)*

Crêpes with Zucchini, Spinach, and Onions *(page 143)*

Croque Madame (aka Mrs. Crunch) *(page 153)*

Niçoise Salad *(page 160)*

Chopped Cobb Salad *(page 162)*

Homemade Pastrami *(page 182)* sandwich and
Shoestring Potatoes *(page 214)*

Deviled Eggs *(page 78)*,
Smoked Salmon and Goat
Cheese Roses *(page 193)*, and
Smoked Trout and Scallion
Mousse *(page 196)*

Crab Salad *(page 199)*

CLASSIC EGGS BENEDICT AND VARIATIONS

SERVES 1

Eggs Benedict is a decadent breakfast composed of two crispy slices of good Canadian bacon on top of two halves of a toasted English muffin. Two perfectly poached eggs sit on top of the Canadian bacon, and the eggs are covered with rich, lemony hollandaise sauce. Serve with Home Fries (page 209), Skillet Hash Browns (page 211), or Stone-Ground Hominy Grits such as Hoppin' John's or Anson Mills (page 207).

2 slices Canadian bacon	½ cup Traditional or Blender
1 English muffin	Hollandaise Sauce (pages 285
2 extra-large eggs	and 286)

1. Sear the Canadian bacon in an 8-inch nonstick skillet over medium-high heat for about 1 minute per side.

2. Split and toast the English muffin.

3. Poach the eggs as directed on page 75.

4. Arrange the muffin halves on a plate. Top each half with the bacon and then the poached eggs. Pour hollandaise sauce over the top and serve immediately.

CLASSIC EGGS FLORENTINE VARIATION (4 SERVINGS): Trim and wash (several times) one bunch of spinach. Steam the spinach, squeeze it dry in a clean kitchen towel, and coarsely chop it with a sharp knife into ¼-inch pieces. Before serving, sauté the spinach in 1 tablespoon unsalted butter. Add a little diced onion or garlic, if you like. Season the spinach with salt and pepper and substitute the spinach for the Canadian bacon.

SMOKED SALMON BENEDICT VARIATION: Substitute thin slices of smoked salmon for the Canadian bacon. Don't cook the smoked salmon as this will ruin its creamy texture and make it more like cooked salmon. For an additional variation, try Smoked Salmon Florentine by adding spinach (see above). The bright orange salmon is beautiful with the green spinach, the white egg, and the pale yellow hollandaise. Make sure the hollandaise isn't steaming hot when you pour it over the salmon or it will cook the salmon.

FRIED GREEN TOMATO BENEDICT VARIATION (4 SERVINGS): Slice a firm green tomato into ¼-inch-thick slices. Soak the slices for 5 minutes in buttermilk. Dredge the slices in yellow or white cornmeal seasoned with salt and pepper. To fry the tomatoes, put ½ cup vegetable oil in a cast-iron skillet and allow the oil to get good and hot (375°F), but not smoking. Fry the tomatoes on both sides for 2 to 3 minutes per side or until golden brown. Remove them from the pan and pat dry with paper towels. To place the poached eggs on the tomatoes, make an indentation in the tomatoes with a spoon for the eggs to sit in or they may roll off to the side.

Similar variations are to substitute the fried green tomatoes for the Canadian bacon, to serve the fried green tomatoes in addition to the Canadian bacon, or to serve Fried Green Tomatoes Benedict with slab bacon.

For a nice southern touch, substitute Bubby's Variation on Mr. Beard's Cream Biscuits (page 54), sliced in half, for the English muffins. Or, instead of hollandaise sauce, try Sausage Gravy (page 186).

SEARED BEEF TENDERLOIN BENEDICT WITH BÉARNAISE SAUCE VARIATION: First make the Béarnaise Sauce (page 287). For the tenderloin, cut ½-inch-thick slices of raw beef tenderloin and season well with salt and pepper (we use very good sea salt, which makes all the difference). Heat a cast-iron skillet to smoking hot and add a very small amount of vegetable oil. Very quickly sear the tenderloin pieces, keeping them very rare. For medium rare, sear for 45 to 60 seconds on each side. Use the seared tenderloin in place of Canadian bacon and top with the béarnaise sauce.

SMOKED TROUT BENEDICT WITH BÉARNAISE SAUCE VARIATION: Substitute one-half fillet smoked trout, warmed for 1 minute in a toaster oven or broiler, for the Canadian bacon. Top with Béarnaise Sauce (page 287) instead of hollandaise.

HUEVOS RANCHEROS

Bubby's SIGNATURE DISH

SERVES 1

W hat makes this Mexican classic special is the Pico de Gallo, a fresh, chunky salsa that also can be used as a dip for vegetables, alongside grilled meats, and to garnish tacos. Cotija is a salty Mexican cheese that is also called queso añejo. It's fine to use canned chipotles, which are actually dried, smoked jalapeños, for this dish. If you're using dried chipotles, cover them with boiling water, let them sit for an hour, remove the stems and seeds, and purée in a food processor or blender. Discard the soaking liquid. Serve with a pitcher of Sangría (page 248).

2 teaspoons vegetable oil

3 corn tortillas

3 extra-large eggs

⅛ teaspoon puréed canned chipotles in adobo sauce

¼ cup Pico de Gallo (page 290)

¼ cup grated Cotija cheese or sharp Cheddar cheese (1 ounce)

1. Preheat the oven to 200°F.

2. Heat 1 teaspoon of the vegetable oil in a large nonstick skillet over medium heat for 30 seconds. Add the tortillas, one at a time, and cook for 30 seconds per side. Remove the tortillas to a very large piece of aluminum foil, wrap them tightly, and place them in the oven to keep hot while you cook the eggs.

3. Heat the remaining 1 teaspoon vegetable oil in the skillet and fry the eggs until just set (sunny-side up or over easy). See page 74.

4. Unwrap the tortillas and arrange them flat on a serving plate. Rub the chipotle purée on the tortillas. Top the tortillas with the eggs. Spoon the pico de gallo over the top and sprinkle with the Cotija. Serve immediately.

SAVORY BACON AND CHEESE BREAD PUDDING

SERVES 6 TO 8

A meal in itself, this is a great dish for a crowd. It can be made ahead, baked, and reheated, or it can be held unbaked until a couple of hours before you plan to serve it.

One 1-pound loaf crusty white
    bread
12 ounces slab bacon, cut into
    ½-inch dice
4 tablespoons (½ stick) unsalted
    butter
1 large garlic clove, chopped
1 cup coarsely diced onions

6 extra-large eggs
3½ cups heavy cream
3 cups grated sharp white Cheddar
    cheese (12 ounces)
2 teaspoons kosher salt
1 teaspoon freshly ground black
    pepper
½ cup chopped fresh parsley

1. Preheat the oven to 350°F.

2. Cut the bread into cubes and place the cubes in a single layer on a large baking sheet. Bake for 5 minutes, until just barely toasted. Remove the bread cubes from the oven and set aside.

3. Cook the bacon in a skillet over medium heat until very crisp. Remove the bacon to a paper towel–lined plate and set aside.

4. Reserve 2 tablespoons of the bacon fat and discard the rest. Add the butter to the bacon fat in the skillet and sauté the garlic and onions for 10 minutes, or until lightly browned. Set aside to cool.

5. Whisk the eggs and cream in a large mixing bowl. Add the bread cubes, bacon, garlic and onions, and 2 cups of the Cheddar cheese. Whisk in the salt, pepper, and parsley.

6. Butter a 9 x 13 x 2-inch baking pan. Pour the mixture into the pan and sprinkle the top with the remaining 1 cup Cheddar cheese. Bake for 45 minutes, or until firm and brown.

FRUITY CLAFOUTI

*A*dapted from a recipe by Julia Child, this country French dessert is made by baking a fresh fruit layer in an eggy pancake, then serving it hot with plenty of confectioners' sugar and lemon or with whipped cream or ice cream. Choose your fruit according to the season: In the winter, use apples, and in the summer, any berries or pitted cherries.

1¼ cups milk

⅔ cup sugar

3 extra-large eggs

1 tablespoon pure vanilla extract

⅛ teaspoon kosher salt

½ cup all-purpose flour

3 cups fresh fruit: your choice of berries; pitted cherries; or chopped, peeled apples

Confectioners' sugar

1. Preheat the oven to 350°F. Lightly butter a 10-inch ovenproof skillet.

2. In the work bowl of a food processor fitted with the metal blade or a blender, purée the milk, ⅓ cup of the sugar, the eggs, vanilla, salt, and flour until smooth.

3. Pour a ¼-inch layer of the batter into the prepared pan. Bake for 10 minutes, or until barely set.

4. Remove the pan from the oven and carefully spread the fruit over the batter. Sprinkle with the remaining ⅓ cup sugar. Spoon or pour the remaining batter evenly over the sugared fruit.

5. Bake the clafouti for 45 to 50 minutes, checking after 45 minutes. The clafouti is done when it is puffed and brown and a knife inserted into the center comes out clean. Sprinkle with the confectioners' sugar and serve warm.

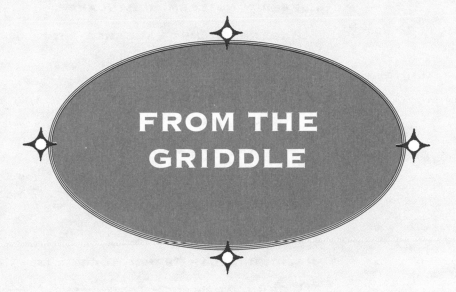

FROM THE
GRIDDLE

Whether you've got your grandmother's well-worn cast-iron frying pan or a state-of-the-art electric griddle, you can expertly turn out such Bubby's brunch favorites as light, fluffy pancakes, old-fashioned cheese blintzes (my mother's), and a sweet collection of French toast variations, including our cherished stuffed French toast filled with cream cheese and dripping with thick blackberry compote and maple syrup.

Each weekend folks line up outside the restaurant for heavenly Bubby's Sour Cream Pancakes (page 120) and old-fashioned, delicious Buttermilk Waffles (page 135), which are crisp outside and delicate within, thanks to the way we mix the batter (with a very light hand). Other popular pancakes at brunch include Banana Walnut Pancakes (page 122), German Skillet-Baked Pancakes (page 129), and Blueberry Johnnycakes (page 130). Besides traditional waffles, we offer wonderful spiced Pumpkin Waffles (page 138), earthy Pecan Waffles with Maple Butter (page 139), and chewy Yeasted Buckwheat Waffles (page 136). Because the batter is made the night before, yeast-raised waffles are a great way to get a head start on your brunch.

Actually, many of Bubby's batters can be prepared several hours ahead of time, which means that you can easily cook up great batches of pancakes, waffles, and French toast for a crowd, or for two, without having to run around like a crazy person when your guests arrive. Most batters hold well for several hours, so there's less mixing and prepping to do at the last minute. Since batters tend to thicken in the refrigerator, you may need to thin them out slightly with a little milk if you make them in advance.

You may want to wipe off the griddle after making several batches of pancakes before proceeding with more, but you probably won't have to use any more butter to grease the griddle after the first batch of pancakes because the griddle will be seasoned and the pancakes should not stick. If you find them sticking, use a little more butter on the griddle. Both waffle and pancake batters can stay out at room temperature for an hour or so with no problems.

Griddle dishes are cooked in a minimum of butter on a superhot surface on medium to medium-high heat in a skillet, a frying pan, a stovetop griddle, or an electric griddle.

Always make a "tester"—a test waffle or pancake—to make sure it has the consistency and texture you want before you proceed with the rest of the batter; this way, if it is too thick, you can add a little milk, about 2 tablespoons at a time, to achieve the right consistency. For optimal flipping, a pancake should be about 4 inches in diameter, though nothing puts a smile on a child's face like a little stack of silver dollar pancakes and those are generally only 2 inches in diameter.

PANCAKES CAN BE MADE INTO A RANGE OF FUN SHAPES THAT WILL BRING A SMILE TO THE FACES OF KIDS AND GROWN-UPS ALIKE.

When cooking pancakes, the time to flip them is when they begin to appear slightly set around the edges and the bubbles on the surface begin to pop. This usually takes 2 to 3 minutes. When I was a kid, I read in some cookbook that when ten bubbles popped, the pancakes were ready to flip, and I have always gone by that rule. Flip just once and keep in mind that the second side will take only about half as long to cook as the first side. Don't press down on the pancakes with your spatula or they'll lose some of their light texture, and don't overcook them or you'll have a great thing turn into a bad thing.

Watch carefully to see if it takes longer than 2 to 3 minutes for the pancake to begin to set, no bubbles are popping, and when the cake is flipped, it is still blond. This means the griddle is not hot enough. Turn it up. The saying "Faster than spit on a griddle" is useful. A drop of water should bounce up and down and then disappear when the proper temperature for the griddle or pan is achieved. It is also important to note that sometimes the first pancake sticks; call this one the sacrificial pancake. This said, there is nothing quite as thrilling as watching a perfect pancake rise up on the griddle after it is flipped.

Waffles are crisper than pancakes and are typically enriched with generous amounts of melted butter. Waffles served alongside a thick slab of bacon or sizzling sausages and topped with either maple syrup or any number of homemade butters, compotes, or fruit preserves are a treat that brings a delighted look to faces of all ages. You'll need a waffle iron, obviously, and keep in mind that you should brush it with butter the first several times you use it, even if its surface is nonstick. Usually a modern waffle iron has a heat indicator light, so pay attention and don't fill the iron with batter until it's hot enough. Typically, the iron is not filled so full of batter that it extends all the way to the ends of the iron. Your reward will be waffles that don't come apart when you open the iron.

Be sure to let your waffle iron heat back up again before you make another waffle. With waffles, too, it is wise to try a "tester" waffle to make sure you're satisfied with the color and texture before making up a big batch. As with pancakes, sometimes the first one sticks a little. Don't be afraid to sacrifice the first waffle.

Ideally, waffles should be eaten as close as possible to when they're made. If absolutely necessary, lightly cover waffles with a clean, lightly damp kitchen towel or aluminum foil and hold them in a preheated 200°F oven for 5 to 10 minutes at most. Waffles can be frozen and heated in a toaster oven or the oven, so if you have extra batter, you might as well cook it, wrap the waffles in aluminum foil, and have them for breakfast during the week. Just make sure to cool them down all the way before wrapping them and putting them into resealable plastic freezer bags.

Crêpes may seem intimidating, but they are, in fact, quite easy to make. The batter can be prepared in the blender up to a day ahead. Always let the batter sit out at room temperature for 30 minutes before using. A special crêpe pan, while handy, is not essential. You can use any small to medium skillet (8 to 10 inches), preferably nonstick.

Another griddled brunch mainstay, French toast, is a great way to use up leftover bread of all kinds. How soft or crisp your French toast turns out depends upon how long it's soaked in the batter. If you prefer a fairly dry, crisp French toast, soak the bread for less time—5 to 10 minutes. Longer soaking means you will have French toast with a moist, creamy interior. Once the French toast is griddled, cover it with a clean kitchen towel and keep it warm for up to 30 minutes in a 200°F oven.

Bubby's Sour Cream Pancakes

MAKES 16 PANCAKES

These pancakes, the signature griddle dish at Bubby's, were inspired by James Beard's excellent recipe. Half the milk called for in Mr. Beard's recipe is replaced with sour cream, resulting in a fluffy, deep golden griddle cake. Mix the dry ingredients and mix the wet ingredients separately ahead of time, but don't make this batter more than three hours in advance or it might deflate. Serve with plenty of butter and maple syrup, Canadian bacon, or one of Bubby's fruit compotes (pages 276 to 278).

2 tablespoons sugar

4 cups all-purpose flour

5 teaspoons baking soda

2½ teaspoons kosher salt

4 extra-large eggs

1½ cups sour cream

5 tablespoons unsalted butter, melted and cooled, plus more for the griddle and for brushing on the pancakes

2¾ cups milk

1. Combine the sugar, flour, baking soda, and salt in a large bowl; set aside.

2. Using a whisk or a mixer set on medium speed, beat the eggs in a bowl for 2 minutes, or until frothy. Beat in the sour cream, butter, and milk. Stop beating as soon as the ingredients are combined.

3. Using a large spoon or rubber spatula, briskly fold the egg mixture into the flour mixture, being careful not to overmix or your pancakes will be tough. It's okay if there are a few little lumps in the batter. (At this point, you can cover the batter and refrigerate it for up to 3 hours, or use it right away.)

4. Preheat a stove-top griddle or a skillet over medium heat, or an electric griddle to 400°F, testing to make sure it's hot enough for a drop of water to bounce on it.

5. Lightly butter the griddle. Using a ladle, form pancakes on the griddle using ¼ cup batter per pancake. Cook the pancakes until a few bubbles have formed on the surface of each one.

6. Flip the pancakes with a spatula and cook until golden brown on the other side. Brush the finished pancakes with a little melted butter before serving.

CHOCOLATE CHIP SILVER DOLLAR PANCAKES VARIATION: Form 2-inch pancakes, using about 2 tablespoons of batter per pancake, on the hot griddle. Place 5 chocolate chips on each pancake before flipping the pancakes over to cook on the other side.

BLUEBERRY BUTTERMILK PANCAKES

MAKES 16 PANCAKES

A generous measure of blueberries—two full cups—ensures a juicy mouthful of berries with every bite. Use fresh berries when they are in season, or frozen if fresh seasonal berries are unavailable. There is no need to thaw frozen berries before using them. You can keep the cooked pancakes, loosely covered with a clean kitchen towel, for 15 minutes in a 200°F oven. Serve with Roasted Asparagus and Leek Frittata (page 96).

2 tablespoons sugar

4 cups all-purpose flour

5 teaspoons baking soda

2½ teaspoons kosher salt

4 extra-large eggs

3½ cups buttermilk

5 tablespoons unsalted butter, melted and cooled, plus more for the griddle and for brushing on the pancakes

2 cups fresh or frozen blueberries

1. Combine the sugar, flour, baking soda, and salt in a large bowl; set aside.

2. Using a whisk or a mixer set on medium speed, beat the eggs in a bowl for 2 minutes, or until frothy. Beat in the buttermilk and butter.

3. Using a large spoon or rubber spatula, briskly fold the egg mixture into the flour mixture, being careful not to overmix or your pancakes will be tough. It's okay if there are a few little lumps in the batter. (At this point, you can cover the batter and refrigerate it for up to 3 hours, or use it right away.)

4. Preheat a stove-top griddle or skillet over medium heat, or an electric griddle to 400°F, testing to make sure it's hot enough for a drop of water to bounce on it.

5. Lightly butter the griddle. Using a ladle, form pancakes on the griddle using ¼ cup batter per pancake. Add the blueberries. Cook the pancakes until a few bubbles have formed on the surface of each one.

6. Flip the pancakes with a spatula and cook until golden brown on the other side. Brush the finished pancakes with a little melted butter before serving.

BANANA WALNUT PANCAKES

MAKES 16 PANCAKES

These extra-special pancakes are filled with toasted walnuts and topped with caramelized bananas—a perfect combination. While adding syrup may seem over the top, we always slather these with some anyway, for extra decadence. Serve with yogurt and fruit.

For the batter
1 cup coarsely chopped walnuts
2 tablespoons sugar
4 cups all-purpose flour
5 teaspoons baking soda
2½ teaspoons kosher salt
4 extra-large eggs
1½ cups sour cream
5 tablespoons unsalted butter,
    melted and cooled, plus more
    for the griddle and for brushing
    on the pancakes
2¾ cups milk

For the topping
4 tablespoons (½ stick) unsalted
    butter
4 bananas, peeled and cut on the
    bias into ¼-inch-thick slices

1. Make the batter: Place the chopped walnuts in a skillet and toast them over medium heat, stirring occasionally and watching carefully, for 2 to 3 minutes, or until they are fragrant and turn a darker brown color. Remove the walnuts from the pan and set aside to cool. Alternatively, toast the nuts on a baking sheet in a preheated 300°F oven for 10 to 15 minutes.

2. Combine the sugar, flour, baking soda, and salt in a large bowl; set aside.

3. Using a whisk or a mixer set on medium speed, beat the eggs in a bowl for 2 minutes, or until frothy. Beat in the sour cream, butter, and milk. Stop beating as soon as the ingredients are combined.

4. Using a large spoon or rubber spatula, briskly fold the egg mixture into the flour mixture, being careful not to overmix or your pancakes will be tough. It's okay if there are a few little lumps in the batter. (At this point, you can cover the batter and refrigerate it for up to 3 hours, or use it right away.)

5. Make the topping: Melt the butter in a small skillet over medium heat. Add the banana slices and sauté for 3 minutes, or until very brown. Flip the slices and brown evenly on the other side. Turn off the heat and leave the bananas in their pan while you griddle the pancakes.

6. Preheat a stove-top griddle or skillet over medium heat, or an electric griddle to 400°F, testing to make sure it's hot enough for a drop of water to bounce on it.

7. Lightly butter the griddle. Using a ladle, form pancakes on the griddle using ¼ cup batter per pancake. While the batter on the griddle is still very wet, sprinkle the uncooked surface with some of the toasted walnuts. Cook the pancakes until a few bubbles have formed on the surface of each one.

8. Flip the pancakes with a spatula and cook until golden brown on the other side. Brush the finished pancakes with a little melted butter. Serve the pancakes on a platter and top them with the sautéed bananas.

ORANGE RICOTTA PANCAKES

MAKES 12 PANCAKES

The addition of ricotta cheese gives these citrusy pancakes a little more heft. After you cook each batch of pancakes, transfer them to a heatproof platter and keep them warm for up to 20 minutes in a preheated 200°F oven.

4 extra-large eggs, separated	½ cup all-purpose flour
1⅓ cups ricotta cheese	Pinch of salt
1½ tablespoons sugar	Melted butter for the griddle
1½ tablespoons freshly grated	and for brushing on the
orange zest	pancakes

1. Combine the egg yolks, ricotta cheese, sugar, and orange zest in a medium bowl. Using a whisk or a mixer set on medium speed, beat for 2 minutes, or until creamy.

2. Sift the flour over the egg mixture. Using a large spoon or spatula, fold the flour into the egg mixture, being careful not to overmix or your pancakes will be tough.

3. In a bowl with the mixer set on high speed, beat the egg whites with the pinch of salt for about 1 minute, or until they hold stiff peaks. Whisk about one fourth of the egg whites into the ricotta mixture; then fold the remaining whites in gently but thoroughly.

4. Preheat a stove-top griddle or a skillet over medium heat, or an electric griddle to 400°F, testing to make sure it's hot enough for a drop of water to bounce on it.

5. Lightly butter the griddle. Using a ladle, form pancakes on the griddle, using ¼ cup batter for each pancake. Cook the pancakes until a few bubbles form on the surface of each one.

6. Flip the pancakes with a spatula and cook until golden brown on the other side. Brush the finished pancakes with a little melted butter before serving.

RASPBERRY RICCOTA PANCAKES VARIATION: Add 1 cup of raspberries to the batter, stir gently, and form pancakes, using about ¼ cup batter per pancake.

RASPBERRY LEMON RICCOTA PANCAKES VARIATION: Add 1 cup of raspberries to the batter, and substitute freshly grated lemon zest for the grated orange zest.

BUCKWHEAT PANCAKES

The agreeably assertive flavor of buckwheat flour, the nuttiness of wheat germ, and the pleasantly chewy texture of rolled oats combine to make these pancakes hearty and full-bodied. They're really a meal on their own, though nobody would complain if you were to offer Venison Sausages (page 185) or thickly cut Maple-Glazed Bacon (page 177) alongside.

¾ cup rolled oats	3 extra-large eggs
½ cup wheat germ	2½ cups milk
1¼ cups buckwheat flour	1¼ cups sour cream
⅓ cup cornmeal	8 tablespoons (1 stick) unsalted
4 teaspoons baking soda	butter, melted and cooled, plus
4 teaspoons baking powder	more for the griddle and for
¾ teaspoon kosher salt	brushing on the pancakes

1. Combine the rolled oats, wheat germ, buckwheat flour, cornmeal, baking soda, baking powder, and salt in a large bowl; set aside.

2. Using a whisk or a mixer set on medium speed, beat the eggs, milk, sour cream, and butter in another large bowl for 1 minute, or until well incorporated.

3. Add the egg mixture to the flour mixture and beat well.

4. Preheat a stove-top griddle or skillet over medium heat, or an electric griddle to 400°F, testing to make sure it's hot enough for a drop of water to bounce on it.

5. Lightly butter the griddle. Using a ladle, form pancakes on the griddle, using ¼ cup batter for each pancake. Cook the pancakes until a few bubbles form on the surface of each one.

6. Flip the pancakes with a spatula and cook until golden brown on the other side. Brush the finished pancakes with a little melted butter before serving. Serve immediately.

SOURDOUGH PANCAKES

MAKES 16 PANCAKES

My mother used to make these slightly tangy, slightly chewy, wonderfully moist pancakes when we were kids. Now, Bubby's serves these pancakes every weekend. The recipe works best when you have all your ingredients at room temperature. Plan to make the Primary Batter 8 to 12 hours ahead of time. Allow the batter to sit at room temperature for 30 minutes before you make the pancakes, and give it a good stir before using. The Primary Batter will yield 3¾ cups, which you will use in the pancakes, and 2½ cups to return to the starter container, which will feed your starter for a week. Plan on ordering starter for the Primary Batter from any number of online companies. Serve the pancakes with a fruit compote (pages 276 to 278) or sautéed bananas (see Banana Walnut Pancakes, page 122) and Glazed Smoked Ham (page 187).

For the Primary Batter	For the pancakes
Live sourdough starter	3¾ cups Primary Batter
2½ cups lukewarm water (90° to 100°F)	2½ cups sour cream
3¾ cups all-purpose flour	2½ cups all-purpose flour
	5 extra-large eggs
	¼ cup sugar
	4 tablespoons (½ stick) unsalted butter, melted and cooled, plus more for the griddle and for brushing on the pancakes
	1 tablespoon kosher salt

1. Make the Primary Batter: Warm a very large bowl by filling it with hot water. Empty it out (a cold bowl can retard the leavening).

2. Remove the sourdough starter crock from the refrigerator and stir it well. Measure out 2½ cups. Return the remaining starter to the refrigerator.

3. Combine the warm water and starter in the warm bowl and stir until well mixed. Using a whisk or a mixer set at medium-low speed, add the flour slowly, beating continually for 4 to 5 minutes, or until the mixture is smooth and lump-free. Cover the bowl with plastic wrap and place it in a warm, draft-free area for proofing.

4. Proof the batter for 8 or up to 12 hours (see sidebar). During the proofing period, a crust or a liquid may form on the top of the batter. If this happens, just stir it back down into the batter. At the end of the proofing period, stir the batter thoroughly. Take out 2½ cups and return it to the starter container (this feeds your starter). Stir the starter in the container thoroughly and refrigerate it.

5. Make the pancakes: Place the 3¾ cups of Primary Batter into a large warm bowl. Stir in the sour cream. Using a whisk or a mixer set on medium speed, beat in 1¼ cups of the flour.

6. Using a whisk or a mixer set on medium speed, beat the eggs in a separate bowl for 2 minutes, or until frothy.

7. Stir the eggs into the batter. Stir in the sugar, butter, and salt; then stir in the remaining 1¼ cups flour. Don't worry if the batter looks a little lumpy. Cover the bowl with plastic wrap and set it aside for 30 minutes.

8. Preheat a stove-top griddle or skillet on medium heat, or an electric griddle to 400°F, testing to make sure it's hot enough for a drop of water to bounce on it.

9. Lightly butter the griddle. Using a ladle, form pancakes on the griddle using about ⅓ cup batter for each pancake. Cook the pancakes for 3 minutes, or until the edges begin to look set and the top has a few bubbles. The bottom should be golden brown.

10. Flip the pancakes with a spatula and cook for 1½ to 2 minutes, or until golden brown on the other side. Brush the finished pancakes with a little melted butter before serving.

PROOFING STARTER

The proofing period will be for 8 to 12 hours, depending on how active your starter is when taken from the refrigerator. The Primary Batter is ready when it is foamy and full of large bubbles. You can use it immediately or within the next 8 to 12 hours. If your batter has many tiny bubbles in it, it has reached the proper state. If few or no bubbles are present during the 8 to 12 hours after proofing, your starter is not acting properly and you should determine the reason for this before continuing with the recipe. The most likely reason your starter is not working is because it is dead. You will need to get new starter. To keep your starter alive (it is a living organism), you need to feed it once a week. By removing a little starter and adding back an equal amount of flour and water, your starter will thrive for a long, long time.

SWEDISH PANCAKES

MAKES 12 TO 14 PANCAKES

*T*hin, buttery, and delicate, these fall somewhere between crêpes and American pancakes. It's traditional to eat Swedish pancakes topped with lingonberries (or lingonberry jam) or another tart berry, a slice of lemon to squeeze on the pancake, and confectioners' sugar. These pancakes cook quickly because they're so thin. In fact, they're so thin that most guests will want three or four. Serve with your choice of herrings (page 196) or Smoked Salmon (page 191).

3 cups all-purpose flour	½ pound (2 sticks) unsalted butter,
1½ teaspoons kosher salt	melted and cooled, plus more for
6 extra-large eggs	the griddle and for brushing on
¼ cup sugar	the pancakes
	2½ cups milk

1. Combine the flour and salt in a bowl; set aside.

2. Using a whisk or mixer set on medium speed, beat the eggs, sugar, and butter in a large bowl for 3 minutes, or until the batter is pale yellow, smooth, and thick. Add the milk and beat for 1 minute, or until smooth.

3. Add the flour to the egg mixture all at once. Using a whisk or a wooden spoon, stir the batter by hand until smooth. The batter will be fairly thin.

4. Preheat a stove-top griddle or skillet on medium heat, or an electric griddle to 400°F, testing to make sure it's hot enough for a drop of water to bounce on it.

5. Lightly butter the griddle. Using a ladle, form thin pancakes on the griddle, using about ⅓ cup batter for each pancake and leaving about ½ inch of space between them. Since they spread out, you may be able to fit only 1 or 2 on a griddle at a time. Cook the pancakes for 1 minute, or until golden brown on the bottom.

6. Flip the pancakes with a spatula and cook for 1 minute, or until golden brown on the other side. Brush the finished pancakes with a little melted butter before serving.

GERMAN SKILLET-BAKED PANCAKES

MAKES TWO 10- OR 11-INCH SKILLET PANCAKES, SERVES 4

*T*his recipe yields puffy, golden pancakes with minimal effort because they're baked rather than cooked on top of the stove. Lemon cuts the sweetness of these pancakes and imparts its fresh, citrusy flavor. Serve with Venison Sausages (page 185).

For the pancakes
8 extra-large eggs
1 cup all-purpose flour
1 cup half-and-half
8 tablespoons (1 stick) unsalted
    butter, room temperature, plus
    4 tablespoons, melted, for
    brushing on the pancakes

For the topping
4 tablespoons unsalted butter,
    melted
Confectioners' sugar
2 lemons, cut into wedges

1. Preheat the oven to 425°F.

2. In a large blender, combine the eggs, flour, and half-and-half. Blend on medium speed until the batter is fairly thick and smooth, scraping down the sides of the blender container several times.

3. Place 4 tablespoons of the softened butter in each of two 10-inch or 11-inch cast-iron skillets. Place each skillet over low heat and melt the butter.

4. Pour the batter over the melted butter in the skillets, making sure the batter is evenly distributed.

5. Carefully slide the skillets into the oven. Bake the pancakes for 25 minutes, or until puffed and golden.

6. Transfer the pancakes from the skillets to large plates or shallow bowls with a large spatula. Immediately pour 2 tablespoons of melted butter over each pancake. Sprinkle with confectioners' sugar and place wedges of lemon for squeezing on top of the sugared pancakes. Serve immediately.

BLUEBERRY JOHNNYCAKES

MAKES ABOUT 20 JOHNNYCAKES

Johnnycakes, believed to be the precursor of the pancake, date back to the 1700s and are typically made with cornmeal and either water or milk. Though they used to be fairly flat griddle cakes, our johnnycakes contain eggs, butter, and leavening, so they taste somewhat like a cross between pancakes and corn bread. Adding blueberries makes them even better.

1½ cups plus 1 tablespoon all-
    purpose flour
1 cup cornmeal
½ cup plus 1 tablespoon sugar
2½ teaspoons baking powder
½ teaspoon kosher salt
2 extra-large eggs

1½ cups buttermilk
5 tablespoons unsalted butter,
    melted and cooled, plus more for
    the griddle and for brushing on
    the johnnycakes
1½ cups fresh or frozen blueberries

1. Combine the flour, cornmeal, sugar, baking powder, and salt in a large bowl; set aside.

2. Using a whisk or a mixer set on medium speed, beat the eggs in a bowl for 1 minute, or until frothy. Add the buttermilk and butter and mix well.

3. Add the egg mixture to the flour mixture. Beat with a whisk or a wooden spoon for a minute, or just until the ingredients are combined.

4. Preheat a stove-top griddle or skillet over medium heat, or an electric griddle to 400°F, testing to make sure it's hot enough for a drop of water to bounce on it.

5. Lightly butter the griddle. Using a ladle, form johnnycakes on the griddle, using ¼ cup batter for each johnnycake. Sprinkle each johnnycake with 5 or 6 blueberries.

6. When several bubbles pop on the top surface of the johnnycakes, flip them with a spatula and cook until golden brown on the other side. Brush the johnnycakes with a little melted butter before serving.

CLASSIC FRENCH TOAST

MAKES 8 SLICES FRENCH TOAST

You can serve this brunch favorite as soon as it's ready, or keep it warm for up to twenty minutes, loosely covered with a clean, damp kitchen towel in a 200°F oven. Avoid using very soft white bread as it tends to fall apart when dipped into the egg mixture. It's best to use a firm bread such as a large baguette or sourdough loaf. In fact, French toast is a great way to use up slightly stale bread, and you can make this with just about anything from a baguette to brioche to a cinnamon raisin loaf.

4 extra-large eggs

½ cup buttermilk

¼ teaspoon pure vanilla extract

¼ teaspoon ground cinnamon

Pinch of kosher salt

8 slices hearty bread of your choice,
 cut ¾ to 1 inch thick

Butter for the griddle, about 1
 teaspoon per slice

1. Using a whisk or a fork, beat the eggs in a large mixing bowl until frothy. Add the buttermilk, vanilla, cinnamon, and salt. Beat for 1 minute, or until well combined.

2. Dip the bread slices, one at a time, into the egg mixture, turning to coat both sides. Arrange the prepared slices on a baking sheet or platter as you go. Dip and prep all that will fit into the pan at one time. While the first batch is on the griddle, begin dipping the second batch.

3. Preheat a stove-top griddle or skillet over medium heat, or an electric griddle to 400°F, testing to make sure it's hot enough for a drop of water to bounce on it.

4. Butter the griddle generously. Arrange the bread slices in a single layer on the griddle and cook well for 2 to 3 minutes on each side, or until golden brown, turning once with a spatula. If you're using a skillet, you'll need to do this in batches, depending on the size of the skillet. After the toast is flipped, you may need to add more butter to the griddle. As you add the butter, lift the French toast with a spatula so the butter flows underneath the griddling toast. Transfer the French toast to a platter or individual plates and serve.

RAISIN CHALLAH FRENCH TOAST

MAKES 8 SLICES FRENCH TOAST

French Toast is the perfect way to use up day-old bread. If you've made Raisin Challah Bread (page 61), go ahead and use up the leftovers the next morning. Good-quality store-bought thick-cut raisin bread will also work. Cut your challah slices on the thick side, about ¾ to 1 inch thick, so that when you griddle them, the outside will be crisp and the inside will be moist and creamy. Serve with lots of syrup, homemade jam, sautéed bananas (see Banana Walnut Pancakes, page 122), fresh bananas and strawberries, or the fruit compote of your choosing (see pages 276 to 278).

6 extra-large eggs	Pinch of kosher salt
½ cup buttermilk	8 thick (¾ to 1 inch) slices Raisin
¼ cup packed dark brown sugar	Challah Bread (page 61)
½ teaspoon pure vanilla extract	Butter for the griddle, about
Pinch of ground cinnamon	1 teaspoon per slice

1. Using a whisk or a fork, beat the eggs in a large mixing bowl until frothy. Add the buttermilk, brown sugar, vanilla, cinnamon, and salt. Beat for 1 minute, or until well combined.

2. Dip the challah slices, one at a time, into the egg mixture, turning to coat both sides. Arrange the prepared slices on a baking sheet or platter as you go. Dip and prep all that will fit into the pan at one time. While the first batch is on the griddle, begin dipping the second batch.

3. Preheat a griddle or skillet over medium heat, or an electric griddle to 400°F, testing to make sure it's hot enough for a drop of water to bounce on it.

4. Butter the griddle generously. Arrange the bread slices in a single layer on the griddle and cook them for 2 to 3 minutes on each side, or until golden brown. If you're using a skillet, you'll need to do this in batches, depending upon the size of the skillet. After the toast is flipped, you may need to add more butter to the griddle. As you add the butter, lift the French toast with a spatula so the butter flows underneath the griddling toast. Transfer the French toast to a platter or individual plates and serve.

CRUNCHY FRENCH TOAST

MAKES 8 SLICES FRENCH TOAST

*I*f there's anything better than traditional French toast, it's this crisp, golden variation, made by pressing the bread slices in crushed cornflakes before griddling. Be sure to generously coat both sides of the bread with the cornflakes and use plenty of butter on the griddle. Serve with maple syrup, sautéed bananas (see Banana Walnut Pancakes, page 122), fruit compote (see pages 276 to 278), or homemade jam, such as Strawberry Jam (page 280).

2 cups crushed cornflakes	¼ teaspoon pure vanilla extract
½ teaspoon ground cinnamon	Pinch of kosher salt
2 tablespoons granulated sugar	8 thick slices bread (1 inch)
4 extra-large eggs	Butter for the griddle, about
½ cup buttermilk	1 teaspoon per slice
¼ cup packed dark brown sugar	

1. Stir together the cornflakes, ¼ teaspoon of the cinnamon, and the granulated sugar in a pie plate or a large shallow bowl; set aside.

2. Using a whisk or a mixer set on medium speed, beat the eggs in a large bowl until frothy. Add the buttermilk, brown sugar, vanilla, remaining ¼ teaspoon of cinnamon, and the salt. Beat for 1 minute, or until well combined.

3. Dip the bread slices, one at a time, in the egg mixture, turning to coat both sides. Shake the excess egg mixture back into the bowl. Carefully place the bread slices into the cornflake mixture and turn carefully to coat both sides. Arrange the prepared slices on a baking sheet.

4. Preheat a stove-top griddle or skillet over medium heat, or an electric griddle to 375°F, testing to make sure it's hot enough for a drop of water to bounce on it.

5. Butter the griddle generously. Arrange the bread slices in a single layer on the griddle and cook well on each side for 2 to 3 minutes, or until golden brown, turning once with a spatula. If you're using a skillet, you'll need to do this in batches, depending upon the size of the skillet. After the toast is flipped, you may need to add more butter to the griddle. As you add butter, lift the French toast with a spatula so the butter flows underneath the griddling toast.

6. Transfer the French toast to a platter or individual plates and serve it immediately, or keep it warm for up to 30 minutes in a 200°F oven.

CRUNCHY FRENCH TOAST STUFFED WITH CREAM CHEESE AND BLACKBERRY JAM VARIATION:
Before cooking, make sure the bread is cut 1 inch thick. Using a sharp slicing knife, gently make a 2-inch-long incision in the bread by cutting into the edge of the slice and working the knife into the interior. Wiggle the tip of the knife gently as you work it into the slice, being careful not to tear a hole in the bread. Use a pastry bag or spoon to insert about 1 tablespoon blackberry jam (or another berry jam, if you prefer) and 2 tablespoons of room-temperature cream cheese. Continue the instructions for breading and cooking the Crunchy French Toast. Serve with maple syrup.

BUTTERMILK WAFFLES

MAKES 6 TO 8 WAFFLES

*S*ince the invention of the nonstick electric waffle iron, making homemade waffles is a breeze. *You can freeze these waffles for up to a month. Baking them in a preheated 350°F oven will quickly restore them to their irresistibly crisp, buttery state.*

2 cups all-purpose flour

1 tablespoon baking powder

1 teaspoon baking soda

½ teaspoon kosher salt

4 extra-large eggs

2 cups buttermilk

8 tablespoons (1 stick) unsalted

butter, melted and cooled, plus

more for the waffle iron

1. Combine the flour, baking powder, baking soda, and salt in a large bowl; set aside.

2. Using a whisk or a mixer set on medium speed, beat the eggs in a bowl for 2 minutes, or until frothy. Beat in the buttermilk.

3. Stir the egg mixture into the flour mixture. Beat for 2 minutes, or until smooth. Pour in the butter and beat until well combined.

4. Preheat a waffle iron to medium or 375°F. Lightly butter the waffle iron, unless your iron is well seasoned.

5. Pour about ¾ cup batter—or enough to cover about two-thirds of the grid surface—onto the iron.

6. Close the lid of the waffle iron and allow the waffle to cook for 3 to 5 minutes. You'll know the waffle is ready when steam stops coming out of the sides of the waffle iron and when the top of the waffle iron is easy to lift. If the top seems to stick a little, give the waffle another minute and try again. Gently dislodge the waffle from the waffle iron with the tines of a fork. The waffle should be golden brown.

7. Be sure to let the iron heat up again; then repeat with the remaining batter. Serve warm. (The waffles may be kept warm in a preheated 200°F oven for up to 10 minutes.)

BLUEBERRY BUTTERMILK WAFFLE VARIATION: Sprinkle ¼ cup fresh or frozen blueberries per waffle onto the batter after measuring it onto the waffle iron and before closing the lid.

Yeasted Buckwheat Waffles

*T*he yeast, in addition to letting the batter sit for at least six hours, gives these waffles a chewy consistency and a slightly pungent flavor. One note on preparation: Since this batter needs to stand overnight, be sure to prepare it a day in advance. You can freeze these waffles, well wrapped, for up to a month. Simply heat them until nice and crispy in a preheated 350°F oven for 5 to 10 minutes.

One ¼-ounce package active dry yeast
½ cup warm water (100°F)
2 cups warm milk (100°F)
8 tablespoons (1 stick) unsalted butter, melted and cooled, plus more for the waffle iron

1 teaspoon kosher salt
1 teaspoon sugar
2 cups buckwheat flour
2 extra-large eggs
Pinch of baking soda

1. Whisk together the yeast and water in a large bowl. Allow the mixture to stand for about 5 minutes, or until the yeast is dissolved and the mixture is bubbly

2. Add the milk, butter, salt, and sugar and whisk until combined. Whisk in the flour until smooth. Cover the bowl with plastic wrap and allow the mixture to stand overnight, or for at least 6 hours, at room temperature.

3. Shortly before making the waffles, stir the batter so that it deflates. Add the eggs and baking soda.

4. Using a whisk or a mixer set on medium speed, beat the batter for 1 minute, or until smooth. Don't worry if the batter seems thin. The waffles will rise as they cook.

5. Preheat the waffle iron to medium or 375°F. Lightly butter the waffle iron, unless your iron is well seasoned.

6. Pour about ¾ cup batter—or enough to cover about two-thirds of the grid surface—onto the iron.

7. Close the lid of the waffle iron and allow the waffle to cook for 3 to 5 minutes. You'll know the waffle is ready when steam stops coming out of the sides of the waffle iron and when the top of the waffle iron is easy to lift. If the top seems to stick a little, give the waffle another minute and try again. Gently dislodge the waffle from the waffle iron with the tines of a fork. The waffle should be golden brown.

8. Be sure to let the iron heat up again; then repeat with the remaining batter. Serve warm. (The waffles may be kept warm in a preheated 200°F oven for up to 10 minutes.)

WHOLE GRAIN APPLE WAFFLES

MAKES 6 TO 8 WAFFLES

*I*f *you didn't think waffles could taste good and be good for you at the same time, these will change your mind. Besides the taste of fresh applesauce, the addition of flaxseed meal, wheat germ, and whole wheat pastry flour imparts a wholesome flavor. If you choose to buy applesauce rather than making it from scratch, the waffles will still be very good, but nothing compares with homemade applesauce made with crisp autumn apples.*

1 cup whole wheat pastry flour
½ cup flaxseed or cornmeal meal
¼ cup wheat germ
¼ cup all-purpose flour
1 tablespoon plus 1 teaspoon
   baking powder
1 tablespoon sugar
½ teaspoon kosher salt
2 extra-large eggs

1¾ cups milk
¼ cup canola oil
1 tablespoon unsalted butter, melted
   and cooled, plus more for the
   waffle iron
¼ cup applesauce, homemade (page
   279) or store-bought
1 teaspoon pure vanilla extract

1. Combine the whole wheat pastry flour, cornmeal, wheat germ, all-purpose flour, baking powder, sugar, and salt in a large mixing bowl; set aside.

2. Using a whisk or a mixer set on medium speed, beat the eggs in a bowl for 1 minute, or until frothy. Add the milk, canola oil, and butter. Beat for 1 minute, or until well combined. Stir in the applesauce and vanilla.

3. Add the flour mixture to the egg mixture. Beat for 1 minute, or until smooth.

4. Preheat a waffle iron to medium or 375°F. Lightly butter the waffle iron, unless your iron is well seasoned.

5. Pour about ¾ cup batter—or enough to cover about two-thirds of the grid surface—onto the iron.

6. Close the lid of the waffle iron and allow the waffle to cook for 3 to 5 minutes. You'll know the waffle is ready when steam stops coming out of the sides of the waffle iron and when the top of the waffle iron is easy to lift. If the top seems to stick a little, give the waffle another minute and try again. Gently dislodge the waffle from the waffle iron with the tines of a fork. The waffle should be golden brown.

7. Be sure to let the iron heat up again; then repeat with the remaining batter. Serve warm. (The waffles may be kept warm in a preheated 200°F oven for up to 10 minutes.)

PUMPKIN WAFFLES

MAKES 6 TO 8 WAFFLES

*T*hese golden, delicious-smelling waffles are an autumn treat, and they are even better when topped with a fall-fresh Cinnamon Pear Compote (page 277). They're tender and especially aromatic, thanks to the various spices. Buy plain canned pumpkin purée, not the prepared pumpkin pie filling, which contains sugar and added spices. Serve with Fresh Cranberry Juice (page 240).

2½ cups all-purpose flour	4 extra-large eggs
1 tablespoon baking powder	2 cups buttermilk
1 teaspoon ground cinnamon	1 cup canned pumpkin purée
1 teaspoon ground ginger	½ cup packed dark brown sugar
½ teaspoon baking soda	4 tablespoons (½ stick) unsalted
½ teaspoon kosher salt	butter, melted and cooled, plus
¼ teaspoon freshly ground nutmeg	more for the waffle iron
Pinch of ground cloves	1 teaspoon pure vanilla extract

1. Combine the flour, baking powder, cinnamon, ginger, baking soda, salt, nutmeg, and cloves in a large mixing bowl; set aside.

2. Using a whisk or a mixer set on medium speed, beat the eggs in a large bowl for 1 minute, or until frothy. Add the buttermilk, pumpkin purée, brown sugar, butter, and vanilla and beat until smooth.

3. Gradually mix the flour mixture into the egg mixture. Beat until smooth.

4. Preheat a waffle iron to medium or 375°F. Lightly butter the waffle iron, unless your iron is well seasoned.

5. Pour about ¾ cup batter—or enough to cover about two-thirds of the grid surface—onto the iron.

6. Close the lid of the waffle iron and allow the waffle to cook for 3 to 5 minutes. You'll know the waffle is ready when steam stops coming out of the sides of the waffle iron and when the top of the waffle iron is easy to lift. If the top seems to stick a little, give the waffle another minute and try again. Gently dislodge the waffle from the waffle iron with the tines of a fork. The waffle should be golden brown.

7. Be sure to let the iron heat up again; then repeat with the remaining batter. Serve warm. (The waffles may be kept warm in a preheated 200°F oven for up to 10 minutes.)

PECAN WAFFLES

MAKES 6 TO 8 WAFFLES

In place of maple syrup, try homemade Maple Butter (page 274) with these deliciously nutty waffles. Buttermilk makes these waffles especially crisp and light.

3½ cups all-purpose flour

2 tablespoons baking powder

2 teaspoons baking soda

1 teaspoon kosher salt

8 extra-large eggs

4 cups buttermilk

½ pound (2 sticks) unsalted butter,
   melted and cooled, plus more for
   the waffle iron

½ cup chopped pecans

1. Combine the flour, baking powder, baking soda, and salt in a large bowl; set aside.

2. Using a whisk or a mixer set on medium speed, beat the eggs in a bowl for 1 minute, or until frothy. Add the buttermilk and beat until well combined.

3. Gradually add the flour mixture to the egg mixture and beat until smooth. Pour in the butter and beat well.

4. Preheat a waffle iron to medium or 375°F. Lightly butter the waffle iron, unless your iron is well seasoned.

5. Pour about ¾ cup batter—or enough to cover about two-thirds of the grid surface—onto the iron. Sprinkle with some of the pecans.

6. Close the lid of the waffle iron and allow the waffle to cook for 3 to 5 minutes. You'll know the waffle is ready when steam stops coming out of the sides of the waffle iron and the top of the waffle iron is easy to lift. If the top seems to stick a little, give the waffle another minute and try again. Gently dislodge the waffle from the waffle iron with the tines of a fork. The waffle should be golden brown.

7. Be sure to let the iron heat up again; then repeat with the remaining batter and pecans. Serve warm. (The waffles may be kept warm in a preheated 200°F oven for up to 10 minutes.)

FRENCH CRÊPES

MAKES 16 TO 18 CRÊPES

C *rêpes can be sprinkled with confectioners' sugar and served flat, like regular pancakes; or rolled up around fruit, Nutella (chocolate hazelnut butter), or chocolate; or topped with fruit, fruit compotes, whipped cream, or jam. You can make this batter ahead of time and refrigerate it in an airtight container for up to two days. Use a crêpe pan, which has a very long handle and slightly sloping slides, or a small to medium nonstick skillet. Prepared crêpes can be frozen for up to a month and defrosted at room temperature for a couple of hours. For best results, place crêpes between layers of waxed paper or parchment paper before freezing. Rewarm them by removing the waxed paper and baking them, tightly covered, in a baking pan in a preheated 300°F oven for 10 to 15 minutes.*

2 cups all-purpose flour
2 teaspoons kosher salt
4 extra-large eggs
2 cups milk

12 tablespoons (1½ sticks) unsalted butter, melted and cooled, plus more for the pan

1. Combine the flour and salt in a bowl; set aside.

2. Using a whisk or a mixer set on medium speed, beat the eggs in a large bowl for 1 minute, or until frothy. Add the milk and butter and beat for 1 minute, or until well combined.

3. Gradually add the flour mixture to the egg mixture and blend well with a large wooden spoon. Allow the batter to rest for 20 to 30 minutes.

4. When ready to cook, gently stir the crêpe batter. Very lightly butter the pan and use a paper towel to wipe off any excess.

5. Starting in the very center of the pan, slowly pour in enough batter to just coat the entire bottom of the pan. Carefully tilt and rotate the pan so the batter completely covers the bottom.

6. Cook the crêpe for about 1 minute, or until the bottom is light brown and comes off the pan easily. Flip the crêpe with a rubber spatula or your fingers, and let it cook on the second side for about 30 seconds, just until browned (the first side cooked will be darker). Slide the crêpe onto a plate.

7. Continue to cook the crêpes, stacking them evenly one on top of the other, until all the batter is used up. As you cook, keep the crêpes warm in a 200°F oven, covered with a damp kitchen towel.

8. To serve, peel the crêpes from the pile, lay them out flat, and spoon on your choice of filling.

Cinnamon Pear Crêpes Variation: Make Cinnamon Pear Compote (page 277) and place ¼ cup onto each crêpe. Fold over and griddle until the crêpe is very hot. These crêpes are also great drizzled with chocolate sauce (see Chocolate and Sautéed Banana Crêpes, page 145).

Apple Cheddar Crêpes Variation: Make Applesauce (page 279) and place about ¼ cup onto each crêpe. Sprinkle with ¼ cup grated Cheddar cheese per crêpe. Fold over and griddle until the crêpe is very hot.

Nutella Crêpes Variation: Spread about 2 tablespoons Nutella (chocolate hazelnut butter) onto each crêpe. Fold over and griddle until the crêpe is very hot.

CRÊPES WITH BROCCOLI AND GRUYÈRE

SERVES 4

G*ruyère is one of the best cheeses to use in a crêpe because it is flavorful and melts nicely. Here, broccoli adds color and texture. You can prepare both the filling and the crêpes ahead of time and assemble the crêpes at the last minute. If you make crêpes in advance, the crêpes can be wrapped airtight and frozen for up to two months. Serve with Mixed Greens with Shallot Vinaigrette (page 169).*

2 teaspoons olive oil	2 cups very well cooked, chopped
½ teaspoon minced garlic	broccoli (mixture of florets and
Kosher salt and freshly ground	stems, must be cooked soft)
black pepper to taste	2 cups grated Gruyère cheese (8 ounces)
4 cooked French Crêpes (½ recipe,	¼ teaspoon unsalted butter, plus
page 140)	extra for warming the crêpes

1. Heat 1 teaspoon of the olive oil in a medium skillet over medium-high heat for 30 seconds. Add the garlic and sauté for 2 minutes, or until soft. Add the broccoli and season with salt and pepper. Set aside to cool.

2. Shortly before serving, arrange the crêpes dark side down (the first side cooked is darker) on a clean work surface. Place ½ cup broccoli and ½ cup Gruyère cheese onto the center of each crêpe. Fold one-third of the bottom up; then fold each side in toward the center to make an envelope. Fold the top of each crêpe down to seal it.

3. Heat the crêpes in the butter in a crêpe pan or on a griddle. Alternatively, bake them in a preheated 400°F oven until the cheese is melted and the crêpes are very warm.

SAVORY CRÊPES VARIATIONS: Consider assorted cheese, meat, and vegetable combinations. With ham, you could use Brie, Swiss, or Cheddar cheese, or that old standby Gruyère. For Ham and Cheese Crêpes, you'll need a thin layer of thinly sliced ham and ¼ cup or so grated cheese for each crêpe. Arrange the crêpes dark side down on a clean work surface. Fill the crêpe and fold one-third of the bottom up; then fold each side in toward the center to make an envelope. Fold the top of each crêpe down to seal it. Griddle until the cheese is melted.

For Asparagus Cheddar Crêpes, place ¼ cup cooked, finely chopped asparagus onto each crêpe. Sprinkle with ¼ cup grated Cheddar cheese, fold over as per directions above, and griddle until crisp and until the cheese has melted.

CRÊPES WITH ZUCCHINI, SPINACH, AND ONIONS

MAKES 6 CRÊPES

A delicious and painless way to sneak more vegetables into the brunch, these crêpes are good for when brunch tilts more in the direction of breakfast. You can make the filling a day in advance and store it, tightly covered, in the refrigerator. Warm it over low heat before using it as a filling.

1 zucchini, halved lengthwise, ends removed, and very thinly sliced	3 tablespoons unsalted butter, plus extra for warming the crêpes
1 tablespoon kosher salt, plus more to taste	1 small red onion, finely diced
1 bunch spinach, washed three times, stems removed	Freshly ground black pepper to taste
	6 cooked French Crêpes (½ recipe; page 140)

1. Sprinkle the zucchini with the salt and let stand for 10 minutes to draw out the water. Pat dry with paper towels.

2. Cook the spinach in a skillet with ¼ cup of water until completely wilted. Cool under cold running water and squeeze dry in a clean kitchen towel. Chop the spinach into ⅛-inch pieces.

3. Melt the butter in a skillet over medium heat. Add the onion and sauté for 3 minutes, or until translucent. Add the zucchini and cook until it begins to soften, about 1 minute. Add the spinach and cook for about 4 minutes. Season with salt and pepper. Set aside to cool to room temperature.

4. Shortly before serving, arrange the crêpes dark side down on a clean work surface. Place about ⅓ cup filling on the center of each crêpe. Fold one-third of the bottom up; then fold each side in toward the center to make an envelope. Fold the top of each crêpe down to seal it.

5. Heat the crêpes in a little butter in a crêpe pan or on a griddle. Alternatively, bake them in a preheated 400°F oven until the crêpes are very warm.

CREAMY MUSHROOM CRÊPES

A nice vegetarian option, these crêpes have a substantial, almost meaty texture thanks to the mushrooms. They're rich enough to be a main course and especially flavorful, thanks to the fresh herbs. Serve with Mixed Summer Berry Parfait (page 231).

1 tablespoon unsalted butter	¼ cup chopped fresh parsley
2 tablespoons finely chopped shallot	Kosher salt and freshly ground
8 ounces mushrooms, cleaned,	black pepper to taste
trimmed, and thinly sliced	6 hot cooked French Crêpes
¼ teaspoon dried tarragon	(½ recipe; page 140)
¼ cup heavy cream	

1. Melt the butter in a medium skillet over medium heat. Add the shallot and let it cook for 1 minute. Add the mushrooms and tarragon and cook, stirring occasionally, until most of the liquid from the mushrooms has evaporated.

2. Stir in the cream and allow it to reduce for about 10 minutes, or until the mixture is very thick. Add the parsley and salt and pepper to taste.

3. Spoon 3 tablespoons of the mushroom cream onto each hot crêpe, roll up the crêpe, and serve.

CHOCOLATE AND SAUTÉED BANANA CRÊPES

MAKES 4 CRÊPES

A sophisticated dessert or even a sweet main course, these crêpes feature two favorite flavors of kids everywhere: bananas and chocolate. Using bittersweet chocolate cuts the sweetness of the banana and makes these crêpes quite elegant.

8 ounces bittersweet chocolate

3 tablespoons heavy cream

1 tablespoon sugar

2 tablespoons unsalted butter, plus
   extra for warming the crêpes

2 bananas, peeled and thinly sliced
   on the bias

4 cooked French Crêpes (½ recipe;
   page 140)

1. In the top of a double boiler over simmering water, melt the chocolate, cream, and sugar. Stir and remove from the heat.

2. Melt the butter in a skillet over medium heat. When it is sizzling, add the banana slices and cook until brown on both sides.

3. Divide the banana slices among the crêpes. Drizzle each crêpe with 2 tablespoons of the chocolate sauce and fold one-third of the bottom up; then fold each side in toward the center to make an envelope. Fold the top of each crepe down to seal it.

4. Heat a little butter in a sauté pan over medium heat. Add the crêpes and warm for about 1 minute, just until they are hot. Serve immediately.

MOM'S BLINTZES

MAKES 12 TO 14 BLINTZES

A traditional Jewish variation on the crêpe, the blintz can be filled with anything from berries to cheese to mashed potatoes. My mother fills hers with cream cheese and farmer cheese and serves them with a fruit compote. Serve three blintzes per person, accompanied by Blackberry Compote (page 276), strawberry compote (see page 276), sautéed bananas (see Banana Walnut Pancakes, page 122), or Strawberry Jam (page 280). A bit of advice from Mom: Be sure to have all your filling ingredients at room temperature before beginning this recipe, otherwise, it's difficult to mix everything evenly. Serve with Sliced Melon and Raspberries with Port Syrup (page 228).

For the crêpes	For the filling
2 cups all-purpose flour	8 ounces cream cheese, at room temperature
2 teaspoons kosher salt	8 ounces farmer cheese, at room temperature (you can substitute ricotta, though it is very different; it's best to use farmer cheese if you can find it)
4 extra-large eggs	
2 cups milk	
3 tablespoons unsalted butter, melted and cooled	
1 to 2 teaspoons softened butter for cooking the crêpes	4 tablespoons (½ stick) unsalted butter, at room temperature
	2 extra-large egg yolks, at room temperature
	¼ teaspoon kosher salt
	2 teaspoons fresh lemon juice

1. Make the crêpes: Combine the flour and salt in a large mixing bowl; set aside.

2. Using a whisk or a mixer set on medium speed, beat the eggs in a bowl for 1 minute, or until frothy. Beat in the milk and butter.

3. Add the flour mixture to the egg mixture and beat until smooth. Let the batter sit at room temperature for about 30 minutes to allow the gluten to soften a little and to ensure that the crêpes flow onto the pan as thinly as possible.

4. Make the filling: Combine the cream cheese, farmer cheese, 2 tablespoons of the butter, the egg yolks, salt, and lemon juice in a large bowl. Using a whisk or a mixer set on medium speed, beat until smooth. Set aside.

5. Preheat the oven to 400°F.

6. Heat the butter in an 8-inch nonstick skillet over medium heat until sizzling. You will not have to grease the pan again after the first crêpe comes out. Lifting the hot pan in one hand, ladle about 2 tablespoons of the batter into the very center of the pan. Swirl the batter around to coat the bottom of the pan completely, but with the thinnest layer of batter possible.

7. Cook the crêpe for 45 seconds to 1 minute. Flip the crêpe and cook it on the other side for no more than 30 seconds. The crêpe should be firm and still pretty blond, not brown. Stack each crêpe evenly one on top of the other on a plate as you continue to make them.

8. When all the batter has been used up, arrange the crêpes on a clean work surface. Place about 2 tablespoons of the filling on the bottom third of each crêpe. Fold the bottom up over the filling. Tuck in the sides and roll up.

9. Melt the remaining 2 tablespoons of butter in a large skillet over medium heat. Arrange the blintzes in a single layer in the skillet. Cook on one side until golden brown; then flip and cook until golden brown on the other side. If the blintzes seem to be sticking, the pan may not be hot enough. Turn the heat up a notch. You should not need to add any more butter. Serve immediately.

SANDWICHES AND SALADS

At Bubby's, brunch consists of a fairly even mix of breakfast and lunch options. When I serve brunch at home, I like to offer the same range of choices. Usually the hour of the day dictates which way the menu tilts. Given how much we love our greens and our overstuffed sandwiches, it makes sense that both salads and sandwiches are very popular sections of the brunch menu.

Grilled and quartered, or simply layered on the best possible bread, sandwiches are a perennial favorite. They are best assembled at the last minute, but they're ideal for brunch since fillings and spreads can be prepped ahead of time. A sandwich is only as good as the bread it's made on, so get the best loaf you can find. I like to use a variety of breads, from raisin pumpernickel to seven-grain bread to crusty white, sliced nice and thick. A typical loaf of bread weighs a pound to one and a half pounds, which will yield about eighteen regular slices and fourteen to sixteen thick slices. One way to keep sandwiches that must be made in advance fresh is to wrap them with wax paper, butcher paper or a brown paper bag cut flat. Secure the wrapping with toothpicks, and the sandwiches won't get stale.

If you're hosting an outdoor brunch—a beach picnic, for instance—pack your sandwich fillings separately and assemble the sandwiches once you arrive. You can avoid soggy sandwich syndrome by spreading the bread with a very thin layer of butter or mayonnaise before putting on the main filling. As a general rule of thumb, if you make sandwiches in advance, serve and eat them within four hours.

As a brunch main course, salads are very host friendly. Most of the prep can be done ahead, from making the dressing to chopping the vegetables to washing and drying the greens. Salads also are versatile, so if you can't find or don't like one type of green, vegetable, or grain, it's simple enough to substitute something else and still end up with great results.

Because salads rely for the most part on greens as a base, acquiring the freshest ones is very important. Use lettuces of all kinds as soon as possible after you buy them. Always remove any wilted leaves, and store greens in open plastic bags in the refrigerator's vegetable bin. Some of my favorites are romaine, arugula, watercress, Belgian endive, and even iceberg lettuce for its crispness.

The easiest way to clean most greens is to fill the sink with cold water and to swish the greens around in order for the grit to sink to the bottom. You can also do the same in a big bowl of cold water. After the lettuces have soaked for a bit, lift them out of the water, leaving any dirt behind. Some greens, such as spinach, may require two or three changes of water. It's always good to take a bite of the greens to make sure that all the dirt is gone. Drying is easy if you have a salad spinner, or you can wrap clean greens in paper towels and gently remove all the water. Refrigerate the clean lettuce to keep it nice and crisp. Cleaned greens will keep in the refrigerator for up to three days.

Dressings nearly always contain oil of some sort and here, too, it's crucial to use the best you can find. The flavor of really good quality extra-virgin olive oil is worth the extra price. The other dressing essential, vinegar, comes in many varieties. Stock your kitchen with sherry vinegar, cider vinegar, and wine vinegars for salad dressings and keep balsamic vinegar on hand, too, although because its flavor can quickly become overpowering, sprinkle it on judiciously.

With the addition of chicken or tuna or your favorite meat or fish, just about any salad becomes a main course. Salads can easily be prepared for a crowd because recipes are easy to double and triple, and dressings can be served on the side.

Brunch is about relaxing, and relaxing the rules, and that means the cook gets to decide what to toss—and what not to toss—into a salad and what to layer into a sandwich. Always use the best possible ingredients, but there's no need to follow a recipe to the letter. This chapter's meant to be fun, flexible, and full of options.

WITH BOTH SANDWICHES AND SALADS, FEEL FREE TO CHANGE OR ADD ACCORDING TO WHAT YOU LIKE AND WHAT LOOKS GOOD AT THE MARKET.

MR. CRUNCH, AKA CROQUE MONSIEUR

SERVES 1

This sandwich is a French import made by dipping a basic ham and cheese sandwich into a beaten egg before sautéing it in butter. It's like a savory French toast sandwich. It's best made in a cast-iron skillet since cast iron distributes the heat very evenly. Ask the deli clerk to slice the ham very thin, and use good-quality French bread.

1 extra-large egg, well beaten

2 tablespoons milk

1 teaspoon mayonnaise, homemade (page 284) or store-bought

2 slices good French bread (½ inch thick)

4 ounces thinly sliced smoked ham

2 slices Gruyère cheese (⅛ inch thick)

2 teaspoons unsalted butter

1. Using a whisk or fork, beat the egg and milk together in a small bowl or a deep pie plate; set aside.

2. Spread ½ teaspoon of the mayonnaise on each slice of bread.

3. Arrange the ham and cheese on 1 slice of bread. Top with the other slice of bread, mayonnaise side down.

4. Heat a large cast-iron skillet over medium heat until very hot.

5. Melt 1 teaspoon of the butter in the hot skillet. Holding the sandwich together carefully between your fingers, dip both sides of the sandwich into the egg batter. Let any excess drip off.

6. Lay one side of the dipped sandwich in the skillet. Cook for 3 to 4 minutes, or until golden brown on the bottom. Using a spatula, flip the sandwich at the same time that you add the remaining teaspoon of butter to the skillet. Lift the sandwich to allow the butter to run underneath as it melts. Brown the sandwich on the second side for 4 to 5 minutes.

7. Cut the sandwich in half or quarters and serve immediately.

CROQUE MADAME VARIATION: For croque madame, proceed with the above recipe. Keep the sandwich warm on a plate while you melt 1 teaspoon butter over low heat in the same skillet until sizzling. Crack an egg into the skillet and fry it, flipping once, until it is fairly firm. Add a little salt and pepper to taste. Arrange the fried egg on top of the sandwich, cut in half, and serve.

TRADITIONAL BLT

SERVES 1

This classic sandwich relies on good ripe tomatoes, thickly sliced bacon, and top-quality crusty bread. Although you might normally shun iceberg lettuce, this is one instance where its crunchiness is welcome. Feel free, of course, to substitute another lettuce such as romaine.

4 slices good-quality thick-cut
   bacon (⅛ inch thick)
2 slices crusty bread (½ inch thick)
1 tablespoon mayonnaise,
   homemade (page 284) or
   store-bought

½ ripe tomato, cut into 4 slices
1 or 2 iceberg lettuce leaves,
   washed and thoroughly dried

1. Cook the bacon in a single layer in a skillet over medium heat. Turn occasionally, until browned and crisp, 5 to 7 minutes. Drain on a paper towel–lined plate; set aside.

2. Spread one side of each slice of bread with the mayonnaise.

3. Arrange the bacon slices, tomato slices, and lettuce on 1 slice of bread. Top with the other slice of bread, mayonnaise side down.

4. Cut the sandwich in half or in quarters, secure each piece with a toothpick, and serve.

GRILLED BACON, APPLE, AND CHEDDAR SANDWICH

SERVES 1

Tart apple, smoky bacon, and rich Cheddar cheese all come together for a flavorful autumnal treat with this unique sandwich. Certain elements of this sandwich should be thick—the bacon and the bread—and others should be thin—the apple and the Cheddar. Use a crisp, tart apple such as Granny Smith, Mutsu, or Honeycrisp. Use the best bacon you can find as well. I like to make this sandwich in a cast-iron skillet because it makes for a uniformly deep golden crust, which I cherish above all else in a grilled sandwich.

4 slices thick-cut bacon (⅛ inch thick)

1 tablespoon unsalted butter

¼ crisp, tart apple, such as Granny Smith, Mutsu, or Honeycrisp, peeled, cored, and cut into ⅛-inch-thick slices

1 tablespoon mayonnaise, homemade (page 284) or store-bought

2 slices crusty bread (½ inch thick)

2 thin slices sharp white Cheddar cheese (about 2 ounces)

1. Cook the bacon in a single layer in a skillet over medium heat. Turn occasionally, until browned and crisp, 5 to 7 minutes. Drain on a paper towel–lined plate. Pour the bacon fat out of the skillet.

2. Melt 1 teaspoon of the butter in the same skillet over medium-high heat. Add the apple slices and sauté for a minute or two, until they become slightly soft. Transfer the apple slices to a plate and wipe out the skillet.

3. Spread a very thin layer of mayonnaise on each slice of bread. Arrange the bacon in a single layer on 1 slice of bread. Arrange the apple slices over the bacon. Arrange the cheese slices over the apple slices, and top with the other slice of bread, mayonnaise side down.

4. Melt 1 teaspoon of the butter in the skillet over medium heat. Carefully lay the sandwich in the pan. Cook for 2 to 3 minutes, or until golden brown on the bottom. Using a spatula, flip the sandwich at the same time that you add the remaining 1 teaspoon butter to the skillet. Lift the sandwich to allow the butter to run underneath it as it melts. Brown the sandwich on the second side until it is golden brown and the cheese is melted, another 2 to 3 minutes.

5. Remove the sandwich from the skillet, cut it in half, and serve.

OPEN-FACE GRILLED CHICKEN, MAYTAG BLUE CHEESE, AND TOASTED PECAN SANDWICH

SERVES 2

Maytag Blue cheese, made by the same family that became world famous for its appliances, is handmade from cow's milk and has a peppery, piquant flavor. Start this sandwich about an hour in advance so the chicken has time to marinate. This is an easy recipe to double or triple for a larger group, and the chicken can be made ahead. I like to serve this sandwich on raisin pumpernickel bread, but feel free to use another favorite loaf.

One 6-ounce boneless, skinless
   chicken breast, cut in half
   lengthwise
2 tablespoons olive oil
Kosher salt and freshly ground
   black pepper to taste
Dash of Worcestershire sauce

2 tablespoons chopped pecans
2 slices raisin pumpernickel bread
2 tablespoons mayonnaise,
   homemade (page 284) or
   store-bought
2 tablespoons Maytag Blue cheese
8 watercress sprigs

1. Combine the chicken, olive oil, salt, pepper, and Worcestershire sauce in a bowl. Cover with plastic wrap and set aside for 30 minutes so the chicken can marinate.

2. Toast the pecans in a small skillet over medium heat for 2 minutes, or until golden brown, stirring occasionally. Alternatively, roast the pecans in a preheated 300°F oven for 15 minutes, or until they smell toasted. Transfer the pecans to a plate and set aside to cool.

3. Grill the chicken under the broiler or on an outdoor grill for 10 to 12 minutes, or until thoroughly cooked, turning once. Whether broiling or grilling, for the best flavor make sure the heat is high so you will get a nice caramelized brown color on the chicken. Allow the chicken to rest for at least 10 minutes to allow the juices to settle in the meat. Using a very sharp knife, slice the chicken as thinly as possible on a bias.

4. Spread each slice of bread evenly with the mayonnaise. Divide the chicken slices between the 2 slices of bread. Sprinkle with bits of the blue cheese and then sprinkle on the toasted pecans.

5. With a sharp knife, quarter each sandwich. Garnish each quarter with a sprig of watercress and serve.

ROAST BEEF SANDWICH WITH
HORSERADISH CREAM

SERVES 4

*T*wo keys to a great roast beef sandwich are rare roast beef and good, crunchy, warm sourdough bread. We added some spicy horseradish cream to give it a kick.

For the horseradish cream	For the sandwiches
¼ cup heavy cream	1 fresh sourdough baguette, cut
¼ cup sour cream	into 4 pieces, split lengthwise
½ cup prepared horseradish	1½ pounds thinly sliced roast beef
1 teaspoon Worcestershire sauce	12 slices ripe tomato
1 teaspoon freshly ground black	(from 3 tomatoes)
pepper	4 romaine lettuce leaves
Kosher salt to taste	

1. Make the horseradish cream: Using a mixer set on high speed, beat the heavy cream so it holds its shape, about 1 to 2 minutes. Fold in the sour cream, horseradish, Worcestershire sauce, pepper, and salt.

2. Preheat the oven to 350°F.

3. Make the sandwiches: Warm the baguette in the oven for about 2 minutes.

4. Put 1 tablespoon of the horseradish cream on each bottom half of bread. Fold one-quarter of the sliced roast beef over the horseradish, then put another 1 tablespoon horseradish cream on top of the beef for each sandwich. Over this, arrange 3 tomato slices and a leaf of romaine on each sandwich. Top with the remaining bread halves.

5. Cut each sandwich in half, secure each half with a toothpick, and serve.

TURKEY, EMMENTHALER, AND RUSSIAN DRESSING ON RYE

SERVES 1

This is a real deli-lovers sandwich, topped with Emmenthaler, which is a good sharp Swiss cheese. You'll have enough Russian dressing for six sandwiches; you can keep the extra for a week in the refrigerator.

For the Russian dressing
2 tablespoons sugar
¼ cup ketchup
1 tablespoon fresh lemon juice
1½ teaspoons white wine vinegar
¼ teaspoon kosher salt
¼ teaspoon paprika
½ teaspoon celery seed
1 teaspoon Worcestershire sauce
2 tablespoons grated onion
¼ cup vegetable oil

For the sandwich
4 ounces thinly sliced turkey
   breast
2 thin slices Emmenthaler cheese
1 romaine lettuce leaf
2 slices good rye bread

1. Make the Russian dressing: Heat the sugar and 1 teaspoon of water in a saucepan over low heat until the sugar is dissolved. Transfer to a mixing bowl.

2. Stir in the ketchup, lemon juice, vinegar, salt, paprika, celery seed, Worcestershire sauce, and onion. Gradually whisk in the vegetable oil until all the ingredients are incorporated. Taste, and adjust the seasonings as needed.

3. Make the sandwich: Layer the turkey, Emmenthaler cheese, romaine, and 2 tablespoons of the Russian dressing on 1 slice of bread. Top with the other slice of bread.

4. Cut the sandwich in half, and serve.

TUNA SALAD SANDWICH WITH APPLES AND WALNUTS

SERVES 4

This dish can be served as a sandwich filling or as a stand-alone salad accompanied by favorite lettuces and veggies. We use canned tuna packed in spring water because it's lighter than tuna packed in oil, and we make sure the apple is tart and crisp. Granny Smith apples are fine, but also Mutsu, Honeycrisp, or any good local crispy, tart apple will do. Add half the dressing at first and see if you need more—it's up to you how well coated you want the tuna and apples to be.

¼ cup chopped walnuts

¾ cup mayonnaise, homemade (page 284) or store-bought

2 teaspoons sugar

1 teaspoon cider vinegar

Kosher salt and freshly ground black pepper to taste

2 crisp, tart apples, such as Granny Smith, Mutsu or Honeycrisp, peeled, cored, and cut into ⅛-inch cubes

3 small cans (about 18 ounces total) canned tuna in spring water, drained and separated into chunks

6 tablespoons finely diced red onion

¼ cup chopped fresh parsley

8 slices multi-grain bread

1. Toast the walnuts in a small nonstick skillet over medium heat for 2 minutes, or until golden brown, stirring occasionally. Alternatively, roast the walnuts in a preheated 300°F oven for 10 minutes, or until they smell toasted. Remove the walnuts to a plate and set aside to cool.

2. Whisk together the mayonnaise, sugar, and cider vinegar in a small bowl. Add salt and pepper to taste. Adjust the seasonings as needed.

3. Combine the walnuts, apples, tuna, red onion, and parsley in a bowl. Toss with half the dressing. Add more dressing, if desired.

4. Spread the salad over 4 slices of bread. Top with the other 4 slices. Cut each sandwich in half, and serve.

NIÇOISE SALAD

Bubby's
SIGNATURE DISH

SERVES 4 TO 6

When a dish is called Niçoise (French for "as prepared in Nice"), it's a safe bet that it contains tomatoes, tuna, green beans, and black olives. Though you could use jarred roasted peppers, the salad is best if you roast your own. And use the best-quality canned tuna that you can get—it makes a huge difference. Start this signature salad at least one hour in advance, so you can have eleven-minute boiled eggs ready and chilled. Ditto with the beans—they should be chilled after blanching. You may use either fresh green beans or the skinny French haricots verts in this recipe. All told, this is a beautiful salad, especially when the ingredients are cut carefully and arranged in groups. This dressing, good on greens of all kinds, will keep well, tightly covered, in the refrigerator for up to a week.

For the Niçoise dressing
1 garlic clove, minced
2 tablespoons capers, rinsed and drained
⅓ cup red wine vinegar
1 cup olive oil
Kosher salt and freshly ground black pepper to taste

For the salad
1 red bell pepper
8 ounces fresh green beans or haricots verts, trimmed
4 extra-large eggs
1 head romaine lettuce
1 fennel bulb
1 teaspoon fresh lemon juice
4 canned artichoke hearts, drained and halved
½ cup good Niçoise olives, pitted
1 ripe tomato, cut into 6 wedges
1 cup very good quality canned tuna packed in olive oil

1. Make the Niçoise dressing: Combine the garlic, capers, vinegar, and olive oil in a 1-quart jar with a lid. Shake the dressing very well. Season with salt and pepper. Refrigerate until serving time.

2. Preheat the broiler.

3. Make the salad: Place the bell pepper under the broiler, about 4 inches from the heating element, for 2 to 3 minutes, checking often so it doesn't burn. When one side is nicely blackened, use tongs to turn the bell pepper until it is evenly blackened on all sides. Remove the bell pepper from the broiler. Alternatively, place the bell pepper directly in the flame of the burner on a gas stove and turn it as each side gets blackened. While it is still hot, place it in a paper bag and let it sweat for 10 minutes. Then work the burned skin off with your fingers. I don't like to rinse the bell pepper under water because it removes the flavorful oil. You'll inevitably be left with a little skin on the pepper, which is fine, but remove as much as possible. Split the bell pepper lengthwise and remove the core and seeds. Slice the flesh into ¼-inch-wide julienne strips and set aside.

4. Bring a medium saucepan of lightly salted water to a boil. Cook the beans for 3 to 4 minutes, or until they are just slightly tender but still nice and green. Drain. Plunge the beans into a bowl of ice water to stop the cooking and drain again. Set aside.

5. Cook the eggs in a 6-quart saucepan of simmering water for 11 minutes. (If you like a slightly wet center, cook for 10 minutes; for a completely cooked egg, try 12 minutes.) Run cold water over the eggs in the saucepan. Remove the eggs from the water and peel them under running water. Cut in half lengthwise and set aside.

6. Remove and discard the tough outer leaves and the tough bottom part of the romaine. Split the head lengthwise into sixths with a sharp knife. Wash the romaine wedges, shake out the excess water, and pat the wedges dry with paper towels. Trim the center core, leaving just enough to hold the wedges together. Wrap the wedges in paper towels and refrigerate.

7. Trim away the fronds and hollow stalks of the fennel bulb, and cut away the bottom. Cut the bulb in half and remove the center core. Cut the bulb either crosswise or lengthwise into very fine slices. Place the fennel in a bowl with the lemon juice and 2 cups of water. This will keep the fennel from browning. Alternatively, cut the fennel bulb into sixths, removing the center core, and coat with a little olive oil, salt, and pepper. Roast or grill the pieces for 5 to 10 minutes, or until tender. (You can serve the fennel in this salad hot, at room temperature, or chilled.)

8. Arrange the romaine wedges cut side up in the center of a platter. Arrange the green beans, eggs, fennel, artichokes, olives, tomato, and tuna in separate groups around the edges. Arrange the roasted bell peppers around the whole salad.

9. Just before serving, drizzle the Niçoise dressing over the salad. Alternatively, pour the dressing into a cruet or pitcher and let guests dress their own salads.

CHOPPED COBB SALAD

SERVES 6 TO 8

Cobb Salad was born in the 1920s at Hollywood's Brown Derby restaurant, where a restaurant manager by the name of Bob Cobb created it as a way to recycle leftovers. The classic vinaigrette dressing really makes this salad, which traditionally contains finely chopped chicken, bacon, hard-boiled eggs, cheese, and lettuce. All the ingredients are chopped and arranged to give a colorful presentation. I like the chicken when it's grilled because it adds a smoky flavor and a pleasing crunchiness. If you prefer, you can also sear the chicken over high heat. Store Cobb dressing in the refrigerator and use leftovers within several days.

For the dressing
¼ cup red wine vinegar
¼ teaspoon sugar
1 teaspoon fresh lemon juice
2 teaspoons kosher salt
¾ teaspoon freshly ground black pepper
¾ teaspoon Worcestershire sauce
¼ teaspoon dry mustard
1 small garlic clove, finely minced
¼ cup olive oil
¾ cup canola oil

For the salad
Two 6-ounce boneless, skinless chicken breasts
Kosher salt and freshly ground black pepper to taste
4 extra-large eggs
6 slices bacon (⅛ inch thick)
1 head romaine
1 bunch watercress
2 heads Belgian endive
1 bunch arugula
2 ripe avocados, halved, peeled, pitted, and cut into ½-inch dice
2 medium tomatoes, cored and chopped into ¼-inch pieces

1. Make the dressing: Combine ¼ cup of water, the vinegar, sugar, lemon juice, salt, pepper, Worcestershire sauce, mustard, and garlic in a large bowl. Stir well until combined.

2. Slowly pour in the olive oil and canola oil. Using a whisk, mix the dressing vigorously until creamy and thick. Taste, and adjust the seasonings as needed.

3. Make the salad: Grill or broil the chicken breasts under a broiler or on an outdoor grill, or sear them in a very hot pan, for 3 to 4 minutes on one side, then for 2 to 3 minutes on the other side, until nicely seared on the outside and cooked thoroughly on the inside. Season with a little salt and pepper. Let the chicken rest for 10 minutes so the juices have a chance to distribute throughout the meat. Chop the chicken into ½-inch pieces.

4. Bring a pot of water to a boil. Add the eggs, reduce the heat, and simmer for 12 minutes. Remove the eggs from the water and run under cold water. Peel them under the running water. Finely chop the eggs; set aside.

5. Cook the bacon in a single layer in a skillet for 5 minutes, or until crisp, turning it once or twice. Drain on paper towels. Chop the bacon into a small dice.

6. Wash the romaine, watercress, Belgian endive, and arugula thoroughly in several changes of water. Spin them dry in a salad spinner or pat them dry with paper towels. Chop into ¼- to ½-inch pieces.

7. Toss the greens together on a large platter. They will serve as a base for the other ingredients. Arrange the chicken, eggs, avocados, tomatoes, and bacon into individual piles around the greens.

8. Just before serving, drizzle the dressing over the salad. Alternatively, pour the dressing into a cruet or pitcher and let guests dress their own salads.

CHICKEN SALAD WITH GRAPES

SERVES 6 TO 8

*T*his salad is easy to put together and makes a nice presentation when mounded on a platter. If you can find smoked chicken, by all means use it, but otherwise, a good roast chicken will suffice. The contrasting colors and flavors of the fruits and nuts, with a slightly sweet dressing, make this especially pleasing as a brunch entrée. If you would like to make sandwiches, toasted seven-grain bread is a good choice. If you'd like to get a head start on the salad, the whole thing can be made a day ahead and refrigerated until ready to serve.

¼ cup chopped walnuts

¼ cup mayonnaise, homemade
    (page 284) or store-bought

1 tablespoon distilled white vinegar

¼ cup maple syrup

Kosher salt and cayenne pepper
    to taste

4 cups chopped roasted or smoked
    chicken

¼ cup chopped fresh parsley

½ cup red or green seedless grapes,
    halved

1. Toast the walnuts in a small nonstick skillet over medium heat for 2 minutes, or until golden brown, stirring occasionally. Alternatively, roast the walnuts on a baking sheet in a preheated 300°F oven for 15 minutes, or until they smell toasted. Transfer to a plate and allow to cool.

2. Whisk together the mayonnaise, vinegar, and maple syrup in a small bowl until well blended. Season with salt and cayenne pepper as needed.

3. Combine the chicken, parsley, grapes, and walnuts in a large bowl. Spoon the dressing over the chicken mixture and toss so that the chicken is well coated.

4. Mound the salad onto a serving platter garnished with salad greens, and serve.

BUBBY'S CAESAR SALAD

SERVES 6 TO 8

This salad is practically a meal in itself, especially if you fan out a beautifully grilled sliced chicken breast or some shrimp on top. Because it contains raw egg, this dressing, which can be made ahead, should be refrigerated and used within three days.

For the dressing	For the croutons
2 garlic cloves	2 tablespoons olive oil
1 to 2 anchovy fillets (depending on how anchovy-y you like it)	2 cups sourdough bread cubes (½ inch)
2 extra-large egg yolks	2 teaspoons chopped fresh parsley
Juice of 1 lemon	Pinch of kosher salt
¼ cup red wine vinegar	
1 tablespoon Dijon mustard	For the salad
1 cup olive oil	1 head romaine lettuce
Kosher salt and cayenne pepper to taste	¼ cup freshly grated Parmesan cheese, plus more for the top of the salad

1. Make the dressing: In the work bowl of a food processor fitted with a metal blade, purée the garlic. Add the anchovy fillets and egg yolks and process for about 30 seconds, or until well mixed. Add the lemon juice, vinegar, and mustard. Process for about 15 seconds. With the motor running, pour in the olive oil in a slow stream, pulsing until well incorporated. Season with salt and pepper. Pour the dressing into a jar or another covered container and refrigerate until serving time.

2. Make the croutons: Heat the olive oil in a large skillet over medium heat until very hot. Add the bread cubes and cook, stirring occasionally, for about 3 minutes, or until golden brown. Alternatively, brown the bread cubes on a baking sheet coated with olive oil in a preheated 350°F oven for 6 to 8 minutes. Sprinkle with the chopped parsley and cook for 1 minute. Remove the croutons to a large plate and sprinkle with a little salt.

3. Make the salad: Remove and discard the tough outer leaves and the tough bottom part of the romaine. Wash the lettuce under cold running water. Spin it dry in a salad spinner or pat it dry with paper towels. Chop into 2-inch pieces. Place the romaine into a plastic bag or a bowl with a damp kitchen towel on top of it, and refrigerate until well chilled and crisp.

4. Place the romaine in a large mixing bowl. Add the croutons and Parmesan cheese. Spoon about ½ cup of Caesar dressing over the salad and toss gently. Add extra dressing as needed. Mound the salad onto a large platter or in a large serving bowl, and sprinkle the top with a little grated Parmesan cheese before serving.

GREEN GODDESS SALAD

SERVES 6 TO 8

A chef at the Palace Hotel in San Francisco in the 1920s is said to have created this to honor George Arliss, an actor appearing there in a play entitled The Green Goddess. The dressing is made with an abundance of herbs and can be served with fish or shellfish as well as salads. Be sure to use fresh herbs: Dried just don't deliver the same flavor. For this salad to look its best, place it in a bowl that's twice the size of the greens so you'll have plenty of room to toss.

For the dressing
1 garlic clove, finely minced
4 anchovy fillets, finely minced
2 cups mayonnaise, homemade
(page 284) or store-bought
1 cup chopped scallions (green part
only)
2 teaspoons chopped fresh parsley
2 tablespoons cider vinegar, or to
taste
1 teaspoon chopped fresh tarragon
Kosher salt and freshly ground
black pepper to taste

For the salad
1 head romaine lettuce
1 bunch watercress
1 bunch arugula
1 fennel bulb
Olive oil for roasting the fennel
Kosher salt and freshly ground
black pepper for roasting the
fennel
1 large carrot, peeled and shredded
1 cucumber, peeled and thinly sliced
1 cup cherry tomatoes

1. Make the dressing: In the work bowl of a food processor fitted with a metal blade, combine the garlic and anchovy fillets. Pulse for 30 seconds, or until puréed. Add the mayonnaise, scallions, parsley, vinegar, and tarragon. Pulse several times until the mixture is creamy. Season with salt and pepper. Pour the dressing into a jar or other covered container and refrigerate until serving time.

2. Make the salad: Cut the romaine into ½-inch pieces. Wash the romaine, watercress, and arugula thoroughly in several changes of water. Spin them dry in a salad spinner or pat them dry with paper towels. Place them into a large serving bowl, cover with a damp paper towel and refrigerate until ready to serve.

3. Preheat the oven to 400°F.

4. Trim away the fronds and the hollow stalk of the fennel bulb and cut away the bottom. Cut the fennel bulb into sixths, remove the center core, and coat the pieces with a little olive oil, salt, and pepper. Roast on a baking sheet for 10 to 15 minutes, or until tender. When the fennel is cool enough to handle, chop it into ¼-inch pieces.

5. Remove the bowl of greens from the refrigerator and add the fennel. Add the carrot, cucumber, and cherry tomatoes.

6. Toss the salad with about ¾ cup of the green goddess dressing. Add extra dressing if desired. Alternatively, pour the dressing into a small cruet or pitcher and let guests dress their own salads.

MIXED GREENS WITH SHALLOT VINAIGRETTE

SERVES 4

A simple green salad, this one is made special by the unusually good vinaigrette. The dressing can be made up to three days ahead and stored, tightly covered, in the refrigerator.

For the vinaigrette
⅓ cup minced shallots
2 tablespoons fresh lemon juice
2 tablespoons red wine vinegar
1 teaspoon freshly grated lemon
    zest
1½ teaspoons Dijon mustard
½ cup olive oil
2 tablespoons chopped fresh parsley
Kosher salt and freshly ground
    black pepper to taste

For the salad
6 cups greens of your choice,
    washed, dried, and crisped

1. Make the shallot vinaigrette: Combine the shallots, lemon juice, vinegar, lemon zest, mustard, olive oil, parsley, salt, and pepper in a jar with a lid and shake vigorously.

2. Make the salad: Arrange the greens in a large bowl and toss with the vinaigrette. Serve immediately.

THE MEAT OF THE MATTER:

BRUNCH MEATS AND FISH

At brunch, meat and fish play a strong supporting role to eggs and griddle specialties. Sumptuous home-smoked salmon; crisp, thick strips of bacon; slices of dry-aged New York strip steak, roasted to rosy-pink perfection, enhance everything from waffles to omelets to pancakes. Whether smoked, roasted, or fried, the meat and fish part of brunch is practically essential.

The meats and seafood we feature at brunch are so varied that there's literally something for everyone. At Bubby's, meat and fish are usually served more as a condiment on the brunch plate, rather than as a front-and-center hunk of protein.

For fish lovers, Bubby's brunch serves both salmon and trout that are smoked right there at the restaurant, along with a scrupulously fresh Crab Salad (page 199), Smoked Salmon and Goat Cheese Roses (page 193), and fabulous fried oysters that are rolled in cornmeal for extra crunch.

Meatier options include a petite New York strip or tenderloin that is panfried and served alongside eggs, Biscuits with Sausage Gravy (page 186), Pork Belly Hash (page 179), and several varieties of bacon, including Maple-Glazed Bacon (page 177), which is a snap to make at home.

At Bubby's, we smoke our own chicken and make our own sausages (both pork and venison). Our age-old preparation for Smithfield Ham (page 188) is a memorable signature offering. Piquant Corned Beef Hash (page 183), a Bubby's classic, is a robust skillet concoction involving diced potatoes, onions, and beef, seasoned with an abundance of black pepper and laced with horseradish. Though not for the light eater, it is nonetheless a timeless favorite for legions of Bubby's brunchers.

Smoking and curing meat and fish at home may be a little out of your comfort zone, but the results are worth it. To make pastrami at home, you'll need at least a week of curing and a day of smoking. For homemade smoked salmon, give yourself two days. As for the Smithfield ham, you have to soak it for three days, change the water regularly, and then cook it.

Yes, it takes time and patience to smoke your own salmon, make your own pastrami, or cook a Smithfield ham to perfection. But there is a certain joy that comes from knowing that you actually can accomplish these projects. When you undertake a major cooking feat such as home smoking, you get to see what the process is, and you have a little flexibility to customize your own dish. You also get more value when you do it yourself. For instance, good smoked salmon can cost you upward of twenty-four dollars a pound. You'll spend a fraction of this when you smoke it yourself.

Tastewise, the rewards are great when you smoke and cure your own meat and fish. The homemade version of just about anything lacks the preservatives that commercially prepared food often has. While such endeavors every once in a while can be extremely rewarding for both you and your guests, you may not choose to embark on them all that often—or at all, and that is perfectly okay, too. It's a time-saver to be able to buy smoked and cured meats from a reputable purveyor, and there are plenty of choices about where to shop.

Whether cured or not, meat and fish perfectly complement so many other dishes. Pancakes, waffles, and French toast taste better when they're on the same plate as Bubby's homemade sweet Italian sausages, and Bubby's smoked salmon is perfect with a bagel and a schmear of cream cheese. It's impossible to have eggs Benedict without Canadian bacon, a Hangtown Fry without the addictive fried oysters, or steak and eggs without the peppery New York strip. And a celebratory spring brunch cries out for a generous platter of fresh crab salad to accompany a vegetable frittata and some just-baked fruit muffins.

In this chapter, you'll not only learn how to smoke, season, and sauté a variety of meat and fish dishes, you'll also see what to serve with them so that they

CHOOSING A MEAT OR FISH TO SERVE AT BRUNCH IS EASY ENOUGH— JUST GO WITH YOUR FAVORITES—YOU SIMPLY CAN'T GO WRONG.

brighten any brunch menu. But if you don't have time to smoke and grind your own meats, I recommend buying your meats at a reputable butcher or gourmet store. I like Ottomanelli's in New York City for many meats (www.ottomanellibros.com). One of my favorite commercial brands for sausages is Aidells (www.aidells.com).

Good-quality store-bought breakfast sausage links are a convenient way to add a protein accompaniment to many brunch dishes, especially when you don't have the time or inclination to make homemade sausage. They cook quickly and can be panfried or baked in the oven.

So whether you choose chorizo or smoked salmon, the protein part of just about any brunch is as flexible as the rest of the meal. Unlike dinner, where meat is often front and center, at brunch it's more of an accent, playing a supporting role to any number of egg or griddled dishes.

Choosing a brunch meat or fish is stress-free since there really aren't any hard and fast rules. Just pair whatever protein you love with your other favorite dishes, and your guests can serve themselves as much or as little as they like. It's all fun and casual, in keeping with the brunch theme.

BACON 101

JUST THE SMELL OF COOKING BACON IS enough to draw everyone into the kitchen and to make even the most dedicated herbivore reconsider the carnivorous pleasures that cured pork presents. There are many excellent bacons to try, and the supermarket bacon most of us grew up with isn't nearly as good as some other varieties. Bacon still in a slab tends to be better than commercially sliced bacon and gives you more control over the thickness.

At Bubby's, we serve a very thick cut of bacon. We buy bacon in a slab and slice it ourselves, but you can ask your butcher to cut it thick for you. We like it at least ⅛-inch thick. In addition to traditional slab bacon, here are a few other varieties to try.

PANCETTA: Italian bacon, pancetta is not typically smoked; instead, it is cured with spices and salt. Used very often in Italian cooking, it's a favorite in sauces because it has a flavorful and slightly salty taste. You can buy pancetta in a roll or sliced by your butcher. Slice pancetta and cook it in a pan just as you would regular bacon.

CANADIAN BACON: Made from smoked, cured pork loin, Canadian bacon has become a staple with brunch, especially in the classic preparation for eggs Benedict. But it is just as good as an accompanying brunch meat, like Smithfield ham, slab bacon, or sausage. At Bubby's, we have our Canadian bacon smoked by our local hog man. This Canadian bacon is far and away superior to the store-bought kind. It is smokier, juicier, and more interesting in texture. More like ham than regular bacon, Canadian bacon comes from the tender, lean eye of the pork loin. While more costly than regular bacon, it is also leaner and it shrinks less so you get more servings to the pound than with regular bacon. It is worth it to find a local smokehouse. There are several good places online to buy real Canadian bacon, such as Authentic Peameal Back Bacon from Canada, or Burgers' Smokehouse in California, Missouri (www.peamealbacon.com and www.smoke house.com).

To prepare Canadian bacon, slice or cut the cylindrical chunk anywhere from ⅛- to ¼-inch thick. Get a large skillet hot enough to sizzle a drop of water, put a little butter in the pan, and lay the Canadian bacon slices evenly in the skillet. Sizzle until crispy on one side, then turn and let the other side get nice and crispy. Serve hot.

IRISH BACON: Similar to Canadian bacon in that it is a cured pork loin, Irish bacon is generally not smoked and comes with a layer of fat around it, unlike Canadian bacon, which is usually quite lean. When cooking Irish bacon, fry it in a pan, but don't make it entirely crispy. Irish bacon is not so popular in America, and it can be difficult to find. One place to buy Irish bacon and other

Irish meat products is Tommy Moloney's (www.tommymoloneys.com).

THERE ARE A FEW OPTIONS FOR COOK-ing bacon. Something to consider is how crisp you like the bacon. Some people prefer it so crisp that others would consider it burned, while many like chewy bacon that still has a few ripples of visible fat on it. No matter which method you choose to cook bacon (and there are several), after cooking it, be sure to drain the slices on paper towels to maximize crispness. Here are the methods that I prefer for cooking bacon.

BAKED BACON: Preheat the oven to 375°F. Lay out the bacon slices in a single layer on a rimmed baking sheet. Bake for 8 to 10 minutes; then remove the pan from the oven and flip the bacon slices with tongs. When you flip the bacon, take a moment to pour off some of the grease, being very careful that it doesn't spill or splatter. This way you won't end up with a very full pan of bacon fat at the end. (If you like to cook with bacon fat, reserve the fat in a jar in the freezer.) Return the pan to the oven and continue to bake for another 3 to 4 minutes, or until the bacon is nice and crisp. Drain on paper towels before serving. Baking is a good method to use when preparing bacon for a crowd since you can cook a lot more at a time than with the panfrying method.

PANFRIED BACON: Place the bacon strips in a single layer in a large skillet. Cook the bacon over medium heat. Turn the slices over when they've nicely browned on one side, and continue frying until nice and crispy. Remove the bacon from the skillet to a paper towel–lined plate. All told, plan on anywhere from 8 to 15 minutes, depending on how much bacon you're cooking, how thick it is cut, and the size of the pan.

MAPLE-GLAZED BACON: Maple glazing works best with the baking method. About halfway through the cooking, when you flip the bacon slices, carefully drain off all the fat. Evenly drizzle the partially cooked bacon slices with good-quality maple syrup (about 1 teaspoon per slice) and return the pan to the oven. Continue baking for 5 to 7 minutes, until crispy and caramelized, keeping a close eye on it so as not to burn it.

Pork Belly Cured in Maple Syrup

SERVES 8 TO 10

Pork belly is not bacon because it is not cured. Pork belly is what bacon is made from. It is a delicious breakfast meat all by itself, especially when allowed to sit overnight with a little salt, pepper, and maple syrup before slowly cooking in a low oven. Most of the pork bellies in America are cured and smoked for bacon. However, raw bellies are rich, succulent, and very versatile. It may be difficult to find fresh pork belly at the supermarket, but the meat manager can probably special-order it. Otherwise, visit a reputable butcher and look for the leanest pork belly that you can find. (Even lean ones have generous amounts of fat.) It's most convenient to cook pork belly when it is trimmed into pieces smaller than a whole belly. A three-pound piece is manageable at home. Start this project a day ahead of when you want to serve the meat, since the pork belly needs to marinate overnight, and then cook for about three hours.

2 cups grade A maple syrup	¼ cup coarsely ground black pepper
⅓ cup kosher salt	3 pounds pork belly

1. Combine the maple syrup, salt, and pepper in a large bowl. Stir well to combine.

2. Place the pork belly in the syrup mixture and turn it so that all sides of the meat are coated. Wrap the bowl securely in plastic and refrigerate it for at least 8 hours or overnight.

3. The following day, transfer the marinated (cured) pork belly to a 4-quart casserole dish, allowing some of the marinade to drip off into the dish.

4. Preheat the oven to 200°F.

5. Pour 4 cups of water around the pork belly in the casserole dish. Tightly cover the dish with a lid or aluminum foil. Bake the pork belly for 2 to 3 hours, or until a meat thermometer registers 180°F when inserted into the center.

6. Remove the pork belly from the liquid, drain thoroughly, and set aside to cool. Discard the liquid.

7. When the pork belly has cooled, use a sharp slicing knife to cut it into ¼-inch-thick slices. Cut each slice in half. Arrange the slices in a skillet and cook over medium heat until they are sizzling. Serve the pork belly with your choice of eggs.

PORK BELLY HASH

SERVES 8 TO 10

With its golden crust and slightly sweet, subtly spiced flavor, this dish is especially good with eggs. Though much of the fat in pork belly is rendered during cooking, you'll still have enough to achieve a nice caramelized color in this flavorful hash. Make this a day ahead of time if you like—it's wonderful the second day. Serve pork belly hash with over easy, scrambled, or poached eggs (see pages 74 to 75).

3 pounds cooked Pork Belly Cured
   in Maple Syrup (page 178), cut
   into ¼-inch dice
2 large green bell peppers, cored,
   seeded, and cut into ¼-inch dice

2 large red bell peppers, cored,
   seeded, and cut into ¼-inch dice
½ recipe Home Fries (page 209)

1. Combine the pork belly, the green and red bell peppers, and the home fries in a bowl and mix well.

2. Sauté the pork belly–home fry mixture in a skillet over medium heat for 5 to 10 minutes, without stirring. When a nice brown crust has formed, flip the hash with a large spatula and allow the other side to get nice and crusty, about 5 more minutes.

HOMEMADE CORNED BEEF

Bubby's
SIGNATURE DISH

SERVES 12

Corning beef is a lengthy process, but it is very rewarding. It requires brining a brisket for a week and then, for corned beef, boiling the brined brisket for a couple hours. For brining, always use a nonreactive (ceramic, enamel, stainless steel, or glass) airtight container. It needs to be large enough to hold a brisket submerged in liquid brine. You will also need two ovenproof "turkey bags" or oven bags. Most supermarkets or box-type stores such as Walmart and Costco carry these. The bags will keep the fridge smells out of your beef as it cures/brines. Always note the date when you start to brine the meat so you'll know when it's ready.

Keep in mind that this is a big piece of meat. Corned beef is meant to be used for leftovers. If you are going to corn a brisket, serve it for dinner and make hash with the leftovers. You could also make a corned beef and cabbage dinner. If you make Homemade Pastrami (page 182), make sandwiches with the fresh stuff, and serve pastrami and eggs with the leftovers. These meats will keep for up to a week in the refrigerator.

For the pickling spices
1 teaspoon black peppercorns
1 teaspoon yellow mustard seeds
1 teaspoon coriander seeds
1 teaspoon crushed red pepper
   flakes
1 teaspoon allspice berries
½ teaspoon ground mace
1 small cinnamon stick, crushed or
   broken into pieces
2 bay leaves, crumbled
1 teaspoon whole cloves
1 teaspoon ground ginger

For the brine
1 cup kosher salt
12 garlic cloves, crushed
3 tablespoons pickling spices
   (above)
8 whole bay leaves
2 tablespoons juniper berries

For the corned beef
One 4-pound grass-fed brisket
¼ cup pickling spices (above)

1. Make the pickling spices: Combine the peppercorns, mustard seeds, coriander seeds, red pepper flakes, allspice berries, mace, cinnamon, bay leaves, cloves, and ginger in a medium bowl. Measure out 3 tablespoons for the brine and ¼ cup for the cooking, and set the rest aside. (The pickling spices will keep in a sealed container at room temperature for up to 6 months.)

2. Bring 4 quarts of water to a boil. Remove the pot from the heat and stir in the salt. When the salt is completely dissolved, set the pot aside to cool to room temperature.

3. When cooled, stir in the garlic, pickling spices, bay leaves, and juniper berries; set aside.

4. Prepare the corned beef: Trim the brisket so there is only about ¼-inch of fat. Remove the deckle, which is the small separate piece that is separated from the main piece by a layer of fat. (The deckle is much fattier than the rest of the brisket. If you are buying meat from a good butcher, ask him to remove the deckle and grind it for a burger.)

5. Place the trimmed brisket in a doubled turkey bag or oven bag. Place the bagged brisket in a casserole dish large enough to hold the meat and the brine. Pour the brine into the bag and seal very well by twisting the inner bag tightly, folding it over, and then twisting the outer bag and tying it tightly.

6. Marinate the meat in the refrigerator for 1 week.

7. To cook the corned beef, remove it from the brine and place it in a pot just large enough to hold it. Discard the brining liquid. Add enough water to the pot to cover the meat. Add ¼ cup of pickling spices and bring to a boil over medium heat.

8. Reduce the heat to low, cover the pot, and simmer the corned beef gently for 2½ hours, or until fork-tender. Check the water level in the pot occasionally. There should always be enough water to cover the meat, so replenish the water as needed.

9. Remove the corned beef from the cooking liquid. Allow the hot corned beef to cool at room temperature for about 30 minutes before slicing, or wrap the fully cooled corned beef in plastic wrap and refrigerate until ready to use.

HOMEMADE PASTRAMI

*Y*ou'll need a slow-cooking barbecue smoker to make this pastrami. Use apple wood, cherry wood, or another subtle wood to bring out the flavor in the meat. Homemade pastrami keeps for five to six days as opposed to commercial pastrami, which uses preservatives to extend its shelf life. Extra rub will keep for four to five days in the refrigerator. Besides pastrami sandwiches, you can make pastrami and eggs, or pastrami hash, in which case you just substitute pastrami for the corned beef (see page 183). Be sure to start this well in advance since the meat must marinate overnight.

For the rub	For the pastrami
5 tablespoons kosher salt	One 4- to 6-pound brined brisket
¼ cup paprika	(see Homemade Corned Beef,
3 tablespoons coriander seeds	page 180)
3 tablespoons black peppercorns	
2 tablespoons yellow mustard seeds	
1 tablespoon juniper berries	
3 tablespoons packed dark brown sugar	
8 garlic cloves, minced	

1. Make the rub: Using a spice grinder, grind the salt, paprika, coriander seeds, peppercorns, mustard seeds, and juniper berries. Pour into a small bowl, and add the brown sugar and garlic; set aside.

2. Make the pastrami: Remove the brisket from the brine. Rinse it well under cold running water for 1 minute. Place it in a large stainless steel bowl filled with cold water and soak it for 30 minutes, changing the water every 10 minutes. Remove the meat from the water and pat it dry with paper towels.

3. Using 2 tablespoons of rub per pound of meat, rub the brisket very well. Wrap the brisket in plastic wrap, refrigerate, and allow it to marinate for at least 8 hours or overnight.

4. In a slow-cooking barbecue smoker (you need to keep the temperature controlled the entire time), start a fire using your choice of fuels—charcoal, wood, or a combination of the two. Bring the smoker temperature up to 275°F. Before putting the pastrami in, add fresh wood so there is plenty of smoke. Immediately add the pastrami. Let the temperature fall to 250°F, but keep adding fuel as needed to maintain 250°F. Smoke the pastrami until the internal temperature reaches 180°F, approximately 1 hour per pound.

5. Remove the pastrami from the smoker. Let it sit for 10 minutes before slicing.

CORNED BEEF HASH

The rib-sticking, classic hash recipe, updated with fresh parsley and chopped red bell pepper, doesn't need much more than a couple of eggs (your choice of style) on top to round out a brunch. It's an ideal way to use up leftover mashed potatoes, but if you don't have any on hand, you can simply dice, boil, and mash an extra potato or two. The recipe calls for both cooked diced potatoes and mashed potatoes.

2 potatoes, peeled and cut into ½-inch dice

8 tablespoons (1 stick) unsalted butter

2 onions, finely diced

2 garlic cloves, minced

1 red bell pepper, cored, seeded, and finely diced

1 cup cooked mashed potatoes

4 cups diced Homemade Corned Beef (page 180), or use an equivalent amount of store-bought corned beef

½ cup finely chopped fresh parsley

2 tablespoons prepared horseradish

1 tablespoon Worcestershire sauce

½ teaspoon freshly ground black pepper

1. Bring a saucepan of lightly salted water to a boil. Add the diced potatoes and cook for 10 minutes, or until soft.

2. Melt the butter in a large skillet over medium heat. Add the onions, garlic, and bell pepper and sauté for 5 minutes or until soft.

3. Reduce the heat to low, stir in the mashed potatoes, and cook the mixture for a minute or two, or until warmed through.

4. Stir in the diced potatoes, corned beef, parsley, horseradish, Worcestershire sauce, and pepper. Cook the hash over low heat until it is steaming hot, stirring occasionally.

5. To prepare an individual serving, sauté 1 cup hash in a little butter in a nonstick pan until crispy. To serve a group, flip the steaming hot hash over with a metal spatula once a nice brown crust has formed on the bottom. Allow the other side to get nice and crusty, about 5 more minutes. Use a spatula to cut the hash into portions and transfer to individual plates. Serve hot.

SWEET ITALIAN SAUSAGES

MAKES SIXTEEN 2-OUNCE PATTIES

With the fresh, zesty taste of basil and garlic, these juicy sausages are a perfect homemade accompaniment to a variety of egg dishes. Ask the butcher to grind up the pork butt, and make sure the pork is well chilled (32°F) before starting on this recipe. The meat and fat need to stay very cold during the grinding and mixing process. Otherwise, the sausage comes out mealy because the fat doesn't maintain its form and melts into the meat.

1½ pounds well chilled coarsely ground pork butt

⅓ pound well chilled coarsely ground fatback

¼ cup dry white wine

2 garlic cloves, crushed

6 fresh basil leaves, minced, or ¼ teaspoon dried basil

¼ teaspoon fresh oregano, minced, or ⅛ teaspoon dried oregano

¼ teaspoon fresh rosemary, minced, or ⅛ teaspoon dried rosemary

3 teaspoons fennel seeds

2 teaspoons kosher salt

1 teaspoon freshly ground black pepper

1. Combine the pork butt, fatback, and white wine in a large bowl and mix well. Make sure to keep the mixture cold. If it is a warm day, you can place the mixing bowl over a second mixing bowl of ice water.

2. Add the garlic, basil, oregano, rosemary, fennel seeds, salt, and pepper to the pork mixture. Using your hands, mix very well. Form the mixture into sixteen 2-ounce patties, each one about the size of a very small hamburger patty.

3. Heat a large skillet over medium heat until a drop of water sizzles on it. Arrange the sausages in a single layer in the skillet. Fry the sausages, turning them once, until golden brown and crusty on the outside and the interior loses its pink color, about 4 minutes total.

SPICY ITALIAN SAUSAGE VARIATION: Reduce the amount of fennel to ½ tablespoon and add ½ to 1 tablespoon crushed red pepper flakes.

VENISON SAUSAGES

Bubby's
SIGNATURE DISH

MAKES TWENTY-FOUR 2-OUNCE PATTIES

These robust, aromatic sausages pair well with many egg dishes. For best results, most of these ingredients should be chilled before you start. The fat needs to stay separate during the mixing process or the sausages will be mealy. Properly handled ingredients, especially the fat and meat, are the key to good sausages. Both the meat and the fatback should be brought down to 32°F, so place them into the freezer for about an hour. Fatback, which is the fresh unsmoked layer of fat that runs along the pig's back, is sold at butcher shops. Don't confuse it with salt pork: They're not the same thing. The easiest way to get ground juniper berries is to grind them in a spice grinder.

If you don't cook all the sausages in one meal, the patties freeze well for several weeks as long as they are well wrapped. The best thing is to wrap the patties individually in plastic wrap, wrap six to eight of the plastic-wrapped sausages in aluminum foil, then put the foil packages in a resealable plastic freezer bag and mark the bag with the date they were frozen.

1 pound ground venison shoulder or flank, well chilled	½ teaspoon garlic powder
	1½ teaspoons onion powder
8 ounces ground pork shoulder, well chilled	1½ tablespoons grated fresh ginger
8 ounces ground fatback, well chilled	¼ teaspoon freshly ground juniper berries
1½ tablespoons kosher salt	1 teaspoon dry mustard
3 teaspoons freshly ground black pepper	6 extra-large egg whites (about ½ cup)
	1 teaspoon arrowroot

1. Combine the venison, pork shoulder, and fatback in a very large bowl.

2. Add the salt, pepper, garlic powder, onion powder, ginger, juniper berries, dry mustard, egg whites, and arrowroot. Using your hands, mix together very well.

3. Mix in 1 cup ice water a little bit at a time, until the sausage is firm enough to form into patties but not too dry. Form the mixture into 24 patties, each about the size of a tiny hamburger patty.

4. Heat a large skillet over medium heat until a drop of water sizzles on it. Arrange the sausages in a single layer in the skillet. Fry the sausages, turning them once, until golden brown and crusty on the outside and the interior loses its pink color, about 4 minutes total.

BISCUITS WITH SAUSAGE GRAVY

SERVES 6 TO 8

*B*échamel, a basic French white sauce made with butter and cream or milk, is combined with a generous amount of homemade sausage, then poured over warm, flaky biscuits. It's as addictive as it is undeniably rich. For extra decadence, put poached eggs (see page 75) on top of the biscuits. Make the biscuits ahead of time and freeze them for up to two months. Rewarm in a preheated 350°F oven for 10 to 15 minutes.

About 12 ounces sausage, casings
    removed
1½ cups Béchamel Sauce (page 288)
¼ cup chopped fresh parsley
Kosher salt and freshly ground
    black pepper to taste

6 to 8 Bubby's Variation on
    Mr. Beard's Cream Biscuits
    (page 54), cut in half

1. Sauté the sausage in a large skillet over medium heat, breaking up the sausage with a fork as it cooks, until it has lost its pink color and is thoroughly cooked, about 5 minutes. Drain off any fat. Cool slightly.

2. Warm the Béchamel in a heavy saucepan over medium heat. Stir in the sausage and parsley. Taste, and season with salt and black pepper if needed.

3. Place both halves of the biscuits on plates. Ladle some sausage gravy over each biscuit and serve immediately.

GLAZED SMOKED HAM

SERVES 12 TO 16

*T*his hard-to-resist ham makes a great centerpiece at a brunch. Moist and succulent within, it has a delicious crusted exterior that is both sweet and spicy. Leftovers are delicious in sandwiches as well as in many egg dishes.

For the ham
One 12-pound bone-in cured
  ham

For the rub
2 cups packed dark brown sugar
¼ cup kosher salt
1 tablespoon ground cinnamon
¼ cup dry mustard
2 tablespoons freshly ground black
  pepper
½ teaspoon ground cloves
1 cup Dijon mustard for coating the
  ham

1. Preheat the oven to 325°F.

2. Score the ham about ½-inch deep with a sharp knife, making diamond patterns along the surface.

3. Make the rub: Combine the brown sugar, salt, cinnamon, dry mustard, pepper, and cloves in a bowl.

4. Rub the ham all over with the Dijon mustard, making sure to get into the scored cuts. Generously coat the ham with the rub, making sure some gets into the scored cuts and using up all the rub.

5. Pour 3 cups of water into the bottom of a roasting pan that is large enough to hold the whole ham. Place the ham in the center of the roasting pan. Cover the ham with aluminum foil.

6. Roast the ham for about 2½ hours, basting it every 20 minutes with the caramelizing glaze, until it is nice and brown. As the scored cuts open, be sure to baste often, brushing with the glaze. Add more water if needed to prevent the glaze from burning.

7. Remove the ham from the oven and allow it to cool for 15 minutes before slicing.

MAPLE-GLAZED SMOKED HAM VARIATION: Pour 1 tablespoon maple syrup over a 3-ounce portion of ham steak. Bake in a preheated 425°F oven for 7 minutes. This will yield one serving.

SMITHFIELD HAM

SERVES 20

*S*mithfield ham is the American answer to prosciutto. To be called a Smithfield ham, the ham must be cured and processed in Smithfield, Virginia. It is aged for twenty-four months and offers a unique taste. (You can buy Smithfield ham online at www.smithfieldhams.com. Order the uncooked bone-in version.)

It requires some serious effort to prepare a proper Smithfield ham, but it is very worth it. The instructions are odd, even counterintuitive, but this is the way it is done! Smithfield ham is easiest to prepare when it's cold enough to leave the ham outside. That means it has to be below 40°F all day and night. Otherwise, you have to refrigerate the ham while soaking it, and unless you have a walk-in refrigerator, it is nearly impossible.

When you are ready to prepare the ham, remove it from the bag. Place it in a sink or a very large pot of water and scrub it with steel wool to remove the outside mold and grime. Don't let the mold (a result of aging) worry you. Once it is scrubbed, place the ham in a pot large enough that it can be covered with plenty of water. The ham needs to soak for three days and the water changed every twelve hours, at least. Now you're ready to cook the ham. The best way to serve Smithfield ham is with eggs and fresh biscuits.

For the ham
One 12-pound Smithfield ham, scrubbed and soaked (see headnote)

For the rub
2 cups packed dark brown sugar
¼ cup kosher salt
1 tablespoon ground cinnamon
¼ cup dry mustard
2 tablespoons freshly ground black pepper
½ teaspoon ground cloves
1 cup Dijon mustard for coating the ham

1. Score the ham about ½-inch deep with a sharp knife, making diamond patterns along the surface; set aside.

2. Make the rub: Combine the brown sugar, salt, cinnamon, dry mustard, pepper, and cloves in a bowl.

3. Rub the ham all over with the Dijon mustard, making sure to get into the scored cuts. Generously coat the ham with the rub, making sure some gets into the scored cuts and using up all the rub.

4. Line a roasting pan with heavy-duty aluminum foil, leaving plenty of extra foil to seal up the ham with a second top layer of foil. Put the ham on the bottom layer of foil. Now put a layer of foil on top of the ham. Begin sealing the top to the bottom by crimping the two layers of foil together. Before you finally close up the seal, pour in 5 cups of water. Seal completely. Place the ham into a cold oven.

5. Heat the oven to 500°F. Once the oven temperature reaches 500°F, bake the ham for 15 minutes. Turn off the oven and leave the ham inside for 3 hours. *Do not open the oven door or you will let out the heat.*

Turn on the oven again and heat to 500°F. When the oven reaches 500°F, bake the ham for 10 minutes. Turn off the oven and let the ham remain in the oven for 8 hours or overnight. Again, *do not open the oven door or you will let out the heat.* Remove the ham from the oven.

6. Slice the ham very thin, like prosciutto, using a very sharp knife and cutting against the grain.

SMITHFIELD HAM WITH RED-EYE GRAVY VARIATION: Melt 1 tablespoon unsalted butter in a small pan over medium heat. Stir in 2 ounces thinly sliced ham, and cook for several minutes, or until crisp. Transfer the ham to a plate. Stir ½ cup brewed strong coffee into the pan and cook, uncovered, for 10 minutes, or until the gravy is reduced by half. Return the ham to the gravy and simmer until very hot. Season with freshly ground black pepper. This will yield one serving.

ROASTED NEW YORK STRIP STEAK

A thick steak is essential in order to get nice rare slices for your buffet brunch. Be sure to let the steak rest for at least 15 minutes before slicing. This allows the juices to disburse throughout the meat and not go running all over the cutting board.

One 2- to 2½-pound New York strip steak (2 inches thick)	Kosher salt and coarsely ground black pepper to taste 1 tablespoon vegetable oil

1. Preheat the oven to 475°F.

2. Season the steak on both sides with salt and pepper.

3. Heat a 10-inch ovenproof skillet to the smoking point (very hot) over medium-high heat. Add the oil and the steak. Sear the steak on both sides for 3 to 4 minutes per side. The surface of the steak will be a dark brown color. Sear the edges for 1 to 2 minutes, or until they are brown.

4. Place the skillet in the oven for about 5 minutes, or until the steak reaches the desired doneness. To check for doneness, use an instant-read thermometer. The internal temperature should be 135°F for rare and 145°F for medium-rare.

5. Allow the steak to rest for 15 minutes. To slice the steak, place it on a cutting board and cut it on a slight bias, leaving the slices still touching so that the meat stays juicier as you cut. Fan out the slices in an attractive pattern on a platter or the cutting board. Serve immediately.

SMOKED SALMON

*S*moking a whole side of salmon may seem like a lot of effort, but it is worth it, especially if you are having more than eight people for brunch. Not only is the salmon better tasting than many commercial products available, it is also about 80 percent less expensive.

Smoked salmon is cold smoked. In other words, it is not smoked in a hot smoker; the smoke does not cook the fish. The fish is cooked through the brining process. Cold smoke imparts a subtle smoky flavor. With practice, you can develop your own levels of curing and smoke. This is an ancient way of preserving food, and there are myriad subtleties to achieve.

Smoked salmon keeps in the refrigerator for up to two weeks. The process of curing and smoking salmon takes a couple of days. You need a refrigerator with enough room to let the salmon sit inside, unobstructed. The process involves curing, rinsing, crusting, smoking, and saturating in oil. Bubby's uses a combination of maple syrup, sugar, and kosher salt to cure salmon. Besides these ingredients, you'll also need a vented tin can, a piece of charcoal, apple wood chips, a barbecue grill large enough to hold a whole salmon fillet, and 4 quarts of canola oil.

4 cups kosher salt

2 cups sugar

2 cups maple syrup

One 4½- to 6-pound whole side of salmon fillet (big bones and feather bones removed, skin intact)

4 quarts canola oil

1. Line a rimmed baking sheet with plastic wrap.

2. Stir together the salt, sugar, and maple syrup in a medium bowl. Measure and pour about 1 cup of this mixture, called the cure, onto the prepared baking sheet.

3. Arrange the salmon skin side down on top of the cure. Pour the remainder of the cure over the flesh of the salmon, wrap the salmon in plastic wrap, and refrigerate it for 8 to 12 hours. How long it sits depends on how salty you prefer your salmon. If you like it very, very salty, you could leave it in the cure, refrigerated, for 24 to 36 hours. Your taste for this will develop with experience.

4. Remove the salmon after curing and gently place it in a bowl big enough to hold the fish and fit in your sink. It doesn't have to lie flat, but be gentle with it so as not to break the fillet. Fill the bowl with cold water and set it aside for 10 minutes. Change the water and set it aside for an additional 10 minutes. Remove salmon from the bowl and pat dry with a clean kitchen towel.

5. Place the salmon on a large platter in the refrigerator. If possible, make sure the salmon is right in front of the refrigerator fan. This will help the cure to form a crust on the salmon. Allow the salmon to sit in the refrigerator for 12 to 24 hours, depending upon how salty you like your smoked salmon to be. At Bubby's, we cure for 24 hours.

6. The next step is cold smoking. With two hands, gently place the salmon on the grill rack of your slow-cooking barbecue smoker. Make a smoking can from a 16- to 30-ounce can. Carefully punch three 1-inch holes into the sides near the bottom of the can. You can use a hammer and some nails to do this. The holes will facilitate the smoking process by bringing oxygen to the hot charcoal. Then, hold one piece of charcoal in a pair of tongs and place it over a flaming burner until it is white-hot. With the white-hot charcoal in the tongs, carefully place the charcoal into the vented can.

7. Place the smoking can open side up below and off to one side of the salmon. Do not place it directly under the salmon or the salmon will begin to cook from the heat given off when you add the wood chips. Carefully place ¼ cup apple wood chips in the can on top of the charcoal so it begins to smoke.

8. Close the barbecue grill and let the salmon sit in the "cold smoke" for 45 to 90 minutes, depending on how you like your smoked salmon to taste, without opening the smoker.

9. Remove the salmon from the grill and place it in a deep pan. Slowly pour the canola oil over the salmon until the salmon is completely covered. Allow the salmon to sit, refrigerated, in the oil overnight (10 to 12 hours). This oil replaces the moisture that was lost during the curing process, giving the salmon the oily texture associated with smoked salmon.

10. Remove the salmon from the oil. Brush off any excess oil. Wrap the salmon very well in plastic wrap, and keep it refrigerated until you are ready to slice it.

11. To slice the salmon: Chill the salmon in the freezer for 1 hour before slicing. Then, lay it flat on a cutting board and, holding a sharp, thin-bladed slicing knife nearly parallel to the surface, begin cutting off slices as thin as you can. Place the slices on a plate as you go, carefully laying them out so they can be easily peeled up. Or place a layer of wax paper or parchment between the slices, as you prefer. As you cut, make the slices as paper thin as possible and with as much surface as possible, angling slightly down toward the skin. Practice makes perfect.

SMOKED SALMON AND GOAT CHEESE ROSES

MAKES 12 ROSES

A beautiful and elegant starter to have on the table when guests arrive, these are easy to prepare. Toothpicks are optional; you can also just seal the rolls with a firm hand. Make these up to six hours in advance, if you like, and store them, tightly covered, in the refrigerator. These are meant to be eaten in one bite from your hand.

4 ounces Smoked Salmon (page 191), sliced as thinly as possible with as much surface area as possible

6 ounces chèvre-style goat cheese, at room temperature
1 bunch fresh chives, very thinly sliced

1. Lay the smoked salmon slices out, one at a time, on a cutting board. Cut each slice into 1½ x 3-inch strips.

2. Spread 1 teaspoon of goat cheese down the center of each strip. Holding the strip at one end, roll it up on the diagonal, so you wind up with a cone shape. Use your fingers to coax the edges of the large end of the cone in an outward direction. The idea is for it to look like a rose.

3. Stick a toothpick crosswise through the base end of each "rose" if you feel you want to hold it together, or just present the roses without the toothpicks, making sure they are securely sealed so your guests can pick them up.

4. Arrange the roses on a platter. Before serving, sprinkle the sliced chives in the center for a nice splash of green color.

SMOKED TROUT

*T*he taste of homemade smoked trout is incomparable, making this recipe well worth the effort. Trout, like all fish, must be brined before smoking, so plan on several hours' worth of brining time before you actually do the smoking. Unlike salmon, trout is hot smoked. Obviously, you'll need a smoker for this recipe. The choice of wood is up to you: At Bubby's, we strictly use apple wood.

Once you've got smoked trout on hand, you may serve it as is or make it into some delicious Smoked Trout Cakes (page 195), a Smoked Trout Scramble (page 101), or Smoked Trout and Scallion Mousse (page 196). Figure that you need to start this recipe about five hours in advance. The salmon is best when smoked the day before you plan to serve it, so that the flavors can blend. To serve, cut the smoked trout into fairly large 2-inch chunks and arrange them as part of a smoked fish platter, along with Smoked Salmon (page 191) and herring (page 196).

2 tablespoons kosher salt	½ cup maple syrup
2 teaspoons coarsely ground black pepper	6 whole trout, filleted (3 pounds)

1. Combine 2 cups of water, the salt, pepper, and maple syrup in a 3- or 4-quart bowl. Place the trout in this brining mixture, cover, and refrigerate for about 4 hours.

2. Place a wire rack on a baking sheet.

3. Drain the trout and discard the brining liquid. Arrange the trout skin side down on the wire rack. Refrigerate until you are ready to start the smoking process, up to 6 hours.

4. Heat the smoker to 225°F, using charcoal, apple or cherry wood, or a combination of charcoal and wood. Lightly oil the grate of the smoker so the trout won't stick.

5. Arrange the trout skin side down directly on the grate. Be sure to leave a good inch of space between the trout so that more of the surface area will be exposed to the smoke. Make sure that the heat source is not directly under the fish.

6. Place the grate in the smoker; then add more wood to the smoker to ensure that there's plenty of smoke to flavor the fish. It is important to maintain a temperature of 225°F, so add charcoal, 1 piece at a time, or wood as needed to keep the heat.

7. Smoke the trout for 30 to 40 minutes, or until firm and a little flaky. Remove the trout from the smoker and allow it to cool to room temperature. Wrap the trout tightly in plastic wrap and refrigerate it until you're ready to use it. Peel the skin from the fillets before serving.

SMOKED TROUT CAKES

A smoky and appealing cousin of the crab cake, these are excellent served on their own, perhaps as part of a salad, or alongside one of Bubby's egg dishes.

2 large baking potatoes, peeled and
   cut into large chunks
½ onion, grated
1 pound Smoked Trout (page 194)
2 tablespoons chopped fresh parsley

1 cup all-purpose flour
½ cup mayonnaise, homemade
   (page 284) or store-bought
2 tablespoons canola or vegetable
   oil for frying the cakes

1. Bring a large saucepan of lightly salted water to a boil over medium heat. Cook the potatoes for 15 minutes, or until they are fairly soft but still firm enough to retain their shape. Drain and set aside to cool. Dice the potatoes and place them into a mixing bowl.

2. Add the onion to the potatoes in the mixing bowl. Break the trout into small chunks by hand and add it to the mixture. Add the parsley, flour, and mayonnaise and blend well.

3. Using your hands, form the mixture into 4 ovals and flatten them slightly.

4. Heat the vegetable oil in a large skillet over medium heat for 1 minute. Fry the trout cakes for 2 to 3 minutes, or until they are golden brown on one side; then flip and cook on the other side for 2 to 3 minutes, until golden brown and crisp. Serve immediately.

SMOKED TROUT AND SCALLION MOUSSE

Make this ahead of time so it has time to chill, and store it, well wrapped, in the refrigerator. It's great for sandwiches or spreading on crackers. It goes well on a brunch table with other fish options, such as pickled herring. If you're making tea sandwiches, top with Horseradish Cream (page 157).

4 smoked trout fillets (about 1 pound)	1 teaspoon fresh lemon juice
4 ounces cream cheese, at room temperature	½ cup chopped scallion (green parts only)
¼ cup finely diced red onion	2 tablespoons chopped fresh parsley
2 tablespoons Worcestershire sauce	Kosher salt and freshly ground black pepper to taste

1. In the work bowl of a food processor fitted with a metal blade, combine the trout fillets, cream cheese, red onion, Worcestershire sauce, and lemon juice. Process for about 1 minute to incorporate all the ingredients. Process for another minute, or until smooth.

2. Fold in the scallion, parsley, salt, and pepper.

3. Place the mousse in a ramekin, cover with plastic wrap and chill for at least an hour or for up to a week ahead of time.

4. Spoon the mousse into a 2-cup dish and serve it with your choice of crackers or with rye bread. For a more decorative presentation, spoon the mousse into a bowl, packing it in tightly, and then unmold it onto a plate. Or make tea sandwiches by spooning a layer of mousse onto thin slices of bread and topping it with horseradish or horseradish cream. Cut each slice of bread into quarters.

A WORD ABOUT PICKLED HERRING

The practice of pickling herring has been around for centuries. Herring in wine is the typical Jewish preparation. The boneless fillets are first cured in salt to remove the moisture. Then they are rinsed and cured again in a combination of vinegar, wine, sugar, salt, and onions. They keep for months. Herring in cream sauce is basically herring in wine with sour cream added at the end. Other preparations, such as herring in mustard, curry, or dill, are all variations on herring in cream sauce. Matjes herring is a more Scandinavian approach. The herrings are cured in salt, rinsed, then cured again in vinegar, sugar, salt, and spices such as cloves, cinnamon, and a little nutmeg.

CORNMEAL-CRUSTED FRIED OYSTERS

SERVES 4 TO 6

*F*ried oysters are essential in a Hangtown Fry, which also includes eggs and fried bacon. The dish is thought to have been created during the California gold rush in a camp called Hangtown, near Sutter's Mill in the Coloma Valley. The town acquired its gruesome name because of frequent hangings, often carried out by vigilantes. For this recipe, you can either shuck the oysters yourself or buy fresh shucked oysters from your fishmonger.

For the coating
1½ cups cornmeal
1½ tablespoons kosher salt
1½ teaspoons freshly ground black
    pepper
¾ teaspoon garlic powder
1½ teaspoons paprika

For the oysters
4 cups canola oil
24 shucked oysters

1. Stir together the cornmeal, salt, pepper, garlic powder, and paprika in a bowl; set aside.

2. Pour the canola oil into a 10-inch skillet to the depth of 1 inch. Place the skillet over medium-high heat and heat the oil until it reaches 350°F on a food thermometer.

3. Meanwhile, toss the oysters in the seasoned cornmeal until well coated. Using a slotted spoon or a set of tongs, gently place the coated oysters into the hot oil, making sure they are completely submerged.

4. Fry the oysters, turning occasionally so they cook evenly, for 1 to 2 minutes, or until lightly golden.

5. Using a slotted spoon, remove the oysters to a paper towel–lined plate to drain. Blot the oysters with additional paper towels to remove any excess oil. Serve immediately.

CRISPY CRAB CAKES

A luxurious treat, sweet, crisp crab cakes can be made with lump or backfin crabmeat. Frying the crab cakes just before you plan to serve them will ensure that they don't get soggy upon standing. Serve crab cakes with scrambled eggs, inside a crusty baguette, or with lemon wedges and Rémoulade Sauce (page 284).

1 pound fresh jumbo lump
   crabmeat, picked clean of all
   shells and cartilage
2 extra-large eggs, lightly beaten
¼ cup mayonnaise, homemade
   (page 284) or store-bought
1 teaspoon Old Bay Seasoning

½ teaspoon freshly ground black
   pepper
2 teaspoons Worcestershire sauce
1 teaspoon dry mustard
½ cup dry bread crumbs or Saltine
   cracker crumbs
Canola oil for frying

1. Using a rubber spatula, combine the crabmeat, eggs, mayonnaise, Old Bay, pepper, Worcestershire sauce, and dry mustard in a large bowl. Gradually add the bread crumbs. The mixture should just bind together but not be too bready. You may not need to use all the crumbs. Refrigerate the mixture for 30 minutes.

2. Using your hands, shape the mixture into eight 3-ounce or sixteen 1½-ounce cakes (depending on your desire for larger or smaller crab cakes) and flatten them slightly.

3. Pour the canola oil into a 10-inch skillet so that it reaches a depth of about ½ inch. Place the skillet over medium heat until it gets nice and hot. Gently place the crab cakes in the hot oil and cook for 4 to 5 minutes, until golden brown on the bottom. Turn and cook for another 3 to 4 minutes. Using a slotted spoon, remove the crab cakes to a paper towel–lined plate to drain. Serve immediately.

CRAB SALAD

*T*his is an elegant salad in which an abundance of colorful, crunchy vegetables really picks up the flavor of the crab. Spiked with lemon juice and lightly bound with mayonnaise, it can be an entrée served over fresh greens or a great sandwich filling.

1 pound fresh crabmeat, picked
    clean of all shells and cartilage
3 tablespoons finely chopped red
    onion
1 tablespoon finely diced red bell
    pepper
2 tablespoons shredded carrot
1 tablespoon finely chopped celery

½ teaspoon finely chopped fresh
    tarragon
¼ cup finely chopped fresh parsley
½ teaspoon fresh lemon juice
½ cup mayonnaise, homemade
    (page 284) or store-bought
Kosher salt and freshly ground
    black pepper to taste

1. Place the crabmeat in a large bowl. Stir in the red onion, bell pepper, carrot, celery, tarragon, and parsley. Toss gently.

2. Stir together the lemon juice and mayonnaise in a small bowl.

3. Spoon the mayonnaise mixture onto the crab salad and toss lightly to mix. Season with salt and pepper. (If you're not serving the salad right away, cover and refrigerate it for up to 6 hours.)

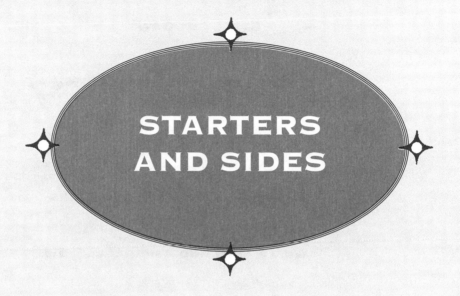

STARTERS AND SIDES

B runch doesn't follow rules about a certain order of courses the way other meals might, though some dishes naturally lend themselves to being openers. Some fall quite smoothly into the role of side dishes, though at brunch, many sides and starters are interchangeable. Sometimes they might even constitute a meal, especially when you combine several of them.

Bubby's Granola (page 206), for instance, a signature dish that is full of nuts, rolled oats, and raisins, is crunchy and wholesome and crisp—practically a meal on its own. Served with some good yogurt or one of the fruit compotes in this book (pages 276–278), or perhaps a lovely fresh fruit salad, granola becomes a seriously substantial brunch.

Granola is typically eaten cold, but Bubby's serves potsful of nourishing, steaming hot cereals for brunch as well. To understand just how satisfying oatmeal or grits can be is to cast aside any childhood memories you may have of gluey, lumpy porridge. At Bubby's, the highest-quality whole grains are cooked with care, seasoned with fresh spices and dried fruits, and sweetened with honey or fruit.

Cereals can be made out of any whole grain, but my favorites are oats and corn. Of all the grains, oats are one of the highest in protein and are extremely filling. Most of the oats we eat are rolled oats, which means that they have been rolled into flakes. Traditional rolled oats have thicker flakes than the quick oats, and Bubby's granola is made with rolled oats. For making cereal, though, I prefer steel-cut oats since they are chewier and have a much better flavor. Steel-cut oats are produced by putting oats through a machine that turns the whole kernels into tiny bits. They simply taste better, and a bowl of Steel-Cut Oats (page 208) with brown sugar or some fresh fruit is incomparable.

When dried corn is treated to remove the hull and the germ, it becomes hominy. And when hominy is ground into meal, the result is hominy grits. Few hot breakfast dishes are as soothing as our Stone-Ground Hominy Grits (page 207). It is traditional to serve grits with butter and salt (not sweetened with brown sugar or syrup, as one might do with cream of wheat). At Bubby's, they're also seasoned with Tabasco for a little extra kick. The crowning glory, if you desire it, is the addition of cheese.

Also in this chapter you will find Bubby's signature potato dishes. Nothing goes better with eggs and bacon than a side of home fries or hash browns, and in addition to the basic recipe, there's a favorite variation of mine, a recipe for Smothered Hash Browns (page 211), in which the potatoes are blanketed with caramelized onions and cheese.

BOTH HOME FRIES AND HASH BROWNS ARE CLASSIC DINER FAVORITES THAT PAIR WELL WITH JUST ABOUT ANY BRUNCH ENTRÉE.

Choosing potatoes for your brunch can be a little tricky since there are so many varieties, but once you understand that potatoes fall into two basic groups, you'll soon be a seasoned potato-picking expert. Boiling potatoes—low in starch and high in moisture—are best in dishes where you need them to hold their shape. Baking potatoes—high in starch, low in moisture—have a dry and fluffy flesh when cooked. Of the baking potato varieties, russets or Idahos make great mashed potatoes and are also ideal for home fries and hash browns. For Potato Pancakes (page 213), also called latkes, you will want to use good starchy Idaho baking potatoes. All-purpose potatoes have a moderate starch and moisture content and are, as the name says, a good all-around workhorse, perfect for, say, potato salad.

When choosing potatoes, avoid any that show signs of sprouting. Don't store them in plastic, and don't put them in the refrigerator. And think little: the smaller potatoes often have better texture and flavor.

Potatoes can be cleverly turned into many different kinds of dishes because they easily assume so many shapes (sliced, diced, grated) and are enhanced by such a variety of flavorings (butter, cream, cheese, and, well, more butter) that the possibilities are nearly endless—as you'll see from the selection of recipes here.

The potato is not the only front-and-center vegetable at brunch. Bubby's tosses beet greens, Brussels sprouts, and broccoli rabe with everything from bacon to mint to sesame seeds for a variety of intriguing sides (or starters, as you see fit). Also included here are some deliciously random dishes, including old-fashioned comfort food such as Creamy Buttermilk New Potato Salad (page 223) and Savory-Sweet Roasted Acorn Squash Pudding (page 224). Because in the end, comfort food is what brunch is all about.

BUBBY'S GRANOLA

SERVES 15 TO 18

This homemade cereal is hearty, wholesome, and filled with nutritious ingredients such as walnuts, rolled oats, raisins, and sunflower seeds. Granola is very flexible, so you can add whatever fruits and nuts are your personal favorites. This granola is great with milk or yogurt, or even as a topping on pancakes. Because raisins can make the granola soggy, we add them right before serving. The granola keeps well for a long time, so this is a big batch—it makes three pounds. Just keep it in an airtight container and eat it for breakfast all week, as we do at Bubby's, or cut it in half to feed a smaller crowd.

½ cup vegetable oil, plus more for the baking sheets	¾ cup pecan pieces
	¾ cup walnut pieces
¾ cup honey	¼ cup sesame seeds
⅓ cup molasses	⅓ cup pumpkin seeds
Pinch of kosher salt	⅓ cup sunflower seeds
2 pounds (10 cups) rolled oats	2 cups raisins

1. Preheat the oven to 350°F. Lightly oil two baking sheets.

2. Combine the vegetable oil, honey, molasses, and salt in a small heavy saucepan over low heat. Cook for 1 to 2 minutes, or until well blended and very hot. Remove the mixture from the heat.

3. Combine the rolled oats, pecans, walnuts, sesame seeds, pumpkin seeds, and sunflower seeds in a large bowl.

4. Pour the honey mixture over the oat mixture and toss briskly to combine. Be sure all the oats, nuts, and seeds are thoroughly coated.

5. Spread out the granola evenly on the prepared baking sheets. Bake for about 30 minutes, stirring every 5 minutes or so, until golden (not dark) brown. Be careful not to overbake it.

6. Remove the pans from the oven and allow the granola to cool completely. It will be crispy when it cools. Transfer the granola to a large container with a lid. Store, tightly covered, at room temperature. Just before serving, add the raisins.

STONE-GROUND HOMINY GRITS

SERVES 6 TO 8

For the best grits, choose good stone-ground hominy grits, found mostly at high-end gourmet shops. Good-quality grits can be yellow, white, even blue, and they have a lively, crunchy texture. Just for the record, most regular folks down South use quick grits. And also for the record, that's what we use at Bubby's. But at home I cook from a bag of stone-ground hominy grits from Hoppin' John's, a small mill in Georgia (www.hoppinjohns.com). The Tabasco in the recipe really adds a zing to the grits, which go especially well with Smithfield Ham with Red-Eye Gravy (page 189).

1 cup old-fashioned white stone-ground grits	⅛ teaspoon freshly ground black pepper, or to taste
2 teaspoons kosher salt, or to taste	2 to 3 dashes Tabasco, or to taste
2 tablespoons unsalted butter	

1. Bring 5 cups of water to a boil in a large pot over medium heat. Stir in the grits and add the salt. Beat the grits vigorously with a wire whisk for 30 seconds or so to avoid lumps. Stir constantly until the grits return to a boil.

2. Reduce the heat to low so the grits are just simmering. Cook, stirring often, for 30 to 40 minutes, or until soft, thick, and creamy.

3. Stir in the butter, pepper, and Tabasco. Taste, and adjust the seasonings with extra salt, pepper, and Tabasco as needed.

4. Cover the grits and keep them warm in a double boiler over low heat for up to 3 hours. Serve warm.

CHEESE GRITS VARIATION: Proceed with the above recipe through step 3. Stir 2 cups of grated sharp white Cheddar cheese into the hot cooked grits, and spoon the grits into a lightly buttered 8 × 10-inch baking pan. Sprinkle another cup of grated sharp white Cheddar cheese over the top. Place the baking pan under the oven broiler, about 4 inches from the heat source, for 1 minute or until golden brown and bubbly. Serve immediately.

STEEL-CUT OATS

*S*teel-cut oats go through a machine that cuts the whole kernels into tiny bits. Sometimes called Scotch or Irish oatmeal, steel-cut oats are chewier and have more texture and flavor than regular rolled oatmeal. They take more time to cook, but steel-cut oatmeal is well worth the wait. McCann's makes the best steel-cut oats that I know. They're available in specialty shops and some supermarkets, as well as at www.mccanns.com. To sweeten the steel-cut oats, add brown sugar, sautéed bananas, raisins, applesauce, berries, or whatever other fruit you like.

2 cups steel-cut oats

3 cups milk

½ teaspoon kosher salt

4 tablespoons (½ stick) unsalted butter

1 teaspoon ground cinnamon (optional)

1. Bring 4 cups of water to a boil in a 6-quart saucepan. Stir in the oats and boil for 3 minutes. Remove from the heat. Cover and allow the oats to stand overnight.

2. When ready to serve, stir the milk, salt, butter, and cinnamon into the oats. Stir and cook the oatmeal over medium-low heat until it comes to a boil.

3. Reduce the heat to a simmer, cover, and cook for 10 to 15 minutes, stirring occasionally. If the mixture looks dry, add a little water.

4. Remove the pan from the heat. Add the sweetener or topping of your choice and serve.

HOME FRIES

*W*hat would bacon and eggs be without a side of home fries? These "homers" are too good to be called simply a "side." Many Bubby's customers prefer to eat them in great quantities with an accompaniment of bacon or sausage.

3 large Idaho potatoes, cut into quarters lengthwise, then cut into ¼-inch-thick slices	2 red onions, thinly sliced
	Kosher salt and freshly ground black pepper to taste
8 tablespoons (1 stick) unsalted butter	¼ cup chopped fresh parsley

1. Bring a large pot of salted water to a boil. Cook the potatoes for 10 to 15 minutes over medium heat, until they are soft but still retain their shape. Drain and set aside.

2. Heat a large (14 inches is ideal) skillet over medium-low heat. Add the butter and let it melt. Add the potatoes and turn up the heat to medium. Cook for about 5 minutes without stirring, allowing a crust to start forming on the potatoes.

3. Flip the potatoes in the pan with a metal spatula and let them cook for 5 minutes.

4. When the potatoes are sizzling but still mostly uncolored, add the red onions. Continue to cook over medium heat without stirring.

5. As the potatoes on the bottom get brown, toss them around the pan with a spatula and continue to cook until golden brown. The home fries should be browned and crispy, but not blackened and burned.

6. When the home fries are nicely browned, season with salt and pepper and add the parsley. Toss well. Serve very hot.

HOME FRIES WITH PEPPERS VARIATION: Add 1 seeded, chopped green bell pepper or 2 seeded, chopped poblano chiles when you add the onions.

ASPARAGUS POTATO HASH

SERVES 6

A robust and filling variation on classic home fries, this pretty vegetable dish gets color and crunch from the asparagus. It pairs especially well with Crispy Crab Cakes (page 198) and Scrambled Eggs (page 75), though potato lovers may decide to eat this as a main course. This is a great way to fit vegetables into a brunch without its being too healthy.

1 bunch asparagus, tough ends trimmed, stems sliced in half lengthwise, cut into 2-inch pieces	6 tablespoons unsalted butter
	1 onion, thinly sliced
2 large Idaho potatoes, cut into quarters lengthwise, then cut into ¼-inch-thick slices	Kosher salt and freshly ground black pepper to taste

1. Bring a large pot of salted water to a boil. Blanch the asparagus for 2 minutes. Drain and set aside.

2. Bring another large pot of salted water to a boil. Cook the potatoes for 10 to 15 minutes, or until they are soft but still retain their shape. Drain and set aside.

3. Heat a large (14 inches is ideal) skillet over medium-low heat. Add the butter and let it melt. Add the potatoes and cook for about 5 minutes without stirring, allowing a crust to start forming on the potatoes.

4. Flip the potatoes in the pan with a metal spatula, raise the heat to medium, and cook the potatoes for 5 more minutes.

5. When the potatoes are sizzling but still mostly uncolored, add the onion. Continue to cook over medium heat without stirring.

6. As the potatoes on the bottom get brown, add the asparagus and sauté until hot. Continue to cook until golden brown. The home fries should be browned and crispy, but not blackened and burned. Season with salt and pepper. Serve hot.

SKILLET HASH BROWNS

SERVES 6 TO 8

While the classic fried potato dish served with bacon and eggs in diners everywhere is excellent on its own, the "smothered and covered" variation is more decadent, blanketing the crusty brown potatoes with caramelized onions and cheese. Thanks must be given here to the Waffle House chain for their inspired innovation!

3 large Idaho potatoes
8 tablespoons (1 stick) unsalted
   butter
2 medium red onions, cut into
   ½-inch dice

Kosher salt and freshly ground
   black pepper to taste
¼ cup chopped fresh parsley

1. Bring a large pot of salted water to a boil. Cook the potatoes whole in their skins for 15 minutes. They should still be fairly firm but easy to pierce with a fork. The idea is that they hold shreds when they are grated, so don't overcook them. Drain and set aside to cool.

2. Using the coarse grating blade on a food processor, or the coarse side of a box grater set over a large plate, grate the potatoes; set aside.

3. Heat a 10- to 12-inch cast-iron skillet or a nonstick skillet over medium-low heat. Add the butter and let it melt. Add the potatoes to the pan, spreading them out so that they form an even 1-inch-thick pancake.

4. Allow the potatoes to get nicely browned for 4 to 5 minutes without stirring, forming a golden crust on the bottom. Watch carefully, and when the potatoes start to brown, use a metal spatula to turn them over once or twice.

5. Add the onions to the potatoes and season with salt and pepper. Continue to cook for another 10 to 12 minutes or so without stirring, forming a golden crust on the bottom. When the hash browns are golden brown, flip them in the pan (intact, as far as this is possible) with a spatula. Add more butter if they seem to be sticking. Season with salt and pepper. Continue to cook until both sides are crispy and golden brown, 5 to 7 minutes.

6. Transfer the hash browns to a serving platter, sprinkle with the parsley, and serve immediately.

SMOTHERED HASH BROWNS VARIATION: Melt 2 tablespoons unsalted butter in a small ovenproof saucepan over low heat. Add 2 diced red onions. Cook until golden brown and caramelized, about

20 minutes, but watch them so they don't burn! Add a little salt and pepper. Follow the recipe through step 5, then scatter the caramelized onions over the top of the hash browns and place 6 slices American cheese or ½ cup grated Cheddar cheese over the top to "smother" them. Bake in a preheated 400°F oven for 2 minutes, or just until the cheese melts. Serve immediately.

SWEET TALK ABOUT ONIONS

Why use red onions in hash browns? They're sweeter than many onion varieties (though their storage life is short) and they offer a little more color to the dish. Among the other sweet specialty onions are the Vidalia, the Georgia Sweet, the White Bermuda, which is mild and sweet, and the Texas Super Sweet. These large yellow onions can grow to the size of a baseball and their storage life is a little longer than the other varieties.

POTATO PANCAKES

SERVES 4 TO 6

*A*lso known as latkes, these crispy, golden treats are a childhood favorite and are best served with caramelized onions, sour cream, and fresh, tangy farmers' market applesauce. Allow yourself about twenty minutes to soak the grated potatoes in the cold water to remove the starch. Otherwise, they become gluey as the starch cooks in the potatoes and they won't get crispy.

3 large Idaho potatoes
2 cups diced onions
¼ cup all-purpose flour
1 tablespoon baking powder

2 teaspoons kosher salt
2 extra-large eggs
Canola oil for frying

1. Using the coarse grating blade of a food processor, or the coarse side of a box grater set over a large plate, grate the potatoes.

2. Using a metal blade attachment of the food processor, purée the grated potatoes until smooth.

3. Remove the potatoes from the food processor and place them in a bowl of cold water. Let them sit for 15 minutes to remove the starch. This prevents them from turning brown.

4. Transfer the potatoes to a fine sieve and drain very well. Using your hands, squeeze out as much liquid from the potatoes as possible.

5. Return the potatoes to the bowl of the food processor and add the onions, flour, baking powder, salt, and eggs. Purée the mixture for 1 minute, or until smooth. Scrape the batter into a mixing bowl so that it will be easier to scoop out to make the pancakes.

6. Preheat the oven to 200°F. Pour the canola oil into a large cast-iron skillet to a depth of about ½ inch. Heat the oil over medium heat.

7. When the temperature of the oil reaches 350°F on a food thermometer, form pancakes, using about 2 tablespoons of batter for each pancake and leaving about ½ inch between them as you place them in the skillet. Allow the pancakes to set and become golden brown on the bottom before turning them with a metal spatula. Turn the pancakes a few times, so they'll get progressively more golden with each turn. Press down when you turn them. Cook for a total of 15 minutes.

8. Remove the pancakes from the skillet and drain well on paper towels.

9. To keep the cooked pancakes warm while you finish making the batch, put them on a paper towel–lined baking sheet, cover them with another layer of paper towels, and hold them in the oven. Blot the potatoes with paper towels again before serving.

SHOESTRING POTATOES

SERVES 6 TO 8

To make this dish, you'll need a mandoline, which is a hand-operated slicing appliance with assorted blades for thick to thin slicing. A metal kitchen utensil known as a spider, which vaguely resembles a spider web with a long handle, is handy when frying because it lets you quickly remove hot food from the oil without removing much of the oil. It's inexpensive and sold in most kitchenware shops. Soaking the julienned potatoes before cooking them removes some of the starch and yields a crisp shoestring effect.

3 large Idaho potatoes, peeled
2 quarts canola oil

Kosher salt to taste

1. Preheat the oven to 200°F.

2. Fit the mandoline with the thin julienne blade. Slice the potatoes lengthwise with the mandoline and place them in a bowl of cold water to remove the starch. Let them soak in the water for about 20 minutes. You want the potatoes to be in very thin slices so that they will cook quickly and emerge nice and crisp. I find that the food processor breaks up the julienne too much, so I don't recommend it.

3. Drain the potatoes in a colander. Spin them in a salad spinner to ensure that they are really dry. It is important to dry them well so the oil doesn't splatter during the frying process.

4. Heat the canola oil in a heavy-bottomed deep 4-quart pot, or a deep fryer, until it reaches 350°F on a food thermometer.

5. Using a frying basket or a long-handled spider utensil, carefully lower about 2 cups' worth of the potatoes into the hot oil. Fry for 8 to 10 minutes, turning the potatoes every minute or two with a slotted spoon or the spider so that they brown evenly.

6. When the potatoes are golden brown, less than 10 minutes, remove them from the oil with the slotted spoon or spider. Drain very well on paper towels.

7. To keep the potatoes warm while you cook the rest of the batch, put them on a paper towel–lined baking sheet, cover with paper towels, and hold in the oven. Repeat with the remaining potatoes.

8. Season with salt before serving.

GINGERED SWEET POTATO HOME FRIES

SERVES 6 TO 8

*S*weet *potatoes make delicious home fries, and with the addition of ginger, these become some-thing really special. Choose small to medium sweet potatoes and use them within a week: They don't keep as long as white potatoes. Store sweet potatoes in a dark, cool place, but don't re-frigerate them.*

2 pounds (about 3 to 4) medium sweet potatoes, peeled and quartered lengthwise, then sliced into ½-inch-wide pieces	1 large onion, cut into ½-inch dice
	¼ cup chopped fresh parsley
	3 tablespoons peeled and finely diced fresh ginger
8 tablespoons (1 stick) unsalted butter	Kosher salt and freshly ground black pepper to taste

1. Bring a large pot of lightly salted water to a boil over high heat.

2. Cook the sweet potatoes for about 15 minutes, or until fairly soft but still holding their shape. Drain and set aside.

3. Heat a 10-inch skillet over medium heat. Add the butter and let it melt. Add the sweet potatoes, onion, parsley, ginger, salt, and pepper. Stir to combine.

4. Cook the potatoes for about 10 minutes, stirring the mixture around in the pan once to make sure all the ingredients are well combined. Cook for another 8 to 10 minutes over medium-low heat, not stirring, until the potatoes are nicely browned and caramelized on one side.

5. Flip the potatoes with a large metal spatula, and allow them to brown and caramelize on the other side. Alternatively, once the potatoes are flipped once, slide them into a preheated 450°F oven for 10 minutes, or until they are nicely browned on both sides. Carefully slide them onto a platter and serve.

STEAMED SESAME SPINACH

SERVES 6 TO 8

With its nutty flavor and beautiful dark green color, this is a good make-ahead brunch dish that tastes best chilled, but it's also good at room temperature. If you prepare it in advance, taste for seasonings before serving; you may need to add a little extra salt or lemon juice.

3 bunches fresh spinach, trimmed	1 teaspoon soy sauce
2 teaspoons sesame oil	¼ teaspoon crushed red pepper
Juice of ½ lemon	flakes
2 tablespoons sesame seeds	

1. Wash the spinach very well by swishing it around in a large bowl of cold water and lifting it out with your hands. Change the water, wipe the bottom and sides of the bowl to get rid of any grit, and repeat this washing process at least twice, or until there is no grit left in the bottom of the bowl.

2. Bring 1 cup of water to a simmer in a large saucepan over low heat. Add the spinach. Toss and cook the spinach for 1 to 2 minutes, or until just wilted.

3. Drain the spinach and run it under cold water to cool it. Using your hands, squeeze the spinach dry in a clean kitchen towel. Chop the spinach into ½-inch pieces.

4. Place the spinach in a large serving bowl. Toss it with the sesame oil, lemon juice, sesame seeds, soy sauce, and red pepper flakes until well combined.

5. Cover and refrigerate for at least 1 hour. Taste and adjust the seasonings before serving.

WILD RAMPS AND ASPARAGUS

SERVES 6 TO 8

A springtime-only treat, wild ramps, also known as wild leeks, resemble broad-leaved scallions and have a flavor that's both oniony and garlicky. Ramps are a great match for asparagus, and the lemon brings out the best of both vegetables. You can prepare this dish ahead of time and chill it, tightly covered, for two to three days in the refrigerator. Serve it chilled or at room temperature.

1 pound wild ramps	Juice of ½ lemon
1 bunch asparagus	Kosher salt and freshly ground
½ teaspoon chopped garlic	black pepper to taste
¼ cup olive oil	

1. Bring a large pot of water to a boil.

2. Wash the ramps very well in several changes of cold water. Trim away the roots. Using a sharp knife, chop both the white and the green parts of the ramps into 2-inch pieces.

3. Trim the asparagus by breaking off the tough stems where they snap. Discard the stems.

4. Cook the asparagus in the boiling water for 2 to 4 minutes, depending on the thickness of the stalks. They should be just tender to the bite, but still firm and green.

5. Drain the asparagus and run them briefly under cold water to cool. Chop into 2-inch pieces.

6. Bring 1 cup of lightly salted water to a simmer in a large skillet over medium heat. Add the ramps and cook, stirring, for about 2 minutes, or until soft.

7. Drain the ramps and run them briefly under cold water to cool. Using your hands, squeeze the ramps in a clean kitchen towel or a paper towel to remove any excess water.

8. Gently toss the asparagus and ramps with the garlic, olive oil, lemon juice, salt, and pepper in a serving bowl until well combined. Cover with plastic wrap and chill well before serving.

SPICY ZUCCHINI WITH MINT

SERVES 6 TO 8

*A*nother great make-ahead dish, this is an appealing way to serve zucchini at room temperature or chilled. Salting the zucchini and letting it sit for about 30 minutes gets rid of excess liquid and keeps this dish from becoming watery. If you make this ahead of time, remove it from the refrigerator about thirty minutes before serving and taste it. You may find that you need extra shakes of salt and pepper, and an extra squeeze or two of lemon juice.

3 zucchini, sliced into ¼-inch rounds	½ cup finely diced red onion
2 tablespoons kosher salt, plus more to taste	Juice of ½ lemon
¼ cup plus 2 tablespoons olive oil	½ cup chopped fresh mint
	½ teaspoon crushed red pepper flakes

1. Place the zucchini in a colander, sprinkle it with the salt, and allow it to sit for 20 to 30 minutes. The salt will extract water from the zucchini, so put a bowl underneath to catch the water. Alternatively, set the colander in the sink so the water drains into the sink.

2. Rinse the zucchini thoroughly under cold running water for about 30 seconds to remove the salt. Firmly pat the zucchini very dry with paper towels.

3. Preheat the oven to 450°F.

4. Toss the zucchini with 2 tablespoons of the olive oil in a large bowl.

5. Arrange the zucchini in a single layer on a baking sheet. Bake for 7 to 10 minutes, until golden brown. Cool for about 10 minutes.

6. Combine the zucchini, red onion, remaining ¼ cup olive oil, lemon juice, mint, and red pepper flakes in a serving bowl until well combined. Taste, and add salt, to taste, if necessary. Cover with plastic wrap and chill for about 1 hour before serving.

BEET GREENS WITH WHITE BEANS

SERVES 6 TO 8

Beet greens, with their dark green leaves and pungent, earthy flavor, are especially tasty with white beans. A nice alternative to beet greens is mustard greens, which are a little spicier. Other options are turnip greens and broccoli rabe. Start this dish a day ahead because the beans need to soak overnight.

2 cups dried white beans	1 teaspoon chopped fresh thyme
2 tablespoons kosher salt, plus	Zest and juice of 1 orange
more to taste	1 teaspoon white wine vinegar
2 bunches beet greens	½ cup olive oil
1 red onion, cut into ⅛-inch dice	¼ teaspoon cayenne pepper
1 garlic clove, minced	

1. Soak the beans overnight in a pot filled with water to cover. Drain and set aside.

2. Bring 10 cups of water to a boil in a large pot over high heat. Stir in the soaked beans and salt. Reduce the heat to medium-low and cook for 45 minutes, or until the beans are soft. Drain and set aside.

3. Meanwhile, wash the beet greens very well by lifting them up and swishing them around in a large bowl of cold water. If any dirt remains in the bottom of the bowl, repeat this process once or twice until the bottom of the bowl is clean. Drain the greens in a colander.

4. Bring 1 cup of lightly salted water to a boil in a 4-quart saucepan over medium-high heat. Reduce the heat to a simmer, add the greens, and cook for 10 minutes, or until soft.

5. Drain the beet greens and run them briefly under cold water to cool. Drain very well and, using your hands, squeeze out any excess water. Chop the beet greens into 2-inch pieces.

6. Mix the beans, beet greens, red onion, garlic, thyme, orange zest, orange juice, vinegar, olive oil, cayenne pepper, and salt, to taste, in a large bowl until well combined. Allow the greens and beans to marinate for at least 1 hour before serving, so the flavors have a chance to marry.

ROASTED BRUSSELS SPROUTS WITH BACON

SERVES 6 TO 8

Bacon is a natural fit with Brussels sprouts because the salt in the cured meat complements the earthiness of the vegetable. This dish is particularly hearty due to the meaty bâtons of bacon. You may have to have a good butcher slice ¼-inch-thick strips from the slab of bacon. As for the Brussels sprouts, choose tightly closed sprouts with no yellowed leaves; the ones that seem heavy for their size are the freshest and best.

12 ounces very thickly sliced bacon (¼-inch-thick)

4 cups Brussels sprouts (about 1¼ pounds)

Kosher salt and freshly ground black pepper to taste

1. Preheat the oven to 400°F.

2. Cut the bacon crosswise into ¼ x 1½-inch strips.

3. Trim the ends from the Brussels sprouts. Split the Brussels sprouts in half lengthwise.

4. Sauté the bacon in a large, heavy ovenproof skillet over medium heat for about 8 minutes, or until crisp. Using a slotted spoon or a pair of tongs, remove the bacon from the skillet and set aside. Discard all but 4 tablespoons of the bacon fat.

5. Toss the Brussels sprouts in the bacon fat in the same skillet over low heat. Season with salt and pepper.

6. Preheat the oven to 400°F.

7. Spread out the Brussels sprouts in a single layer on a large baking sheet. Roast for 5 minutes. Turn the Brussels sprouts over and continue to roast for another 10 minutes, or until soft and slightly brown. Add the bacon strips for the last 3 minutes of cooking. Serve hot or at room temperature.

BROCCOLI RABE WITH RICOTTA SALATA

SERVES 6 TO 8

Don't confuse ricotta salata cheese with ricotta cheese. Made from lightly salted sheep's milk curd that's pressed and dried, firm ricotta salata is a notable cheese that originated in Sicily. It has a pleasant salty flavor that's a little milder than pecorino Romano. Broccoli rabe, sometimes called Italian broccoli, is slightly bitter and earthy and makes an excellent base for a salad. This salad can be made a few hours in advance of serving, and it's easy to double or triple the recipe for a large group.

2 bunches broccoli rabe, trimmed

1 cup chopped green or black olives, preferably Sicilian or kalamata

1 garlic clove, chopped

1 small ripe tomato, cut into ¼-inch dice

½ cup olive oil

Juice of 1 lemon

1 teaspoon balsamic vinegar

Kosher salt and cayenne pepper to taste

4 ounces ricotta salata, shaved with a vegetable peeler or coarsely grated

1. Bring a large pot of salted water to a boil over high heat. Cook the broccoli rabe over medium-high heat for 3 minutes, or just until soft.

2. Drain the broccoli rabe and run it briefly under cold water to cool. Shake out the excess water. Place the broccoli rabe in paper towels and, using your hands, squeeze it dry. Chop into 2-inch pieces.

3. Place the broccoli rabe in a large bowl. Stir in the olives, garlic, tomato, olive oil, lemon juice, and vinegar until well combined. Season with salt and cayenne pepper.

4. Arrange the salad on a serving platter and sprinkle it with the ricotta salata.

BUTTER AND PARSLEY POTATOES

SERVES 6

*V*ery simple to make, this dish goes well with all kinds of brunch meats, such as steak or pastrami, and with eggs. It is easy to double or triple when you're serving a lot of people. Red-skinned potatoes have a moist, less starchy texture than baking potatoes and are ideal for boiling. Use the smallest ones you can find.

1 pound small red new potatoes	¼ cup chopped fresh parsley
4 tablespoons (½ stick) unsalted butter, melted	Sea salt or kosher salt and freshly ground black pepper to taste

1. Bring a large pot of lightly salted water to a boil over high heat. Add the potatoes, reduce the heat to medium, and cook for 10 minutes, or until soft. Drain well. Pat dry with paper towels.

2. Place the potatoes in a serving bowl. Toss gently with the butter, parsley, salt, and pepper until well combined. Serve warm.

SORTING OUT SALTS

So many kinds of salt are in stores now that it's hard to figure out which one to use for what. Keep a box of kosher salt, which is coarse-grained and additive-free, on hand for sprinkling into large amounts of water—when you boil potatoes, pasta, or vegetables, for instance. Most cooks use kosher salt for pretty much everything, and sea salt for finishing. Sea salt tends to be rather gray looking (it literally is the product of the evaporation of seawater), with a very delicate flavor as well as some essential minerals. Fleur de sel is a type of sea salt that's harvested in some areas of France. The salt is marketed as fleur (or "flower") de sel because of the flower pattern it forms as it dries. It looks like flat crystals and has a very delicate flavor. Since it is also expensive, it's best to use it wisely, on salads, meats, fish, or vegetables where it will add texture and really be noticed.

CREAMY BUTTERMILK NEW POTATO SALAD

SERVES 6 TO 8

Buttermilk gives a tangy flavor to this old-fashioned salad, which is great for a brunch picnic. Mixing the potatoes with a firm hand, so that some of the potato is mashed up, makes for a creamy potato salad. You can make this a few hours in advance. Refrigerate, covered, and serve cold. Taste for seasonings before serving.

2 pounds small red new potatoes, halved

½ red onion, cut into ¼-inch dice

1 celery stalk, cut into ¼-inch dice

¼ cup chopped fresh parsley

¼ cup buttermilk

1 cup mayonnaise, homemade (page 284) or store-bought

2 tablespoons white wine vinegar

1 tablespoon sugar

Kosher salt and freshly ground black pepper to taste

1. Bring a large pot of lightly salted water to a boil.

2. Cook the potatoes over medium-high heat for 15 minutes, or until they are soft enough to smash but still hold their shape. Drain and allow to cool slightly.

3. Combine the potatoes, red onion, celery, and parsley in a serving bowl. Using a potato masher or a large wooden spoon, gently mash about one-quarter of the potatoes. Leave the rest as large chunks.

4. Stir together the buttermilk, mayonnaise, vinegar, sugar, salt, and pepper in a separate bowl until well combined.

5. Mix the dressing into the potatoes and stir very well to combine. Taste and adjust the seasonings before serving.

SAVORY-SWEET ROASTED ACORN SQUASH PUDDING

SERVES 6 TO 8

This rich dish is wonderful at a fall brunch. The tawny color of the squash, when it is baked in a casserole, adds a nice touch to a buffet table. This may be prepared ahead of time and re-warmed with good results by heating it for 20 to 30 minutes in a preheated 350°F oven.

1 medium to large acorn squash, halved and seeded

3 tablespoons unsalted butter, melted

2 teaspoons kosher salt, plus more to taste

1 teaspoon freshly ground black pepper, plus more to taste

1 tablespoon all-purpose flour

1 teaspoon ground cinnamon

Pinch of freshly grated nutmeg

1⅓ cups heavy cream

3 extra-large eggs, lightly beaten

2 tablespoons packed dark brown sugar

2 tablespoons granulated sugar

2 tablespoons peeled and minced fresh ginger

1 cup freshly grated Parmesan cheese

1. Preheat the oven to 350°F.

2. Place the squash cut side up in a shallow baking pan large enough to hold both halves. Coat the cut sides of the squash with 1 tablespoon of the butter. Add salt and pepper to taste.

3. Roast the squash for about 45 minutes, or until very soft. Allow the squash to cool slightly in the pan. Using a large spoon, scoop out the flesh and discard the skins. You should have about 2 cups of squash. Use a potato masher to mash the cooked squash to the consistency of mashed potatoes, with a few chunks left in for texture.

4. Reduce the oven heat to 325°F.

5. Combine the squash, the remaining 2 tablespoons butter, the 2 teaspoons salt, the 1 teaspoon pepper, the flour, cinnamon, nutmeg, cream, eggs, brown sugar, granulated sugar, ginger, and Parmesan cheese in a large bowl.

6. Spoon the mixture into a buttered 2½-quart casserole. Bake for about 1 hour, or until the top is set and brown. Allow the pudding to cool for about 30 minutes before serving.

HOPPIN' JOHN

SERVES 6 TO 8

Hoppin' John is the must-have dish for southerners on New Year's Day; it's widely believed that if you eat black-eyed peas on that day, you'll have good luck all year. This a great dish for a crowd and can definitely be prepared ahead of time. Since the black-eyed peas need to soak overnight, start this a day in advance. Serve with my variation on Mr. Beard's Cream Biscuits (page 54).

2 cups black-eyed peas

½ cup olive oil

8 ounces smoked ham or andouille sausage, cut into ½-inch dice

2 red onions, cut into ½-inch dice

3 garlic cloves, chopped

½ red bell pepper, cored, seeded, and chopped

½ green bell pepper, cored, seeded, and chopped

2 celery stalks, cut into ½-inch dice

1 large carrot, peeled and cut into ½-inch dice

1 heaping tablespoon chopped fresh thyme

4 cups cooked white rice

2 medium ripe tomatoes, chopped

1 tablespoon paprika

1 tablespoon kosher salt

1 tablespoon garlic powder

1 teaspoon freshly ground black pepper

1 teaspoon onion powder

¼ teaspoon cayenne pepper

2 teaspoons dried oregano

2 teaspoons dried thyme

¼ cup cider vinegar

½ cup chopped fresh parsley

1. Soak the black-eyed peas overnight in a large pot of cold water to cover. Drain and set aside.

2. Heat the olive oil in a 4-quart saucepan over medium-high heat. Add the ham and cook for about 5 minutes, or until it starts to brown. Add the onions and garlic. Cook for 1 minute. Then add the red and green bell peppers, celery, carrot, and thyme and cook for 2 minutes.

3. Add the black-eyed peas and enough cold water to cover by 1 inch. Stir very well to combine.

4. Reduce the heat to medium-low and bring the mixture to a simmer. Simmer for about 30 minutes, or until the peas are soft.

5. Add the rice and stir in the tomatoes, paprika, salt, garlic powder, black pepper, onion powder, cayenne pepper, oregano, thyme, vinegar, and parsley. Taste, and adjust the seasonings. Serve hot or at room temperature.

CRUMB-CRUSTED BAKED APPLES
AND BAKED PEARS

SERVES 4 TO 6

This is a great fruit dish in the autumn, when the apples and pears are at their peak. Make it a few hours ahead of time, if you like, and leave it at room temperature until ready to serve. You may want to heat it briefly in a 300°F oven before serving. Choose a tart apple, such as Granny Smith, or any good local apple. This could be served as a side dish, as a starter, or even as dessert!

6 tablespoons unsalted butter	3 tart apples, peeled, cored, and
½ cup packed light brown	halved lengthwise
sugar	3 pears, peeled, cored, and halved
¼ teaspoon ground cinnamon	lengthwise
½ teaspoon kosher salt	½ cup soft bread crumbs

1. Preheat the oven to 350°F.

2. Melt 4 tablespoons of the butter in a small saucepan over medium heat. When the butter is melted, add the brown sugar, cinnamon, and salt.

3. Place the remaining 2 tablespoons butter in a 9- or 10-inch pie plate and let it melt in the oven for about 5 minutes. Remove the plate from the oven and arrange the fruit cut side down in the bottom. Evenly distribute the brown sugar mixture over the apples and pears. Sprinkle with the bread crumbs.

4. Return the pie plate to the oven and bake for 25 minutes, or until the fruit is soft when pierced with a fork. Serve hot.

PEACH, PLUM, AND BLACKBERRY
BREAKFAST CRUMBLE

SERVES 6 TO 8

Serve this as a starter: It's nice to have on the table as a beginning for a brunch. You might also serve it as a summery dessert.

For the crumble topping
1 cup all-purpose flour
8 tablespoons (1 stick) unsalted
    butter, chilled
⅓ cup sugar
¼ teaspoon kosher salt

For the filling
1 pound peaches, peeled, pitted, and
    quartered
1 pound plums, peeled, pitted, and
    quartered or sliced
2 cups (1 pint) blackberries
½ cup packed dark brown sugar
1 tablespoon unsalted butter, melted
Juice of 1 lemon
¼ cup all-purpose flour
1 teaspoon freshly grated lemon
    zest
Pinch of kosher salt

1. Make the crumble topping: In the work bowl of a food processor fitted with a metal blade, combine the flour, butter, sugar, and salt. Pulse until the mixture is the texture of bread crumbs; set aside.

2. Preheat the oven to 350°F.

3. Make the filling: Combine the peaches, plums, and blackberries in a mixing bowl.

4. Combine the brown sugar, butter, lemon juice, flour, lemon zest, and salt in another bowl. Gently mix the brown sugar mixture into the fruit mixture.

5. Pour the fruit into a 2-quart baking dish. Sprinkle it evenly with the crumble topping.

6. Bake the crumble on a baking sheet for 50 to 60 minutes, or until thick bubbles emerge from the crumble and the topping is golden brown. Serve warm.

Sliced Melon and Raspberries with Port Syrup

SERVES 6 TO 8

Y*ou can use honeydew, cantaloupe, or any other firm-fleshed melon for this light and luscious brunch dish. The important thing is that your melon be perfectly ripe and juicy, so sniff, pinch, and choose carefully. Make this a couple of hours in advance, so it has time to macerate in the port.*

1 ripe melon, peeled, seeded, and cut into 2-inch pieces	2 cups Port Syrup (page 283)
Juice of 1 lemon	2 cups (1 pint) fresh raspberries

1. Place the melon pieces in a pretty serving bowl. Sprinkle with the lemon juice. Pour on the port syrup.

2. Carefully add the raspberries to the serving bowl, but don't mix them in. They will get mixed in on the plates. Refrigerate for 30 minutes. Serve chilled.

FRUIT SALAD WITH LEMON–POPPY DIPPING SAUCE

SERVES 8 TO 10

Aplatter of fresh fruit served with this lemony dip is a beautiful way to kick off brunch. This fruit salad can also be made into fruit kebobs for a different appearance. Just cut slightly bigger chunks and skewer the fruit onto bamboo skewers. You can prepare the fruit and the dip early and have this all ready when guests arrive. When you make the dip, mince the onion very, very finely or purée it, if you like, and be sure to use a neutral oil, such as canola or corn oil. I find that the onion adds a surprising savory flavor, but it's not at all overpowering.

For the dipping sauce

¾ cup sugar

1 teaspoon Colman's dry mustard

1 teaspoon kosher salt

⅓ cup distilled white vinegar

1½ tablespoons very finely minced onion (as close to liquid as possible)

1 cup canola oil

2 tablespoons poppy seeds

For the fruit

2 crispy, tart apples, peeled, cored, and cut into 1-inch pieces

2 ripe pears, peeled, cored and cut into 1-inch pieces

2 ripe bananas, peeled and cut into ½-inch-thick slices

Juice of ½ lemon

1 medium pineapple, peeled, cored, and cut into 2-inch pieces

1 medium ripe cantaloupe or honeydew melon, peeled, seeded, and cut into 2-inch pieces

1. Make the dipping sauce: Using a whisk, beat the sugar, dry mustard, salt, vinegar, onion, canola oil, and poppy seeds in a bowl until well combined.

2. Spoon the dip into a small bowl, cover with plastic wrap, and chill for 2 hours, or until ready to serve.

3. Prepare the fruit: Toss the apples, pears, and bananas with the fresh lemon juice in order to prevent browning. Arrange the pineapple, cantaloupe, apples, pears, and bananas on a large platter, leaving room in the center for the bowl of dipping sauce. Place the dipping sauce in the center of the platter and serve.

BANANAS, DRIED CRANBERRIES, YOGURT, AND HONEY

SERVES 4

This side dish is a great accompaniment to Bubby's Granola (page 206), Crunchy French Toast (page 133), or, even simpler, seven-grain toast and jam. Try to buy Greek yogurt, which tastes richer and creamier than regular yogurt.

3 ripe bananas, peeled and cut into ½-inch-thick slices	1 cup plain Greek yogurt
1 teaspoon fresh lemon juice	2 tablespoons honey
	½ cup dried cranberries

1. Toss the banana slices with the lemon juice.

2. Stir together the yogurt and honey in a mixing bowl. Add the bananas and gently toss to coat thoroughly with yogurt.

3. Spoon the banana mixture into a serving bowl, sprinkle the dried cranberries on top, and serve.

Mixed Summer Berry Parfait

SERVES 6

The essence of summer, this light and colorful dish goes with just about anything. Prepare the fruit ahead of time, but don't layer it with the yogurt and granola in the parfait glasses until an hour or so before you plan to serve it. Adjust the amount of honey according to your and your guests' preferences.

¼ cup honey

3½ cups plain Greek yogurt

1 cup (½ pint) fresh blueberries

1 cup (½ pint) fresh blackberries

1 cup (½ pint) fresh raspberries

1 cup (½ pint) fresh strawberries,
hulled and cut into halves or
quarters

1 cup fresh pineapple chunks
(1-inch chunks)

2 cups Bubby's Granola (page 206)

1. Whisk together the honey and yogurt in a mixing bowl; set aside.

2. Gently toss together the blueberries, blackberries, raspberries, strawberries, and pineapple in a separate bowl.

3. Layer the ingredients as follows in six parfait glasses: a 2-inch layer of fruit, then ¼ cup yogurt, and then 2 tablespoons granola. Repeat the layers, ending with yogurt and granola. Refrigerate for up to 4 hours. Serve cold.

JUICES, COCKTAILS, AND OTHER LIBATIONS

Brunch begins and ends with drinks, so you want to offer beverages that are memorable and appealing, but not overly filling. They should brighten and complement your menu rather than overpower it, and they should leave guests feeling revived and renewed, not overstuffed, overcaffeinated, or overimbibed.

At Bubby's, we offer a wide range of choices, hot and cold, alcoholic and non, sweet and chocolaty, or fruity and fresh. In the cold weather, our rich hot chocolate, restorative hot toddies, and mulled wine have warmed many souls over the years. Once summer arrives, we make gallons and gallons of pink lemonade. And at every time of year, our fresh cranberry juice, as well as some of the other juice combinations that you will find here, are in high demand.

At home, when planning a brunch, it's easy to consider beverages almost as an afterthought because you're so busy with the rest of the meal. Resist that temptation: Drinks are an essential part of a brunch, and guests feel incredibly pampered when they are offered just-squeezed fruit juices, handcrafted cocktails, and freshly brewed coffee.

Which drinks you choose for your brunch will obviously have to do with the season. Refreshing fruit juice combinations and fresh fruit presses are especially welcome in the hot weather, while our mocha- and hot coffee-based hot drinks are ideal for wintertime brunches.

Allow yourself enough time to assemble a couple of different options for brunch—maybe one or two fresh juices, some type of hot coffee drink, and, depending on your guest list, a festive cocktail or two. To save time and make your job easier during a brunch, these cocktails can often be mixed up in large batches and chilled until it's time to serve.

While many drinks must by their very nature be prepared at the last minute, you can certainly do some of the prep work ahead of time, such as squeezing and slicing citrus fruits, cutting up fruit for garnishes, and making sure you have enough chilled water, seltzer, and sodas on hand. Take a look at your barware, too, to make sure you've got plenty of glasses to go around. Don't automatically assume that everyone will use just one glass. At a brunch, people tend to set down their drinks as they move around and visit with friends, and then they need a freshening up—which usually requires a clean glass, of course.

As you're readying the beverage selection, don't forget to lay in a nice selection of garnishes. Freshly sliced orange, lemon, and lime wheels, half-wheels, or wedges are easy to prepare. You can also make citrus twists by removing a long strip of lemon, orange, or lime peel with a long, sharp paring knife or a zest stripper, which is available at almost any cookware shop. And don't forget about fruits and vegetables. A celery stick's a natural for a Bloody Mary, and green olives—plain or stuffed—can dress up a variety of alcoholic beverages. Cucumber wheels or sprigs of a fresh herb are also nice to use in warm weather. The bright color of fresh fruits—a whole strawberry, or a thin slice of pineapple or watermelon—gives drinks a festive air.

As a brunch host, try to have at the ready some basic bar equipment. Obviously, don't go into a panic if you don't own all of these. Alcoholic drinks are not as big at brunch as they are at dinner, so don't feel compelled to run out and buy gadgets you may not often use. But chances are you'll be happy to have the following in your kitchen: a corkscrew, an ice bucket, a muddler for mashing fruit, a zest stripper, a shot glass, a bottle opener, and a simple cocktail shaker with a strainer top. Short, wide "rocks" or old-fashioned glasses, used for many different beverages, usually hold drinks made with ice, although you could just as easily use the tall, narrow glasses called highballs. Martini glasses typically are used for drinks that are strained before serving, like cosmopolitans. It's always a nice touch to fill your martini glasses with ice water and let them sit for a few minutes before pouring out the water and filling the glasses with the cocktail. Glasses meant for white wine are usually narrower than red wine glasses, and they function as a multipurpose glass since they can be used for various alcoholic drinks in addition to wine.

Ice cubes will pick up the flavors from your freezer, so make fresh ones before you start assembling brunch beverages and toss out the old cubes. And consider whether you want to use ice cubes or crushed ice in your drinks. Since crushed ice melts quickly, you'll probably use it primarily in drinks that guests will consume quickly. Regular ice cubes are best in alcoholic drinks that will be sipped in a leisurely fashion. An old-fashioned ice option that is popular again (at the moment) is chipping or shaving ice from an ice block. If you are serving a fairly large group, this is a great choice. You can have a block of ice delivered from your local ice company. All you need is an ice pick or a shaver and you're set.

In this chapter, you'll learn how to combine juices to make flavorful and lively-tasting combinations. Cocktails are grouped together, and there's a wide range to choose from, including some of my signature cocktails. There's also a whole section on how to grind, brew, and serve great coffee. Lest you think straight-up brewed java is the only option to serve your guests, instructions for how to enhance it with Kahlúa, Baileys Irish Cream, and Irish whiskey are also included.

Whether you are leaning into festive libations or offering more virginal choices, drinks are a fun part of a brunch, so pick out a couple of recipes here that sound enticing. Then offer a toast to your guests (and yourself) as you sit down to a relaxing meal.

ADVANCE PLANNING IS KEY TO THE LIQUID PART OF ANY BRUNCH MENU.

FRESH JUICES 101

Among the fresh juices that we offer at Bubby's are orange, blood orange, grapefruit, pomegranate, pineapple, cranberry, and apple cider. Some of our mixed drinks call for cranberry juice, and in these we use only our own Fresh Cranberry Juice (page 240), sweetened with a light hand.

SQUEEZING FRESH JUICES: Squeezing fresh juice may seem like an unnecessary step, but once you try a freshly squeezed juice, such as cranberry juice, you will never consider using anything else. It requires a vegetable juicer, which extracts juice from solid fruits and vegetables such as apples and carrots. A high-end juicer is expensive (around $250), but it is well worth the price if you use it. Squeezing fresh juice takes some time, but it is always an effort that is appreciated. Follow the instructions on your individual juicer.

SQUEEZING POMEGRANATES AND GRAPES FOR JUICE: Not all fruits go into a juicer, and one that does not is pomegranates. To squeeze these, use a citrus press. (It can be a little messy when the seeds burst, so wear an apron!) Another way to squeeze them that is not so splattery is to remove all the fruit into a big bowl and mash them with your hands, then run this through a sieve. From four or five pomegranates, you will get two or three cups of juice, depending on how fresh and juicy the fruit is.

Another excellent fruit to squeeze in much the same way as you do pomegranates is Concord grapes. Try squeezing them in the fall, when they are in season.

JUICE DUOS: There are infinite ways to showcase fresh fruit juice in drinks. And while a freshly squeezed fruit juice is so naturally good that it's hard to improve on, combining two different juices gives the drink even more appeal. At Bubby's, we're known for our "virginal juice cocktails," which are actually juice duos. Somehow, the flavor combination of two juices is even better than a solo juice.

Here are some of the combinations that we like:

GRAPEFRUIT AND ORANGE: 1 part grapefruit juice and 1 part orange juice

GRAPEFRUIT AND POMEGRANATE: 2 parts grapefruit juice and ½ part pomegranate juice

ORANGE AND CRANBERRY: 1 part orange juice and ¼ part cranberry juice

APPLE CIDER AND CRANBERRY: 1 part fresh apple cider and ¼ part cranberry juice

FRUIT PRESSES: Another way to showcase fruit is with presses. At Bubby's, presses are something we make and serve instead of commercial soda pop. They require only fresh fruit, a splash of simple syrup, ice, and seltzer water. The best thing, besides their inherent deliciousness, is that you can make them as sweet or tart as you like.

To make presses, you will need to know how to make Simple Syrup (page 281), a very basic recipe that keeps for one month in the refrigerator.

These are two of our most popular presses.

LEMON PRESS: Slice 1 lemon in ⅛-inch rounds, keeping them together as you slice. Place the cut lemon into a 20-ounce glass, add 1 or 2 ounces simple syrup, and smash down with a muddler, which is a wooden pestle used by bartenders. If you don't happen to have a muddler, just use a small long-handled spoon. Fill the glass with ice, then fill it to the top with seltzer and stir.

LEMON-LIME PRESS: Slice ½ lemon and 1 lime in ⅛-inch rounds, keeping them together as you slice. Place the cut fruit into a 20-ounce glass with 1 or 2 ounces simple syrup and smash down with a muddler. Fill the glass with ice, then fill it to the top with seltzer and stir.

Here are some other ideas for presses. They use about the same ratios as above, though you could use a little less sugar in these.

Orange press

Blood orange press

Cranberry and lime press

Meyer lemon press

Pomegranate and Meyer lemon press

Pineapple and lime press

Concord grape and lemon press

FRESH CRANBERRY JUICE

MAKES 1 QUART

resh cranberry juice is worth learning to make for its vibrant flavor and color. We use frozen berries most of the year, and they actually make a more consistent juice than fresh, which are available only six or eight weeks of the year. A pound of frozen or fresh cranberries should give you about 2 cups juice. It is important to strain the juice through a very fine sieve. We use a fine chinois, also known as a China cap, to strain our juice. A chinois is actually a conical sieve with a very fine mesh. Use a spoon or even a pestle to press the juice through the chinois.

1 pound fresh or frozen cranberries, thawed if frozen	½ cup sugar
	2 cups hot water

1. Wash and pick over the cranberries, discarding any stems or discolored berries.

2. Squeeze the cranberries through an electric juicer. Strain the juice through a very fine sieve to remove the pulp.

3. Combine the sugar and hot water in a pitcher. Stir briskly until the sugar is completely dissolved. Allow to cool.

4. Pour the cranberry juice into the pitcher and mix well.

5. Serve immediately over ice or refrigerate until serving time.

LEMONADE

*L*emonade is reminiscent of sultry afternoons and evenings spent on a screened-in porch in the days before air conditioning, when it was so hot no one wanted to move off the porch for anything more than a lemonade refill. This is my basic lemonade, which Bubby's make lots of in the summer. You can make it a few days ahead and store it, tightly covered, in the refrigerator. Pink lemonade gets its rosy color not from a chemist's kit, but from fresh cranberry juice. Sweeten this ade with a light or heavy hand, depending upon your taste. One of the great things about homemade lemonade is that you can customize it to how much of a sweet tooth you or your guests have.

1½ cups sugar (or less, to your taste)

2 cups hot water

6 cups cold water

2 cups fresh lemon juice

1. Combine the sugar and the hot water in a very large pot or pitcher. Stir briskly until the sugar is completely dissolved. Allow to cool slightly.

2. Stir in the cold water and the lemon juice, and mix very well.

3. Chill thoroughly in the refrigerator. Serve in glasses over ice.

PINK LEMONADE VARIATION: Stir ½ cup Fresh Cranberry Juice (page 240) into the cold lemonade and mix very well. Chill until serving time.

WATERMELON LEMONADE

MAKES 3 QUARTS

*M*ake this in the summertime, when sweltering days coincide with watermelon season. It's a beautiful and thirst-quenching drink that everyone loves, so make plenty. The watermelon adds a lot of beautiful pink color.

4 pounds watermelon, peeled and cubed (about 8 cups)	8 triangular-shape, ½-inch-thick watermelon slices for garnish
8 cups Lemonade (page 241) or Pink Lemonade (page 241)	

1. Purée the watermelon, seeds and all, in a blender for about 10 seconds, or until just barely liquefied. Strain the liquefied watermelon through a coarse sieve.

2. Combine the watermelon purée and lemonade in a large ice-filled pitcher.

3. Chill thoroughly in the refrigerator. Serve in glasses over ice. Garnish each glass with a small triangle of watermelon.

ROSE HIP AND MINT ARNOLD PALMERS

MAKES 2 QUARTS

*N*amed after the golfer who declared his love for it decades ago, this libation is a classic and refreshing tea and lemonade combination with a special little Bubby's twist: pink lemonade with rose hip and mint teas. Few beverages are more refreshing.

2 bags rose hip tea	1 quart boiling hot water
2 bags mint tea	1 quart Pink Lemonade (page 241)

1. Combine the rose hip tea, mint tea, and boiling water in a large teapot. Steep the tea for 5 minutes. Remove the tea bags and allow the tea to cool slightly.

2. Stir in the pink lemonade.

3. Chill thoroughly in the refrigerator. Serve in tall glasses over ice.

PINK LADY PUNCH

MAKES 2 QUARTS

This is just the kind of recipe found in a Junior League or church cookbook. It is greatly improved upon by using fresh juices and sorbet instead of canned juice and sherbet. But, one can also use the old canned standby.

2 cups Fresh Cranberry Juice
(page 240)
2 cups fresh pineapple juice

1 quart ginger ale
1 quart lemon or orange sorbet

1. Stir together the cranberry juice, pineapple juice, and ginger ale in a large pitcher. Chill in the refrigerator until serving time.

2. To serve, place a scoop of sorbet into a glass and fill with punch.

BLOODY MARY

SERVES 6 TO 8

Nothing says brunch like a perfectly spiked Bloody Mary. Bubby's Bloody Mary is famous for being a cure for hangovers. Mostly, it gives a spicy kick that will help you sweat it out. Using a sixteen-ounce glass leaves you plenty of room for the ice and garnish.

For the Bloody Mary mix
One 46-ounce can V8 vegetable
    juice
1⅓ ounces (2 tablespoons plus
    2 teaspoons) fresh lime juice
1⅓ ounces (2 tablespoons plus 2
    teaspoons) Worcestershire sauce
¼ cup horseradish
3 tablespoons celery salt

1 tablespoon Tabasco
2 tablespoons plus 1 teaspoon Old
    Bay Seasoning

For each serving
1½ to 2 ounces good vodka for each
    10-ounce Bloody Mary
Lime wedge and celery stalk

1. Make the Bloody Mary mix: Stir together the vegetable juice, lime juice, Worcestershire sauce, horseradish, celery salt, Tabasco, and Old Bay Seasoning in a large pitcher. Mix until well combined. Refrigerate until you're ready to pour.

2. For each serving, fill a chilled 16-ounce glass with ice. Pour 1 shot of vodka (1½ ounces) over the ice. Fill the glass to the top with Bloody Mary mix. Garnish the glass with a wedge of lime and a celery stalk.

CLAMARY VARIATION: Steam 1 dozen littleneck clams in a covered pan with ¼ cup water. As soon as the clams open, remove them from the heat. Remove the clams from their shells. Strain the cooking liquid through a fine sieve. Add 1 cup clam juice to 4 cups Bloody Mary mix. Fill six chilled 16-ounce glasses with ice. Pour 1 shot of vodka (1½ ounces) into each glass. Fill to the top with the Bloody Mary–clam juice mixture. Garnish each Clamary with 2 clams and 2 green olives on toothpicks, as well as a celery stalk. Serves 6.

BLOODYTINI

SERVES 1

*T*he quality of the ingredients makes all the difference in this drink, so use the absolutely best vodka and great olives.

3 ounces good vodka	3 large pitted olives, such as
½ ounce (1 tablespoon) dry vermouth	kalamatas
1 ounce (2 tablespoons) Bloody	
Mary mix (page 245)	

1. Combine the vodka, vermouth, and Bloody Mary mix with 1 cup of ice in a shaker, and shake well.

2. Pour the vodka mixture into a martini glass.

3. Spear the olives onto a toothpick and serve as a garnish on the drink.

BLOOD ORANGE MIMOSA

SERVES 1

*I*t used to be that blood oranges came around only at Christmastime and had to be flown in from Malta. Now, however, they are grown in California and Florida and have a much longer season. We show them off in what's become a signature cocktail at Bubby's.

2 ounces (¼ cup) fresh blood	3 ounces Champagne
orange juice	Twist of blood orange zest

1. Combine the blood orange juice and Champagne in a Champagne flute. Stir gently.

2. Garnish with the blood orange twist and serve.

CRANMOSA

SERVES 1

Festive and fruity, this is a natural starter at brunch. For best results and maximum freshness, use freshly squeezed cranberry juice and make the drinks just before you plan to serve them.

2 ounces (¼ cup) fresh orange juice
2 tablespoons (⅛ cup) Fresh
   Cranberry Juice (page 240)

3 ounces Champagne

1. Combine the orange juice and cranberry juice in a Champagne flute. Stir gently.

2. Stir in the Champagne and serve immediately.

PINK GRAPEFRUIT AND CHAMPAGNE COCKTAIL

SERVES 1

This just may be the perfect way to start a celebration. Be sure to use good Champagne, and chill both the Champagne and the grapefruit juice before mixing them.

2 ounces (¼ cup) fresh pink
   grapefruit juice

3 ounces Champagne

Combine the grapefruit juice and Champagne in a Champagne flute. Stir gently and serve immediately.

PINK LEMONADE COSMOPOLITAN

SERVES 1

This cocktail is made with homemade pink lemonade and vodka. A traditional cosmopolitan has cranberry juice and lime juice rather than lemonade. We use Triple Sec, but another orange liqueur such as Cointreau can be used instead.

2 ounces good vodka	Dash of Triple Sec
1½ ounces (3 tablespoons) Pink	Dash of Simple Syrup (page 281)
Lemonade (page 241)	Twist of lemon zest

1. Combine the vodka, pink lemonade, Triple Sec, and simple syrup in a cocktail shaker. Shake well.

2. Pour over ice in a martini glass.

3. Garnish with a lemon twist and serve.

SANGRÍA

SERVES 6 TO 8

This is good for a lunchier-leaning brunch with steak and potatoes. I like to use Tempranillo or Rioja wine in this festive drink, which looks beautiful on the table. Start the sangría a day ahead of time so that the fruit can marinate. Once it's made, sangría will keep for two days in the refrigerator.

One 750-milliliter bottle red wine	1 orange, cut into ⅛- to ¼-inch-thick slices
3 ounces good vodka	
1 cup sugar	1 lime, cut into ⅛- to ¼-inch-thick slices
1 tablespoon freshly peeled and grated ginger	1 apple, cored and cut into ½-inch dice
	1 cup sliced strawberries
1 lemon, cut into ⅛- to ¼-inch-thick slices	1 cup diced fresh pineapple (½-inch dice)

1. Pour the wine into a large pitcher. Add the vodka. Stir in the sugar and ginger.

2. Add the lemon slices, orange slices, lime slices, apple, strawberries, and pineapple. Stir well.

3. Cover, and chill in the refrigerator until serving time.

SERIOUS HOT CHOCOLATE

SERVES 4 TO 6

M*ake this when you have invited serious chocoholics to brunch, and keep in mind that the finest hot chocolate starts with the best possible unsweetened chocolate. I use Callebaut or Scharffen Berger. Sweetened condensed milk is a mixture of sugar and whole milk, and it serves here to both thicken and sweeten.*

6 ounces good-quality unsweetened chocolate, broken into pieces	2 cups heavy cream
	½ cup sweetened condensed milk
2 cups milk	½ cup sugar

1. In the top of a double boiler over simmering water, melt the chocolate.

2. Stir together the milk, cream, sweetened condensed milk, and sugar in a heavy 2-quart saucepan over low heat. Cook until very hot but not boiling.

3. Whisk the melted chocolate into the cream mixture and continue whisking until no chocolate streaks remain and the beverage is smooth and very hot.

4. Pour into mugs and serve.

SPIKED BITTERSWEET HOT CHOCOLATE VARIATION: Add 1½ ounces dark rum to each cup of hot chocolate.

MEXICAN HOT CHOCOLATE

Bubby's SIGNATURE DISH

SERVES 4 TO 6

C innamon is the spice that makes Mexican hot chocolate the exotic warmer that it is, and we also add pinches of cloves and cayenne for good measure. This is especially good following Huevos Rancheros (page 111), but it's a warming treat at just about any brunch.

6 ounces good-quality unsweetened chocolate, broken into pieces	½ cup sugar
	Pinch of ground cloves
2 cups milk	¼ teaspoon ground cinnamon
2 cups heavy cream	2 pinches of cayenne pepper, or
½ cup sweetened condensed milk	to taste

1. In the top of a double boiler over simmering water, melt the chocolate.

2. Stir together the milk, cream, and sweetened condensed milk in a heavy 2-quart saucepan over low heat. Cook until very hot but not boiling. Whisk in the sugar, cloves, cinnamon, and cayenne pepper.

3. Whisk the melted chocolate into the cream mixture and continue whisking until no chocolate streaks remain and the beverage is smooth and very hot.

4. Pour into mugs and serve.

WHEN THE HEAT IS ON

Hot chocolate is not the only winter warmer. There's a whole variety of spiced, sweetened, and heated beverages that contain no milk, no chocolate, and no caffeine. At Bubby's, I've tinkered with some of these traditional hot drinks to come up with some beverages that have become pretty popular in their own right. Here are a couple of examples of our spiced, sweetened, and heated beverages.

- **MULLED SPICED CIDER:** Combine 2 quarts fresh apple cider; 2 cinnamon sticks; 4 whole cloves; ½ orange, cut into quarters; ¼ teaspoon cayenne pepper; and 6 black peppercorns in a large pot. Cover and simmer over low heat for 30 minutes. Remove from the heat and let sit in the fridge for a day to allow the flavors to marry. Reheat and serve hot.

- **HOT HONEYED LEMONADE:** Mix together 1 cup fresh lemon juice, ⅓ cup honey, and 2 cups of hot water in a large saucepan. Stir briskly. Pour the mixture into an insulated container such as a thermos or a slow cooker to keep warm.

- **SPICED ROSE HIP TEA:** In a large saucepan combine 2 whole cloves, 1 cinnamon stick, 6 cups of boiling water, 1 whole lemon, cut in half, and 3 tablespoons honey. Simmer over medium-high heat for 10 minutes. Remove from the heat and add 4 rose hip tea bags. Let steep for 10 minutes. Serve hot.

WARM EGGNOG

Wonderful but very rich, eggnog is best served in small portions. Though good hot or cold, I always serve it hot in the winter. This can be made a day ahead of time and kept in the refrigerator.

1 extra-large egg	½ teaspoon ground nutmeg, plus
¾ cup sugar	freshly grated nutmeg for
¼ teaspoon kosher salt	serving
1 quart milk	1 cup heavy cream
1 tablespoon pure vanilla extract	

1. Using a wire whisk, beat the egg, sugar, and salt in a heavy 4-quart saucepan until well blended. Stir in the milk.

2. Cook the mixture over low heat, stirring constantly, for about 25 minutes, or until it thickens and coats the back of a spoon. Be careful not to boil the mixture or it will curdle.

3. Pour the mixture into a large bowl. Stir in the vanilla, ground nutmeg, and cream. Cover with plastic wrap and refrigerate for 8 hours or overnight.

4. Shortly before serving, warm the eggnog in a 4-quart saucepan until steaming hot but not boiling. Again, be careful not to boil it or it will curdle.

5. Ladle the warm eggnog into mugs and sprinkle each serving with a little freshly grated nutmeg.

SPIKED EGGNOG VARIATION: Stir together ½ cup warm eggnog and 1 ounce good dark rum. Finish with a sprinkling of freshly grated nutmeg. Serves 1.

WASSAIL

his is another Junior League favorite. Make it in the winter and serve it at a cold-weather brunch. You could keep this hot in a slow cooker, turned to the low setting, for several hours.

2 cups Fresh Cranberry Juice (page 240)	6 whole cloves
1 quart Lemonade (page 241)	2 cinnamon sticks

1. Bring the cranberry juice, lemonade, cloves, and cinnamon sticks to a boil in a large saucepan. Reduce the heat. Simmer the wassail, covered, for about 1 hour.

2. Using a slotted spoon, strain out and discard the cloves and the cinnamon sticks.

3. Pour into mugs and serve.

HOT RUM TODDY

SERVES 4

*T*his toddy, a warming way to start brunch on a wintry day, is served in sugar-rimmed mugs and garnished with a stick of cinnamon. To make this for a crowd, mix up the rum and brown sugar and cloves ahead of time and add the boiling water at the last minute.

2 tablespoons granulated sugar	Pinch of ground cloves
3 tablespoons packed dark brown sugar	3 cups boiling water
⅔ cup dark rum	4 cinnamon sticks
	4 lemon slices

1. Spread out the granulated sugar on a small plate.

2. Dip the rims of 4 mugs into cold water and then dip them into the sugar. Set the mugs aside.

3. Stir together the brown sugar, rum, and cloves in a 1-quart pitcher. Whisk in the boiling water and mix well.

4. Pour the toddy into the prepared mugs. Garnish each toddy with a cinnamon stick and a lemon slice. Serve immediately.

MULLED WINE WITH CINNAMON STICKS AND FRUIT

SERVES 6 TO 8

To "mull" wine simply means to flavor it with anything from spices to fruits as it heats. A warming brunch drink on chilly days, this one relies on the best-quality brandy you can find. It's a matter of personal preference as to what kind of wine to use. I like a nice Cabernet or Merlot.

1 liter red wine	Zest of 1 lemon
1 cup good brandy	6 whole cloves
1 orange, halved	4 to 6 cinnamon sticks

1. Combine the wine, brandy, orange halves, lemon zest, cloves, and cinnamon sticks in a 4-quart saucepan over low heat. Simmer for about 2 hours uncovered.

2. Remove the pan from the heat. Using a slotted spoon, strain out and discard the orange, cloves, and cinnamon sticks.

3. Pour the wine into mugs and serve.

COFFEE 101

While hot cider is welcome at fall and winter brunches, when the weather is warm, there is only one hot drink that everyone wants almost every single day of the year—good coffee. Here are a few coffee caveats to keep in mind: For big events, where you need more than ten cups of coffee at a time, you can rent a twenty-five- or fifty-cup coffee brewer from most party rental places. If you are serving more than twenty people, it is also good to rent a smaller brewer to offer decaf to your guests as well.

The smell of coffee can evoke many memories. One of my fondest coffee memories is from summers spent in Berkeley, California, starting in 1975. Walking down Virginia Street from my uncle Howie's house, taking the left on Walnut, an overwhelming smell would immediately fill my nose and a tingle of pre-coffee joy would overcome me. This was my introduction to Peet's Coffee, a coffee so rich and mesmerizing that one is in a trance from blocks away. This may have been one of the seminal moments in my becoming a chef. Compared with the coffee that was served at diners and "family restaurants" in the suburbs where I grew up, the smell of Peet's Coffee was like being yanked out of Plato's cave into the bright, blinding light.

If you've ever had an amazing cup of coffee at a friend's house, chances are you've wondered what the secret could be—a pricey coffeemaker? Expensive coffee? Steamed milk? Actually, good coffee relies on several components: fresh beans that are roasted and ground just right, good filters, good water, and proper equipment.

Choose your coffee and equipment based on your preferences. Do you like dark and heavy or mild and acidic coffee? Or do you like it somewhere in between? As you begin to have strong preferences, it pays to know where your coffee comes from. The world's three biggest coffee-growing regions are Latin America, Africa, and Asia-Pacific. Latin American coffee tends to be subtle and higher in acidity, and it often has a flavor reminiscent of cocoa or nuts. More exotic beans come from regions in Africa such as Ethiopia, where you get into rich dark flavors with hints of fruit and spice. Low acidity, intensely flavored Asia-Pacific coffees, from Java and Sumatra, for example, can be earthy and even herbal.

There are also social and political aspects to coffee. At Bubby's, we use fair trade coffee, which means that the people who pick the coffee in Ethiopia or Java or Guatemala or Brazil are getting a fair wage for their work. We also buy coffee that is shade grown and organic. The reason for buying shade-grown coffee is that big plantations have been clearing rain forest land to make room for coffee growing, which is harmful to the environment and to the natural habitats of many animals.

Whatever beans you choose, they should not only be fresh when you get them, but they should be roasted shortly before you buy them and then stored properly. Proper storage means keeping them in a lightproof sealed bag at room temperature. Light, air, and moisture are coffee's enemies. And while some people freeze their coffee beans, this can cause condensation as the beans thaw, which results in moist beans—not a desirable quality in coffee. Because the beans start releasing gas when they are ground, it is best to grind them yourself just before brewing.

Since beans quickly start to lose their flavor, ideally coffee should be brewed no more than two weeks after the beans are roasted. But, if you buy your beans already ground, use them within three to four days or they will be stale. You will taste the difference. Whole roasted beans will keep nicely in a vacuum pack for a month or so, for ten to fourteen days once opened. Always purchase the amount of coffee you will use in the time before it will go stale.

If you are buying already ground beans, pay close attention to the grind. A too-large grind means the water flows through the beans too quickly and you wind up with weak coffee. If your grind is simply too small for your filter, the filter can get clogged and the water gets held for too long. Result? Muddy coffee.

If your coffee brewer has a basket filter with a flat bottom, you want a relatively coarse grind that will allow the water to flow through it quickly. A slightly less coarse grind works for a French press. Cone-shaped filters require a slightly finer grind to produce excellent results. At home, my machine of choice is a French press. My wife prefers a drip coffee machine because it leaves her hands free for our three children. And believe me, she does not want to have to press down on anything but a button, nor does she want any delay in getting the first cup in the morning. When using drip coffee makers, the secret is to get one that drips the brewed coffee into a thermal carafe rather than into a carafe that sits on a heating element. As the coffee sits on direct heat, it stews and tends to burn, and there goes the flavor. The best carafes are opaque rather than glass, since light can also diminish flavor if the coffee sits around for any length of time.

Water is obviously an essential ingredient in your coffee. You can have the best beans on the planet, but if you use bad water, your coffee is ruined. If the water in your area doesn't taste great, buy a water filter for your faucet and change it on a regular basis, or use bottled water. Always use cold water, freshly drawn, when you brew coffee.

One last thing to pay attention to: filters. Assuming you use paper ones, search out unbleached filters and you will avoid the residual flavors that cheaper ones result in. If your machine has a metal filter, even better, since this won't add flavors to the coffee. Just make sure the metal filter is cleaned well each time you use it.

Finally, coffee is an individual joy. While my memories of Peet's make me want a thick, rich, full-bodied mug of coffee every morning, you and yours may enjoy a lighter, less rich brew. Once you have the beans you like, the brewer you adore, and the water you need, it will still take some trial and error to get your coffee just the way you like it. It is worth the effort, especially if, like so many of us, you enjoy coffee every day. I know I am a little crabby before that first precious cup.

Two more small points: Give your carafe a swirl right before you pour the coffee in order to blend the flavors. And once you brew the coffee, don't keep it on a warming plate for more than 20 minutes; continuous heating makes coffee bitter. If you need to keep coffee hot, invest in a thermally insulated container.

If you want to try your hand at some espresso coffee drinks, the same rules apply. It is very important to have the right equipment. Espresso machines are quite expensive, but the best ones are not necessarily the most costly. Do your research and talk to people who own machines before you buy one. There are stove-top espresso makers that are perfectly okay, but they will not achieve the same results as a very good espresso machine.

Of the many specialty coffee drinks, cappuccino is one of the most popular. The perfect Italian cappuccino is not all foamy, as cappuccinos tend to be at the big coffee chains in America. The milk is steamed to a creamy consistency. The perfect cappuccino is not one-third espresso, one-third milk, and one-third frothy foam.

Having spent a good amount of time sitting in some very snooty cafés in Rome, I feel snooty enough to comment on the subject. There is nothing like a well-made cappuccino. You need a proper machine for it. If you like cappuccino, it is worth doing some research to find a powerful machine that pulls good espresso and steams well. When you have a proper machine, and begin to steam the milk, think about it this way: Fill a metal steamer about one-third full with the milk. Use the steamer until the milk just barely froths, 3 to 5 seconds; then stick the steam nozzle right down inside the milk and steam it until the side of the steamer is just barely too hot to touch. There will be creamy-textured milk in the container. Pull your espresso and then swirl the milk so the creamy hot milk mixes back together if it has settled at all. Then, shaking the steamer to keep the milk creamy and mixed, pour the creamed steamed milk onto the espresso. If you need a reference, come into Bubby's anytime. You will see me obsessing over the coffee, because when all is said and done, this is the thing I get most crazy about!

Here are some other espresso drinks you might enjoy:

MACCHIATO: a shot of espresso with a little foamed milk on top

MOCHACCINO: cappuccino with a little chocolate syrup inside and a little sprinkle of chocolate on top

ICED CAPPUCCINO: one part chilled brewed espresso to two parts cold milk, with a little foamed milk on top

To sweeten cold coffee drinks, I like to offer guests Simple Syrup (page 281), since it is already dissolved. Simple syrup is one part sugar to one part water.

HOW TO MAKE COFFEE ICE CUBES

If you're making iced coffee, the best way to ensure that it doesn't taste weak and diluted is to use coffee ice cubes rather than plain ones. To do this, brew a pot of coffee, let it cool, pour the coffee into an ice cube tray, and freeze it solid. When the cubes are frozen, pop them out and into resealable plastic freezer bags and freeze them for up to a month.

IRISH COFFEE

SERVES 1

Remember that great Irish coffee starts with excellent brewed coffee.

1 teaspoon packed dark brown sugar	1 cup freshly brewed coffee
1½ ounces good Irish whiskey	2 tablespoons heavy cream

1. Stir together the brown sugar, whiskey, and coffee in a large mug.

2. Float the heavy cream on top by pouring it first into a spoon and then gently tilting the spoon so that the cream flows into the mug. Serve immediately.

BAILEYS IRISH CREAM AND COFFEE

SERVES 1

A delicious way to end the meal, especially in cold weather, this drink is better than dessert. Feel free to multiply the recipe for a large group.

3 ounces Baileys Irish Cream	3 ounces brewed hot coffee

1. Combine the Baileys Irish Cream and coffee in a mug.

2. Stir until smooth. Serve hot.

KAHLÚA AND COFFEE

SERVES 1

Y ou can substitute another coffee-flavored liqueur for the Kahlúa and, of course, increase or decrease the amount of liqueur, depending upon your taste.

2 ounces (¼ cup) Kahlúa   6 ounces (¾ cup) brewed hot coffee

1. Combine the Kahlúa and coffee in a mug.

2. Stir until smooth. Serve hot.

HOT CHOCOLATE AND PEPPERMINT SCHNAPPS

SERVES 1

S chnapps is a strong, colorless alcoholic beverage made from potatoes or grains. Peppermint is the most common flavoring in schnapps, which comes from the German word Schnaps, which means "mouthful." If you like chocolate-covered mints, this is the drink for you.

1 cup Serious Hot Chocolate   2 ounces (¼ cup) peppermint
(page 249)   schnapps

1. Combine the hot chocolate and peppermint schnapps in a large mug.

2. Stir until smooth. Serve hot.

TOPPINGS AND SAUCES

Toppings and sauces accentuate the most mundane dishes, elevating them to something extraordinary. Toppings are often a way of enhancing and enlivening a particular dish, making use of a variety of fresh fruits and vegetables that are turned into everything from rich, smooth butters to chunky, flavorful compotes. Syrups also fall into the category of toppings. Though many people think of a bottle of commercial maple syrup as the only entry in this genre, syrups can in fact be made from the essence of a single fruit, or from the reduction of a spirit such as port, or even from just sugar and water (when it becomes the aptly named simple syrup).

Toppings can also be savory solutions when you want to bring out the best in an omelet or a frittata. Very often, savory toppings are made with tomatoes that are seasoned and spiced to produce a roasted tomato sauce or a pico de gallo. Sauces have developed over the millennia, reaching a pinnacle in the kitchen of the great chef Auguste Escoffier, who listed five mother sauces, which form the foundation of sauces in the lexicon of cookery: velouté (clear stock thickened with roux), béchamel (cream sauce), tomato, espagnole (a brown sauce that is not used much today), and hollandaise.

Today's mother sauces might more accurately be described as béchamel, demi-glace (a highly reduced stock), mayonnaise/hollandaise, vinaigrette, and butter sauce, including compound butters and beurre blanc, a white wine butter sauce. Bubby's is more often in touch with the American lexicon, using stewed fruits, compotes, compound butters, or flavored maple syrup.

Toppings and sauces make for beautiful finishing touches on many brunch dishes—a plate of pancakes becomes something special with a lovely fresh fruit compote, some cheese-filled blintzes jump off the plate into your guest's mouth when they are topped with sautéed bananas and blueberries, and topping a slice of fruit bread with raspberry butter lends a touch of magic. While toppings and sauces may take a few extra minutes to make, it's time well spent in terms of having your guests—or maybe just one very special guest—feel pampered to the extreme. These little extras are prepared with very little effort, but they go a long way toward establishing brunch as a reason to celebrate.

Included in this chapter are all those wonderful toppings and sauces, butters and spreads, compotes and preserves. Some are sweet, others savory, but all are easy to make, and many can be made well in advance.

Once you master some basic techniques, you're on your way to creating not only very traditional sauces such as hollandaise and béarnaise, but lighter ones, too, such as Bubby's Roasted Tomato Sauce (page 289). Mayonnaise (page 284) is at its simplest just an emulsion of oil, egg yolks, seasonings, and either vinegar or lemon juice. Though you probably envision a jar when you think of mayonnaise, homemade is completely different—fresh tasting and smooth. Making mayonnaise from scratch is not rocket science, but there are certain parameters to adhere to—and here in this chapter you will find tips for what to do if your mayo breaks. Thankfully, it can nearly always be repaired for use in salads and sandwiches. Mayonnaise is also the base sauce for Aioli (page 284), which is garlic mayonnaise.

THE ADDITION OF HOMEMADE TOPPINGS, SAUCES, AND BUTTERS WILL GIVE AN EXTRA-SPECIAL TOUCH TO ANY BRUNCH ITEM.

Hollandaise—made with butter, lemon juice, and egg yolks—is a very important brunch sauce because without it, we wouldn't have that brunch staple Classic Eggs Benedict (page 109). It's one of the mother sauces of classical cookery, and from it come many variations, such as béarnaise, which is hollandaise enhanced with a reduction of tarragon, white wine, vinegar, and shallots. Hollandaise is also the basis for other sauces you may want to experiment with, such as sauce Choron (tomato) and sauce Maltaise (a blood orange hollandaise that is wonderful with poached salmon).

Many of these classic sauces have a place at brunch. Some of them can seem intimidating, but with practice they become easier. Of course, they have their place at big, formal meals, and the highfalutin chef with fancy pants can do amazing things with sauces that seem impossible to lesser chefs, like us normal people. Sauces can break, curdle, and come out looking nothing like what they should, unless each and every step of the cooking process is controlled right down to the last egg yolk. Broken sauces can be repaired, but who needs that kind of stress when you're trying to ready a relaxing brunch for friends and family?

If some of these skills are new to you, try keeping most of your brunch simple and then choose one new skill to experiment with on your friends. If it's something crucial like Traditional Hollandaise Sauce (page 285), either practice first and be willing to show off your success or toss your failure, or use Blender Hollandaise Sauce (page 286). The traditional method of making hollandaise is more difficult than the blender method, but, honestly, the difference in the results is hardly noticeable.

Sauces aren't only about butter and egg yolks, of course, and some of the signature sauces at Bubby's feature fresh fruit—we call these sauces compotes. When the fruit is truly fresh and good quality, a compote needs only a bit of sugar and some lemon to be memorable. And if fresh berries are out of season when you want to make, say, Blackberry Compote (page 276) or Blueberry Syrup (page 282), using frozen is a great option; frozen berries are often better than out-of-season "fresh" supermarket berries because they are picked and flash-frozen the same day. There are some really good frozen fruits out there, so you can enjoy some of these fruit-based toppings and sauces year-round.

Certain toppings make a dish special. They can be as simple as a sprinkling of brown sugar and toasted nuts or as homey as granola mixed with dried fruit. Some dishes, such as fresh yogurt, may need nothing more than a fresh fruit topping or a drizzle of good honey, or a sprinkling of homemade granola. Suffice it to say that, on many a dish, the topping can bring out the flavors and lend texture and crunch, too.

There are no hard-and-fast rules here about what sauce goes with what dish. I've made suggestions, of course, but as with all things brunch, the rules aren't set in stone. Try different combinations to see which ones you like, and the next time, think about trying something new. See which ones become your own personal tricks of the trade.

FRESH HERB BUTTER

his butter is delicious with eggs, seared fish, steaks, pork chops, chicken, or to spread on savory muffins or scones. When making it, it is important that the butter is still a little firm, but not so cold that it won't whip in the mixer. Take the butter out of the refrigerator a half hour to an hour before making the compound. For best results, don't freeze this butter.

½ pound (2 sticks) unsalted butter, slightly cooler than room temperature, slightly firm	1 tablespoon finely chopped fresh parsley
1 teaspoon finely chopped fresh thyme	1 tablespoon sea salt
1 teaspoon finely chopped fresh rosemary	½ teaspoon freshly ground black pepper
	2 tablespoons finely chopped shallot

1. Cut the butter into 1-inch pieces and place them in the work bowl of a stand mixer fitted with the paddle attachment. Add the thyme, rosemary, parsley, salt, pepper, and shallot. Starting on slow speed, beat until the ingredients begin to incorporate.

2. Turn up the speed to medium-high and whip the butter until all the ingredients are well incorporated. The outside of the mixing bowl should feel cool. If the bowl begins to get too warm, stop the mixer and refrigerate the bowl for 15 minutes before continuing.

3. When all the ingredients are well mixed, use a spatula to scrape the butter onto a large piece of parchment paper or wax paper. Roll the butter into a long tube that is 1 to 2 inches in diameter, and twist the ends to seal in the butter. Chill for at least several hours. Alternatively, scrape the butter into a ramekin and cover it tightly with plastic wrap before chilling.

4. The butter can be refrigerated for 4 to 5 days. When you are ready to serve the butter, cut it into rounds and remove the parchment paper. Alternatively, simply put it on the table in its ramekin.

COMPOUND BUTTERS

When fresh herbs, fruits, or flavorings such as maple syrup are combined with butter, they become what's called a compound butter. Easy to make, these butters are not only great for melting and saucing fish and meat, but they can also be rolled into a log, cut into small, decorative pieces, and served with muffins and quick breads, or even used to top a soup.

Butter is enhanced by the flavors in nuts and citrus, so experiment and make your own combinations. Try using toasted almonds, walnuts, hazelnuts, or cashews, or citrus fruits, such as grapefruit, lemons, blood oranges, Meyer lemons, or tangerines.

When you make a compound butter, be sure to use high-quality fresh unsalted butter. Once the compound butter is made, shaped into a cylinder, and wrapped in parchment or plastic wrap, it can be refrigerated for 3 to 4 days or frozen for several weeks. Just before serving, slice it into thin rounds and unwrap it.

One exception is a fresh herb butter, which needs to be served within 4 to 5 days, or it will lose flavor. If you have time, shape the butter into pretty molds. Otherwise, just put it into a ceramic container or some ramekins and keep it covered until serving time.

ORANGE BUTTER

*O*range butter enhances the flavor of many dishes, from pancakes, waffles, and quick breads to savory roasted chicken, pork, or fish. It takes minutes to make this compound butter, but plan to make it at least thirty minutes in advance so the orange juice reduction has time to cool. Be sure your butter is still a little firm, but not so firm that it won't whip in the mixer. To accomplish this, let the butter sit out at room temperature for a half hour to an hour.

½ cup fresh orange juice	1 teaspoon freshly grated orange
½ pound (2 sticks) unsalted butter,	zest
slightly cooler than room	Pinch of kosher salt
temperature, slightly firm	

1. Place the orange juice in a small saucepan over medium-high heat. Reduce the orange juice to 2 tablespoons, or until very thick and syrupy, 7 to 10 minutes. Let the juice cool to room temperature.

2. Cut the butter into 1-inch pieces and place the pieces into the work bowl of a mixer fitted with the paddle attachment. Add the orange juice reduction, orange zest, and salt. Starting on slow speed, beat until the ingredients begin to incorporate.

3. Turn up the speed to medium-high and whip the butter until all the ingredients are well incorporated. The outside of the mixing bowl should feel cool. If the bowl begins to get too warm, stop the mixer and refrigerate the bowl for about 15 minutes before continuing.

4. When all the ingredients are well mixed, use a spatula to scrape the butter onto a large piece of parchment paper or wax paper. Roll the butter into a long tube that is 1 to 2 inches in diameter, and twist the ends to seal in the butter. Chill for at least several hours. Alternatively, scrape the butter into a ramekin and cover it with plastic wrap before chilling.

5. The butter can be refrigerated for 3 to 4 days or frozen for several weeks. When you are ready to serve the butter, cut it into rounds and remove the parchment paper. Alternatively, simply put it on the table in its ramekin.

ORANGE PECAN BUTTER VARIATION: Stir ½ cup toasted chopped pecans into the butter when you add the orange zest. If you want to make plain Pecan Butter, omit the orange juice and zest.

Strawberry Butter

MAKES 1¼ CUPS

A beautiful pink, intensely flavored butter, this can be made with either fresh or frozen, thawed berries. The butter should be a little cooler than room temperature when you whip it. Take the butter out of the refrigerator a half hour to an hour before you plan to use it, so it can soften.

½ cup chopped fresh or frozen
    strawberries, thawed if frozen
½ pound (2 sticks) unsalted butter,
    slightly cooler than room
    temperature, slightly firm

1 teaspoon freshly grated orange
    zest
Pinch of kosher salt

1. Cook the strawberries in a saucepan over medium heat for about 4 minutes, or until they break down. Continue to cook and reduce the berries, stirring them occasionally, for 7 to 10 minutes, until very thick and syrupy. Let the berries cool for 30 minutes, or until they are at room temperature.

2. Cut the butter into 1-inch pieces and place the pieces into the work bowl of a mixer fitted with the paddle attachment. Add the cooled berries, the orange zest, and salt. Starting on slow speed, beat until the ingredients begin to incorporate.

3. Turn up the speed to medium-high and whip the butter until all the ingredients are incorporated. The outside of the mixing bowl should feel cool. If the bowl begins to get too warm, stop the mixer and refrigerate the bowl for 15 minutes before continuing.

4. When all the ingredients are well mixed, use a spatula to scrape the butter onto a large piece of parchment paper or wax paper. Roll the butter into a long tube that is 1 to 2 inches in diameter, and twist the ends to seal in the butter. Chill for at least several hours. Alternatively, scrape the butter into a ramekin and cover it with plastic wrap before chilling.

5. The butter can be refrigerated for 3 to 4 days or frozen for several weeks. When you are ready to serve the butter, cut it into rounds and remove the parchment paper. Alternatively, simply put it on the table in its ramekin.

BLACKBERRY, RASPBERRY, BLUEBERRY, OR FRESH CURRANT BUTTER VARIATIONS: Substitute equal amounts of blackberries, raspberries, blueberries, or fresh currants for the strawberries. If using currants, add 1 tablespoon sugar to the currants while they are cooking. Another good trick is to replace the fresh berries with ¼ cup berry jam and follow all the same steps. You will still need to heat and cool the jam first.

APPLE BUTTER

MAKES 6 TO 7 CUPS

*A*pple butter, an intensely fruity and concentrated spread, is perfect with your choice of muffins, scones, and quick breads. Use Mutsu, Jonagold, Braeburn, or any other tart/sweet apple. It will keep in the refrigerator for up to a month or you can freeze it in an airtight container for up to six months.

4 pounds tart/sweet apples, such as Mutsu, Jonagold, or Braeburn, peeled and cut into ½-inch dice	2 teaspoons ground cinnamon
	½ teaspoon ground cloves
	2 quarts fresh-pressed apple cider
2 cups sugar	

1. Place the apples in a 3- or 4-quart noncorrodible pot. Stir in the sugar, cinnamon, cloves, and apple cider. Bring the mixture to a boil over medium heat. Cook, uncovered, for 30 minutes, stirring occasionally.

2. Turn down the heat to very low and cover the pot. Continue to cook for 3 hours, until a deep brown color.

3. Uncover the pot and continue cooking the apple butter until the liquid is cooked off and the apple butter is thick. Allow to cool for several hours at room temperature.

4. Spoon the apple butter into jars and cover with a lid.

CINNAMON SUGAR BUTTER

MAKES 1 CUP

U se this sweet spiced butter for the most amazing cinnamon toast. After you toast the bread of your choice, spread on some cinnamon butter and stick it under the broiler for a few seconds to melt. Store the cinnamon sugar butter in the refrigerator for a week or freeze it for several weeks.

8 tablespoons (1 stick) unsalted butter, slightly cooler than room temperature, slightly firm

¼ cup sugar
1½ teaspoons ground cinnamon

1. Cut the butter in 1-inch pieces and place the pieces into the work bowl of a mixer fitted with the paddle attachment. Add the sugar and cinnamon. Starting on slow speed, beat until the ingredients begin to incorporate.

2. Turn up the speed to medium-high and whip until all the ingredients are well incorporated. The outside of the mixing bowl should feel cool. If the bowl begins to get too warm, stop the mixer and refrigerate the bowl for 15 minutes before continuing.

3. When all the ingredients are well mixed, use a spatula to scrape the butter onto a large piece of parchment paper or wax paper. Roll the butter into a long tube that is 1 or 2 inches in diameter, and twist the ends to seal in the butter. Chill for at least several hours. Alternatively, scrape the butter into a ramekin and cover it with plastic wrap before chilling.

4. When you are ready to serve the butter, cut it into rounds and remove the parchment paper. Alternatively, simply put it on the table in its ramekin.

MAPLE BUTTER

MAKES 1¼ CUPS

*U*se grade A maple syrup to make this delicious butter, which is wonderful on toast or pancakes. You can prepare it ahead of time and store it in the refrigerator for three to four days.

½ pound (2 sticks) unsalted butter, slightly cooler than room temperature, slightly firm	½ cup maple syrup

1. Cut the butter into 1-inch pieces and place the pieces in the work bowl of a mixer fitted with the paddle attachment. Add the maple syrup. Starting on slow speed, beat until the butter and syrup start to incorporate.

2. Turn up the speed to high and beat for 1 to 2 minutes, or until the mixture softens. The outside of the mixing bowl should feel cool. If the bowl begins to get too warm, stop the mixer and refrigerate the bowl for 15 minutes before continuing.

3. When all the ingredients are well mixed, use a spatula to scrape the butter onto a large sheet of parchment paper or wax paper. Roll the butter into a long tube that is 1 to 2 inches in diameter, and twist the ends to seal in the butter. Chill for at least several hours.

4. The butter can be refrigerated for 3 to 4 days or frozen for several weeks. When you are ready to serve the butter, cut it into rounds and remove the parchment paper. Alternatively, simply put it into a ramekin and place it on the table.

MAPLE WALNUT BUTTER VARIATION: Add ½ cup toasted, finely chopped walnuts after the syrup is incorporated. You also may want to try Maple Pecan or Maple Almond butters.

SMOKED SALMON–SCALLION CREAM CHEESE

MAKES 1 ⅓ CUPS CREAM CHEESE

A luxurious spread for bagels that is so much better than ordinary cream cheese, this will keep for about a week in the refrigerator. For best results, remove the cream cheese from the refrigerator about an hour or so before you plan to use it, so it will soften.

1 cup cream cheese, softened

3 ounces (⅓ cup) chopped Smoked Salmon (page 191)

4 scallions, (green part only) finely sliced (½ cup)

1. Using a mixer, beat the cream cheese until soft. Beat in the smoked salmon and scallions.

2. Spoon the cream cheese into a crock, cover with a lid or plastic wrap, and refrigerate for at least an hour before serving.

BLACKBERRY COMPOTE

MAKES 1 ½ CUPS

his sauce complements many recipes in the book. It's wonderful with pancakes and waffles and is almost a requirement with Mom's Blintzes (page 146). You can substitute blueberries, strawberries, or just about any berry for the blackberries with excellent results. Be sure to use freshly squeezed orange juice. Alternatively, especially if you make this with other berries, lemon juice is a good substitute for the orange juice. You can even try it with grapefruit juice. The compote can be made a couple of days in advance, if you like, cooled, and stored in the refrigerator in a container with a lid. Before serving, heat the compote over low heat until it is very hot.

2 cups fresh blackberries, picked over	1 tablespoon fresh orange juice
¼ cup sugar	½ teaspoon freshly grated orange zest

1. Stir together the blackberries, sugar, orange juice, and orange zest in a heavy 1-quart saucepan. Bring the mixture to a simmer over medium heat.

2. Reduce the heat to low and simmer for 5 to 10 minutes, or until the mixture coats the back of a spoon.

3. Spoon the compote into a serving dish.

CINNAMON PEAR COMPOTE

MAKES ABOUT 2 CUPS

This versatile fruit sauce is excellent with both Pumpkin Waffles (page 138) and Buttermilk Waffles (page 135). Try stirring it into yogurt, spooning it on top of ice cream, or serving it as you would a fruit cup. Bosc pears work the best here because they are juicy, yet they hold their shape. Use a softer pear and you may wind up with pear sauce, which certainly tastes good, but it isn't as visually appealing as this raisin-flecked chunky compote. If storing for later use, cool the compote completely before covering it with a lid or plastic wrap. This will keep in the refrigerator for up to one week. If the compote is cool, reheat it over low heat to serve hot. Or you can serve it chilled or at room temperature.

6 Bosc pears, peeled, cored, and cut into ¼-inch dice	⅔ cup maple syrup
½ cup raisins	3 tablespoons unsalted butter
½ teaspoon ground cinnamon	Pinch of kosher salt
	2 teaspoons fresh lemon juice

1. Stir together the pears, raisins, cinnamon, maple syrup, butter, salt, and lemon juice in a 2-quart noncorrodible saucepan. Bring the mixture to a simmer over medium heat.

2. Reduce the heat to low and simmer for 10 to 15 minutes, stirring occasionally. The compote is ready when the pears are very soft and beginning to lose their shape.

3. Spoon the compote into a serving dish.

SPICY APPLE COMPOTE

MAKES 2 TO 3 CUPS

This compote has a little kick to it, courtesy of the cayenne pepper. It's excellent with pancakes, oatmeal, or even as a topping on yogurt, and it can be made up to a week ahead. If storing for later use, cool the compote completely before covering it with a lid or plastic wrap. This will keep in the refrigerator for up to one week. If the compote is cool, reheat it over low heat to serve hot. It can also be served warm.

6 tart apples, such as Red Delicious, Golden Delicious, Braeburn, or Granny Smith, peeled, cored, and cut into ½-inch dice

½ teaspoon ground cinnamon

Pinch of freshly grated nutmeg

¼ cup packed light brown sugar

2 tablespoons unsalted butter

Pinch of kosher salt

Pinch of cayenne pepper or freshly ground black pepper

½ teaspoon fresh lemon juice

1. Stir together the apples, cinnamon, nutmeg, brown sugar, butter, salt, and cayenne pepper in a 2-quart noncorrodible saucepan. Bring the mixture to a simmer over medium heat.

2. Reduce the heat to low and simmer for about 10 minutes, stirring occasionally. The compote is ready when the apples are very soft.

3. Remove the compote from the heat and stir in the lemon juice.

4. Spoon the compote into a serving bowl.

APPLESAUCE

MAKES ABOUT 4 CUPS

U se any tart apple for this sauce. I personally like Braeburns, Mutsus, or Jonagolds. In a pinch, use Granny Smiths. It's up to you whether to serve this warm or chilled. Excellent with Potato Pancakes (page 213), it is also called for in the Whole Grain Apple Waffle recipe (page 137), among others. This will keep for up to one week in the refrigerator.

6 tart apples, peeled, cored, and cut into ½-inch pieces	3 tablespoons packed light brown sugar
¼ teaspoon ground cinnamon	1 teaspoon fresh lemon juice
Pinch of ground cloves	

1. Cook the apples in a small saucepan over low heat until they begin to steam. Stir occasionally to keep them from sticking to the bottom of the saucepan.

2. Once the apples start to steam, cover the saucepan and cook over medium-low heat for about 5 minutes.

3. Break up the apples with a wooden spoon. The mixture should be fairly smooth and saucelike, but still contain a few soft chunks. Stir in the cinnamon, cloves, brown sugar, and lemon juice.

4. Serve warm, at room temperature, or cold.

PEAR SAUCE VARIATION: Substitute 6 peeled, cored, and chopped Bosc or Bartlett pears for the apples.

STRAWBERRY JAM

MAKES ABOUT 2 TO 3 QUARTS

Make this in late June or early July when strawberries are abundant at your local farmers' market, and you'll enjoy it for months to come. Pectin, a water-soluble substance used as a thickener in jams and jellies, is available in many supermarkets. Serve this jam with any of Bubby's fruit breads or muffins. You can also substitute blackberries, raspberries, or blueberries for the strawberries. You can mix the berries, too. Though you don't need to sterilize the three 1-quart storage jars, you should wash the berries well. We are not canning here, or sealing, so it's not the same process. This jam will keep for three to four weeks in the refrigerator.

8 cups sugar	1 tablespoon kosher salt
2 quarts whole strawberries, stemmed	¼ cup fresh orange juice
5 tablespoons (2 ounces) dry pectin	¼ cup light corn syrup

1. Stir together the sugar and 1½ cups of water in a large saucepan. Bring to a boil over medium-high heat. Using a ladle or spoon, remove any foam as it forms. Cook until the liquid begins to turn a light brown color and registers 245°F on a candy thermometer.

2. Stir the strawberries into the sugar mixture, and bring the liquid back to a boil. Turn down the heat to low and simmer for 30 minutes.

3. Stir together the pectin, salt, orange juice, and corn syrup in a small bowl. In the work bowl of a food processor or blender, or with an immersion blender, process the mixture very well, so there are no dry clumps of pectin.

4. Whisk the pectin mixture into the strawberry mixture, remove any foam as it forms, and simmer for about 30 more minutes, or until the jam registers 260°F on the candy thermometer. Occasionally skim the surface of the jam to remove any foam that may have accumulated during the cooking. Cool the jam to room temperature.

5. Spoon the jam into 1-quart jars, leaving about 1 inch of room at the top. Fasten the lids and refrigerate until ready to serve.

SAUTÉED BANANA AND RAISIN TOPPING

SERVES 1

This naturally sweet fruit topping is very good on oatmeal, pancakes, or French toast. Be sure the banana you use is nice and ripe.

1 teaspoon unsalted butter	2 teaspoons raisins
1 ripe banana, peeled and cut on the bias into ¼-inch-thick slices	

1. Heat the butter in a small nonstick skillet over medium heat until very hot. Add the banana slices and sauté for 2 minutes, or until golden brown. Turn the slices and continue to cook until golden brown on the other side, 1 or 2 minutes more.

2. When the bananas are golden brown all over, remove them from the pan. Spoon the banana topping over whatever dish you've chosen. Sprinkle on the raisins.

SIMPLE SYRUP

MAKES ABOUT 1½ CUPS

You'll use this syrup in many different ways—it's essential in many drinks. It may be prepared a week in advance, but it should be stored, tightly covered, in the refrigerator.

1½ cups water	1½ cups sugar

1. Stir together the water and sugar in a heavy saucepan and cook over medium heat for about 5 minutes or until the sugar dissolves.

2. Turn up the heat to high and boil the syrup for about 2 minutes, stirring constantly.

3. Transfer the syrup to a covered container and refrigerate for 2 to 3 hours, or until chilled.

BLUEBERRY SYRUP

MAKES ABOUT 3 CUPS

This syrup is excellent on Blueberry Buttermilk Pancakes (page 121) or other berry pancakes. It's also good with waffles, French toast, and johnnycakes. Try this recipe with blackberries or another favorite berry, or a mixture of berries. Boysenberries are great and can usually be bought frozen (but rarely fresh). Red currants are sour and add a real zing to maple syrup. You can do this with any berry you like. Blueberry syrup can be made well in advance and stored for two weeks in an airtight container in the refrigerator. Be sure to reheat it over low heat before serving, because it tastes best hot or warm.

1 cup fresh or frozen blueberries	2 tablespoons unsalted butter
2 cups maple syrup	

1. Combine the blueberries and maple syrup in a heavy 1-quart saucepan. Bring to a boil over medium heat. Reduce the heat to very low and simmer for about 10 minutes.

2. Stir in the butter and cook for 5 more minutes, stirring occasionally.

3. Pour the syrup into a small pitcher and serve immediately.

LEMON SYRUP

MAKES ½ CUP

A very simple-to-make tart-sweet syrup, this sauce is accented with freshly grated lemon zest and freshly squeezed lemon juice for a bright flavor. It's perfect for a wintry fruit salad when the fruit is less than in season, or drizzled on top of pound cake. Make sure your lemons are at room temperature to get the maximum amount of juice out of them.

1 teaspoon freshly grated lemon zest	½ cup fresh lemon juice
	½ cup sugar

1. Stir together the lemon zest, lemon juice, and sugar in a small saucepan over medium heat. Cook for about 5 minutes, stirring constantly, until the sugar dissolves and the syrup looks fairly clear.

2. Pour the syrup into an airtight container and refrigerate for up to a month.

PORT SYRUP

A wonderful syrup to pour over fresh fruit, this is not overpoweringly sweet, thanks to the orange zest. Choose a decent, but not expensive, port for this. Depending upon what you will use it for, opt for the cloves, cinnamon, and pepper. The spicier port syrup is great for reconstituting dried figs, apples, pears, and other dried fruit. You can also use it as a glaze on chicken or pork. Port syrup keeps in an airtight container for a few months in the refrigerator.

1 cup port wine

1 cup sugar

1 tablespoon freshly grated orange
   zest

Pinch of ground cloves (optional)

Pinch of ground cinnamon
   (optional)

Pinch of freshly ground black
   pepper (optional)

1. Stir together all of the ingredients in a small saucepan over medium heat. Cook, stirring constantly, for 5 to 10 minutes, or until the sugar dissolves and the syrup is very hot.

2. Pour the syrup into a container with a lid and allow it to cool to room temperature before covering and storing in the refrigerator.

MAYONNAISE

MAKES ¾ CUP

*H*omemade mayonnaise is so much better than store-bought mayo that you'll become a convert the first time you taste it. It's basically an emulsion of liquid, oil, and egg yolk, the egg being the only nonvariable here. You can choose from a wide range of oils, such as extra-virgin olive or corn oil, but I prefer canola oil because it's not too strong tasting. Though homemade mayo might seem intimidating the first time you make it, the problem is nearly always fixable with the one easy step below. Homemade mayonnaise will keep for up to one week in the refrigerator.

1 extra-large egg yolk	¼ teaspoon Dijon mustard
2 teaspoons fresh lemon juice	½ teaspoon kosher salt
1 teaspoon white wine vinegar	¾ cup canola oil

1. Whisk the egg yolk, lemon juice, vinegar, mustard, and salt in a mixing bowl; set aside.

2. Set a kitchen towel in a stable pan, such as a cast-iron skillet. Set the bowl on the towel. This will keep it stable while you're whisking in the canola oil.

3. Begin whisking the egg yolk mixture and slowly add the canola oil by drizzling it in in a thin stream. Don't go too fast and make sure the oil is being incorporated into the yolk mixture as you go along. Alternatively, you can use a food processor and feed the oil in through the tube portion of the processor.

4. If the mayonnaise breaks, and you will know it if it does because it will go from being a thick paste to being oily and watery, there is a fix: Mix 1 egg yolk with 1 tablespoon of water. Whisking briskly, slowly begin pouring the *broken* mayonnaise into the egg mixture in a thin stream, watching to make sure that it is being incorporated as you go. Then continue, adding the rest of the broken mayonnaise a little at a time until it is all incorporated.

5. Spoon the mayonnaise into an airtight container and refrigerate until ready to use.

AIOLI VARIATION: Stir 1 minced garlic clove and 2 tablespoons chopped fresh parsley into the mayonnaise before spooning it into the container. Serve the aioli with raw vegetables as a dip, as a topping for fish, or on sandwiches.

RÉMOULADE VARIATION: Just before spooning the mayonnaise into the container, fold in 1 tablespoon capers, 1 tablespoon chopped shallot, 1 tablespoon chopped red bell pepper, 1 tablespoon chopped tomato, 2 chopped cornichons, and 1 chopped anchovy fillet. Rémoulade is delicious with a variety of cold meats and seafood. It's also great on sandwiches.

TRADITIONAL HOLLANDAISE SAUCE

MAKES 1 ¼ CUPS

*T*he classic recipe for this very rich sauce goes with everything from meat and fish to eggs and vegetables. It's usually made in a double boiler, but if you don't have one, you can improvise. Make a double boiler by putting one saucepan over another slightly larger one and filling the bottom one with an inch or so of water. Make the sauce in the top saucepan and let the water in the bottom pan simmer—it should not touch the sauce—so the sauce will cook slowly. If your sauce still breaks, transfer it to a bowl. Off the heat in the top of the double boiler, whisk another egg yolk. Gradually pour in the curdled sauce in a stream and whisk vigorously until all the broken sauce has been incorporated into the egg yolk. Make the sauce no more than 30 minutes before you plan on serving it. Do not attempt to reheat or it will break.

3 extra-large egg yolks
½ pound (2 sticks) unsalted butter, melted and cooled until just warm

2 teaspoons fresh lemon juice
½ teaspoon kosher salt
Pinch of cayenne pepper

1. Combine the egg yolks and 1 tablespoon of water in the top of a double boiler. Grasping the bowl with your left hand (if you are right-handed), hold the top of the double boiler over the simmering water in the bottom of the double boiler and begin to whisk vigorously. After a few minutes, the yolks will begin to get pale yellow and thick. To test if the yolks are thick enough to begin whisking in the butter, dip a spoon in. The yolks should be thick enough to coat the back of the spoon before you proceed to the next step.

2. Remove the top of the double boiler from the heat and place it either on a kitchen towel or in a heavy skillet. While whisking the yolks, slowly add a stream of warm melted butter a little at a time, whisking until all the butter is incorporated.

3. Whisk in the lemon juice, salt, and cayenne pepper and taste for additional seasoning. Serve immediately.

BLENDER HOLLANDAISE SAUCE

MAKES 1 CUP

Here's the foolproof version of the sauce. It can get a little hotter or a little cooler than the classic hollandaise without breaking. An added benefit: It takes less than two minutes to make, so you can leave this to the last minute.

2 extra-large eggs	2 teaspoons fresh lemon juice
½ pound (2 sticks) unsalted butter,	½ teaspoon kosher salt
melted and hot	Pinch of cayenne pepper

1. Whip the eggs in a blender on high speed until frothy. With the blender running, slowly drizzle the hot butter into the eggs. Turn off the blender.

2. Add the lemon juice, salt, and cayenne pepper and stir well. Taste, and add extra salt and cayenne pepper if needed.

BÉARNAISE SAUCE

MAKES 1 CUP

Make this superb sauce once in a while when you want to treat your guests to something un-deniably rich and velvety smooth. It is best made as close as possible to when you plan to serve it, though it will hold for about an hour or so before serving. Serve it with Seared Beef Tenderloin Benedict (page 110).

2 tablespoons chopped fresh tarragon, or 1 tablespoon dried

2 tablespoons finely chopped shallot

½ teaspoon freshly ground black pepper

3 tablespoons white wine vinegar (or you can use cider vinegar or sherry vinegar)

3 tablespoons dry white wine

1 recipe Blender Hollandaise Sauce (page 286) or Traditional Hollandaise Sauce (page 285)

1. Stir together the tarragon, shallot, pepper, vinegar, and white wine in a saucepan. Bring to a boil over medium-high heat. Reduce the heat to medium and cook for 5 to 7 minutes, or until most of the liquid has evaporated and a thick paste remains. Cool until just warm.

2. Stir the cooled mixture into the hollandaise sauce and blend very well, either with a whisk or in a blender. Keep the béarnaise in a warm, but not hot, place until serving time. One good spot is on a folded kitchen towel or trivet on the back of the stove when the oven is on.

CHORON SAUCE VARIATION: Add 6 tablespoons Roasted Tomato Sauce (page 289) to 1 recipe Blender Hollandaise Sauce (page 286). Stir very well. Serve as a variation to Classic Eggs Benedict (page 109), or on poached fish or steamed asparagus.

MALTAISE SAUCE VARIATION: Simmer ½ cup fresh blood orange juice with 1 teaspoon freshly grated blood orange zest and 2 tablespoons finely chopped shallot until thick and syrupy (it will measure about 3 tablespoons). Allow the reduction to cool slightly. Stir this into 1 recipe Traditional or Blender Hollandaise Sauce (pages 285 and 286). This is especially good with steamed asparagus or other vegetables, and it's great with poached or seared salmon fillet, too.

BÉCHAMEL SAUCE

MAKES 2 CUPS

A creamy sauce with French origins, this was named after its inventor, Louis de Béchamel, who was Louis XIV's steward. It's a rich indulgence that brings out the flavor in many meat and fish dishes. It is delicious in Sausage Gravy (page 186).

4 tablespoons (½ stick) unsalted butter	Pinch of ground cloves
¼ cup all-purpose flour	1 bay leaf
2 cups milk	Pinch of freshly grated nutmeg
1 garlic clove, crushed	Dash of Worcestershire sauce
1 tablespoon chopped onion	1 teaspoon kosher salt
½ teaspoon freshly ground black pepper	Pinch of cayenne pepper

1. Melt the butter in a heavy 1-quart stainless steel saucepan over medium heat. Stir in the flour and cook, stirring, for about 5 minutes. You want to get rid of the floury taste, but the roux should still be light in color. If it starts to brown, remove it briefly from the heat.

2. Gradually add the milk, whisking vigorously so that no lumps form. Add the garlic, onion, black pepper, cloves, bay leaf, and nutmeg.

3. Reduce the heat to low and simmer, stirring often, for about 20 minutes. Stir in the Worcestershire sauce, salt, and cayenne pepper. Remove and discard the bay leaf. Taste the sauce, and adjust the seasonings with extra salt and cayenne pepper if needed. Serve warm.

ROASTED TOMATO SAUCE

MAKES 4 TO 5 CUPS

An intensely flavored, full-bodied sauce that's good on a variety of dishes, this one will keep for up to one week in the refrigerator. Use ripe local tomatoes and basil for best results.

For the tomatoes
10 to 12 ripe plum tomatoes
¼ cup olive oil
4 garlic cloves
1 teaspoon dried thyme
2 teaspoons kosher salt
1 teaspoon freshly ground black
   pepper

For the sauce
½ cup olive oil
2 garlic cloves, thinly sliced
1 onion, cut into ¼-inch dice
2 teaspoons chopped fresh thyme
½ cup chopped fresh basil
½ cup red wine
Kosher salt and freshly ground
   black pepper to taste

1. Preheat the oven to 450°F.

2. Prepare the tomatoes: Toss together the plum tomatoes, olive oil, garlic, thyme, salt, and pepper in a large bowl.

3. Arrange the tomatoes in a single layer on a baking sheet. Roast the tomatoes for 15 to 20 minutes, or until nicely browned. Allow to cool slightly on the baking sheet.

4. Using your hands, crush the tomatoes into ½-inch pieces, making sure to reserve the juice.

5. Make the sauce: Heat the olive oil in a large saucepan over medium heat. Add the garlic and cook, stirring, for 2 minutes, or until the garlic is barely brown. Stir in the onion and cook for 3 minutes, or until the onion is beginning to brown. Stir in the roasted tomatoes, their reserved juice, and the thyme, basil, and red wine.

6. Simmer the sauce for 20 to 30 minutes, or until thick. Add salt and pepper to taste. Serve warm.

PICO DE GALLO

MAKES ABOUT 3 CUPS

A relish best made when tomatoes are at their peak of summer flavor, this is versatile and zesty. Serve it with Huevos Rancheros (page 111), with chips, or to top an omelet. It would go very nicely with the Spanish Omelet with Chorizo and Avocado (page 79). Once you get started making it, you'll think of many uses. Pico de gallo *means "rooster's beak" in Spanish. This relish apparently got its name because it used to be eaten with finger and thumb, and the action looked like the pecking beak of a rooster.*

3 medium ripe tomatoes, cored, seeded, and chopped	4 garlic cloves, minced
2 fresh jalapeño peppers, seeded and minced	3 red bell peppers, cored, seeded, and chopped
1 bunch fresh cilantro, leaves chopped, stems discarded	1 red onion, chopped
	Juice of 1 lime
	Kosher salt to taste

1. Combine the tomatoes, jalapeños, cilantro, garlic, bell peppers, onion, and lime juice in a large bowl.

2. Stir the mixture to combine all the ingredients. Taste, and add salt as needed.

Orange Vinaigrette

MAKES 1 ¼ CUPS

Wonderful with steamed asparagus, this is also good chilled over a green salad and even with grilled chicken and fish. Try to use extra-virgin olive oil and the freshest garlic you can find. This will keep for about two weeks in the refrigerator.

1 teaspoon finely grated orange zest	3 tablespoons chopped fresh parsley
½ cup fresh orange juice	¾ cup good-quality olive oil
2 tablespoons cider vinegar	Kosher salt and cayenne pepper to taste
1 garlic clove, finely minced	

1. Combine the orange zest, orange juice, vinegar, garlic, parsley, olive oil, salt, and cayenne pepper in a mixing bowl. Whisk vigorously until all the ingredients are well incorporated. Alternatively, you can combine all the ingredients in a jar, tightly cover, and shake until the vinaigrette is well mixed.

2. Store the vinaigrette, tightly covered, in the refrigerator. Serve chilled.

ACKNOWLEDGMENTS

Without my three grandmothers, this book would not have come about: Pearl Stahl, aka Nanny, drove me to cook because she could not; Miriam Silver, aka Grammy, spoiled me with sweet and savory treats; and Lucille Crismon, aka Mema, encouraged me to persevere in addition to making the finest roast beef and Yorkshire pudding I've ever had. My mother, a fine cook, must be acknowledged for forbidding me to play with fire, and so it became my profession to do exactly that.

Rosemary Black gets extra-special mention for her patient understanding of what Bubby's food is and for her graciousness, warmth, and intelligence in interpreting two quadrillion badly written sentences. Thanks to Ben Fink for shooting these photographs in the middle of a very busy brunch, and to the food stylists Jamie Kimm and Suzette Kaminsky for preparing the plates for the photographs in our insane kitchen. Thanks especially to my editor, Pamela Cannon, and to all the helpful people at Ballantine for making this book happen. Our agent, Stacey Glick at Jane Dystel, has been especially patient and deserves extra-special thanks for bringing Rosemary—who is a saint—, Ballantine, and Bubby's together on these pages. Thanks, Stacey!

I can't begin to thank the long list of generous teachers who have taken me under their wings, into their kitchens, and into their hearts. They have shared with me generations of secret recipes, both for food and for sanity, even when I may not have always deserved their generosity. But I will continue to share whatever knowledge was gleaned with whoever cares to have it. With all my heart I thank that higher power that made me love to cook. Every day I am grateful that I get to cook for people, because I always know my place—in the kitchen! And most of all, I thank the amazing people who have worked at Bubby's all these years, Vincent, Christina, Luis, Ricardo, and Antonio Puto, as well as scores of great kids who have worked to make Bubby's what it is.

INDEX

Banana(s) (*cont.*)
    muffins:
        buckwheat and zucchini, 45
        cranberry bran, 44
    sautéed
        and chocolate crêpes, 145
        and raisin topping, 281
    and walnut pancakes, 122–23
Bar equipment, 236
Basil
    and Parmesan scrambled eggs with seared
        ham steak, 103
    with tomato, and buffalo mozzarella
        scramble, 102
Beans, white, with beet greens, 219
Beard, James, 120
    cream biscuits, Bubby's variation on,
        33, 54
Béarnaise sauce, 287
Béchamel sauce, 288
Beef
    corned
        hash, 183
        homemade, 180–81
    New York strip steak, roasted, 190
    pastrami, homemade, 182
    roast, sandwich, with horseradish cream,
        157
    tenderloin, seared, Benedict, with
        Béarnaise sauce, 110
Beet greens with white beans, 219
Bell pepper and caramelized onion torta, 104
Benedict, Mr. and Mrs. Le Grand, 108
Berry(ies)
    from farmers' markets, 43
    summer, mixed, parfait, 231
    See also names of berries
Beverages, 235–61
    cider, mulled spiced, 251
    cocktails, 235–37
        bar equipment for, 236
        blood orange Mimosa, 246
        Bloody Mary, 245
        Bloodytini, 246

        Cranmosa, 247
        pink grapefruit and champagne,
          247
        pink lemonade Cosmopolitan,
          248
        sangría, 248
    coffee, *see* Coffee
    for a crowd, 27
    eggnog, warm, 252
    fruit juices, fresh
        combinations, 238
        cranberry, 240
        squeezing, 238
    fruit presses, 239
    garnishes for, 236
    hot chocolate
        Mexican, 250
        and peppermint schnapps, 261
        serious, 249
    hot rum toddy, 254
    ice cubes for, 236–37
    lemonade, 241
        Arnold Palmers, rose hip and mint,
          243
        honeyed, hot, 251
        watermelon, 242
    mulled wine with cinnamon sticks and
        fruit, 255
    Pink Lady punch, 244
    prep work for, 236
    rose hip tea, spiced, 251
    wassail, 253
Birthday Brunch, 11
Biscuits, cream, Mr. Beard's, Bubby's
        variation on, 33, 54
    with sausage gravy, 186
Blackberry
    compote, 276
    corn muffins, 39
    jam and cream cheese stuffed crunchy
        French toast, 134
    with peach and plum breakfast crumble,
        227
Black-eyed peas, hoppin' John, 225

Drinks, *see* Beverages
Drip coffee makers, 257
Dungeness crabs, 87

Early-Summer Farmer's Market Brunch,
   13
Easter Brunch, 10
Eggnog, warm, 252
Eggs, 71–113
   bacon and cheese bread pudding, savory,
      112
   Benedict
      classic, 109
      making in advance, 108
      variations, 109–10
   boiled, 75
   caramelized onion and pepper torta,
      104
   casserole
      bacon, leek, and onion, 105–6
      sausage and mushroom, 107
   clafouti, fruity, 113
   cooking tips, 73
   deviled, 78
   Florentine, 109
   freshness of, 71–72
   frittata
      baking, 72
      farmer's, 92
      lobster Pecorino, 93–94
      resting of, 73
      roasted asparagus and leek, 96
      zucchini, tomato, and Parmesan, 95
   in the Hole, 76
   huevos rancheros, 111
   omelet
      apple, cheddar, and bacon, 88
      asparagus and white cheddar, 81
      baked, 80
      broccoli, onion, and cheddar, 91
      Cajun, 84–85
      chilled, 80
      crab, 86
      for a crowd, 72

      inside-out, 80
      roasted pear and goat cheese,
         89–90
      sizzling ham and Gruyère, 82
      Spanish, with chorizo and avocado,
         79
      spinach and Brie, 83
      tips, 72
   over easy, 74
   poached, 75
   scramble(d), 75
      andouille and crawfish, 101
      green eggs and ham, 103
      jalapeño and cheddar, 100
      mushroom and leek, 98
      sizzling ham and cheddar, 97
      tomato, basil, and buffalo mozzarella,
         102
      wild ramps and Parmesan, 99
   shirred, 77
   sunny-side up, 74
Emmenthaler with turkey and Russian
      dressing on rye, 158
Equipment, 27–29
Escoffier, Auguste, 265
Espresso drinks
   cappuccino, 258–59
   iced cappuccino, 259
   macchiato, 259
   mochacchino, 259
Espresso machines, 258

Fair trade coffee, 256
Fall Harvest Brunch, 18
Family Reunion Brunch, 17–18
Farmer's frittata, 92
Farmer's markets, 43, 71
Father's Day Brunch, 15
Figs, dried, 58
Filters, coffee maker, 258
First Communion Brunch, 12–13
Fish, *see* names of fish
Food processor, 28
French crêpes, 140–41

Mulled
    spiced cider, 251
    wine, with cinnamon sticks and fruit,
        255
Mushroom
    crêpes, creamy, 144
    and leek scramble, 98
    and sausage casserole, 107

New Girlfriend/Boyfriend/Friend
        Brunch, 8
New potato salad, creamy buttermilk,
        223
New Year's Day Brunch, 5
New York strip steak, roasted,
        190
Niçoise salad, 160–61
Nutella crêpes, 141
Nuts
    in muffins, 35
    See also names of nuts

Oats
    rolled, 203
    steel-cut, 203–4, 208
Old-fashioned glasses, 236
Olive oil, 152
Omelet
    apple, cheddar, and bacon, 88
    asparagus and white cheddar, 81
    baked, 80
    Brie and spinach, 83
    broccoli, onion, and cheddar, 91
    Cajun, 84–85
    chilled, 80
    crab, 86
    for a crowd, 72
    inside-out, 80
    roasted pear and goat cheese, 89–90
    sizzling ham and Gruyère, 82
    Spanish, with chorizo and avocado,
        79
    spinach and Brie, 83
    tips, 72

Onion(s)
    with bacon and leek casserole, 105–6
    with broccoli and cheddar omelet, 91
    caramelized, and pepper torta, 104
    red, 212
    with zucchini and spinach crêpes, 143
Orange juice
    blood orange Mimosa, 246
    butter, 270
    and cranberry juice, 238
    and grapefruit juice, 238
    vinaigrette, 291
Orange zest
    chocolate chip muffins, 41
    ricotta pancakes, 124
Organization, 24
Ottomanelli Brothers, 175
Oyster Breakfast: The Hangtown Fry, 7
Oysters, fried, cornmeal-crusted, 197

Pancake Lover's Brunch, 6–7
Pancakes, 117–18
    banana walnut, 122–23
    buckwheat, 125
    buttermilk, blueberry, 121
    griddle heat and, 118
    orange ricotta, 124
    potato, 213
    size of, 118
    skillet-baked, German, 129
    sour cream, Bubby's, 120
    sourdough, 126–27
    Swedish, 128
Pancetta, 176
Parfait, mixed summer berry, 231
Parker House rolls, 56
Parmesan
    and basil scrambled eggs with seared ham
        steak, 103
    and wild ramp scramble, 99
    and zucchini with tomato frittata, 95
Pastrami, homemade, 182
Peach, plum, and blackberry breakfast
        crumble, 227

ABOUT THE AUTHORS

RON SILVER has had an extensive career as a chef and restaurateur. Prior to opening Bubby's Pie Company in Tribeca in 1990, he specialized in cooking breakfast at New York City's iconic Meatpacking District restaurant Florent. He opened a Brooklyn branch of Bubby's in 2003 and branches in Oradall, New Jersey, and Yokohama, Japan, in 2009. Silver is also the author of *Bubby's Homemade Pies.* He lives in New York.

ROSEMARY BLACK, food editor at the New York *Daily News,* is the author of numerous cookbooks. She has appeared on a variety of radio and television programs, including NBC's *Today* show. She lives in Westchester County, New York.

ABOUT THE TYPE

In 1931 Monotype made this facsimile of the typeface cut originally for John Bell by Richard Austin in 1788, using as a basis the matrices in the possession of Stephenson Blake & Co. Used in Bell's newspaper, "The Oracle," it was regarded by Stanley Morison as the first English Modern face. Although inspired by French punchcutters of the time, with a vertical stress and fine hairlines, the face is less severe than the French models and is now classified as Transitional. Essentially a text face, Bell can be used for books, magazines, long articles etc.